PENGUIN  CLASSICS

THE LIFE OF SAINT TERESA OF ÁVILA

St Teresa was born at Ávila in 1515. Of good parentage, she entered the Carmelite convent of the Incarnation at Ávila in Castile when she was twenty-one. Grieved at being parted from her family, she became a nun with determination but without enthusiasm. She progressed well with contemplation and wrote a good deal about the mystical spiritual experiences she underwent without giving them undue significance. A strong influence upon her was the Dominican priest Domingo Bañez, who taught her that God can be loved in and through all things.

In middle age, she resolved to found a convent under the Carmelite rule. After many setbacks, St Joseph's at Ávila was opened in 1562, the first house of the reformed or 'discalced' (barefoot) Carmelites. During the next twenty years she travelled the length and breadth of Spain founding seventeen convents in all, often in conditions of great hardship.

Frank, affectionate, lively and witty, St Teresa combined the contemplative religious life with a life of great activity and she recorded both aspects in literary form. The most important of her writings are the *Life* of herself up to 1562, written at the request of her confessors; the *Way of Perfection*, intended for the instruction of her own nuns; the *Book of Foundations*, the high-spirited account of the establishment of her convents, and *The Interior Castle*. She died at Alba De Tormes in 1582.

J. M. Cohen translated nine volumes for the Penguin Classics; these have been works by Cervantes, Diaz, Galdos, Montaigne, Pascal, Rabelais and Rousseau. He also edited the Penguin anthologies *Latin American Writing Today*, *Writers in the New Cuba*, the *Penguin Book of Spanish Verse* and the Penguin book of *Comic and Curious Verse*. He compiled the *Penguin Dictionary of Quotations*, the *Penguin Dictionary of Modern Quotations* and published *A History of Western Literature* (Penguin, 1956). J. M. Cohen was born in 1903 and began writing and translating in 1946. J. M. Cohen died in 1989. *The Times'* obituary described him as 'one of the last great English men of letters', while the *Independent* wrote that 'his influence will be felt for generations to come'.

THE LIFE OF
SAINT TERESA OF ÁVILA

BY HERSELF

Translated with an Introduction
BY J. M. COHEN

PENGUIN BOOKS

PENGUIN BOOKS

Published by the Penguin Group
Penguin Books Ltd, 27 Wrights Lane, London W8 5TZ, England
Penguin Books USA Inc., 375 Hudson Street, New York, New York 10014, USA
Penguin Books Australia Ltd, Ringwood, Victoria, Australia
Penguin Books Canada Ltd, 10 Alcorn Avenue, Toronto, Ontario, Canada M4V 3B2
Penguin Books (NZ) Ltd, 182–190 Wairau Road, Auckland 10, New Zealand

Penguin Books Ltd, Registered Offices: Harmondsworth, Middlesex, England

This translation first published 1957
13 15 17 19 20 18 16 14

This translation copyright © J. M. Cohen, 1957
All rights reserved

Printed in England by Clays Ltd, St Ives plc

TO
Simon and Dawn

CONTENTS

CONTENTS

CONTENTS

9

CONTENTS

INTRODUCTION

THE autobiography of Santa Teresa is the story of a most remarkable woman's entry into the religious life, and at the same time a literary masterpiece that is, after *Don Quixote*, the most widely read prose classic of Spain. It is a piece of candid self-revelation, written in the liveliest and most unforced conversational prose. The saint herself states that it was composed in the first place at the request of her confessors, who required some account of her rare experiences to be circulated among those religious of a like bent, and who needed it also, in a day when accusations of heresy were frequent, as proof positive of her complete orthodoxy and utter obedience to the teachings and dictates of the Church. But although she herself protests that she lacked the time and leisure for her unwelcome task, and that she would have been better employed spinning or doing the household work in her poor convent, she was undoubtedly a born writer to whom words came freely and fast, and who took a craftsman's delight in them.

The book as we have it gives an account of Teresa's life up to her fiftieth year, 1565, but it was certainly begun some seven or eight years before the date when it was asked for by her confessors, and was addressed in the first place to those four close spiritual friends whom she mentions in Chapter 16 as her fellow members of 'the Five'. Much of it was, in fact, written at Toledo, during the time that Teresa spent there as the guest of the wealthy Doña Luisa de la Cerda, about whom she tells us in Chapter 34. In its complete form, however, it first began to pass from hand to hand at the beginning of 1565, and soon Father Bañez, the saint's confessor at the time and her firm ally and friend, was reproaching her for putting it about rather too freely. He realized, however, that the fault was not hers. Fashionable Spain was extremely interested in this active and forthright reformer of convents.

Much of the book's immediate success was the result of its sheer good writing. Teresa's thoughts seem naturally to clothe themselves in simple, direct, and picturesque language. Even when she is describing a difficult state of conscience or a very rare supernatural experience, she never fails to find the right homely words, the simple everyday metaphors, that will make it clear to readers whose life has never risen to such levels. Her language flows, as does that of Cervantes, like good talk; and she shares with Cervantes also a taste for proverbs and pithy country sayings. Teresa was a woman of little reading. *The Imitation of Christ* and Saint Augustine's *Confessions* were two of the few books that she knew well. In her youth, as she tells us, she had been fond also of the romances of chivalry;

and perhaps at the same time she read ballads and popular poetry. Latin she could hardly understand; any Latin quotations that occur in the *Life* are spelt so phonetically as to be almost unrecognizable. Her vocabulary, therefore, is that of a plain person; all grand words are suspect to her. Even many religious terms are lumped together in her mind under the heading of 'mystical theology', a theoretical science of which she confessed herself to be ignorant.

If Teresa's spelling of Latin follows its own phonetic rules, so does her writing of Spanish. Her punctuation was weak, even to the point of non-existence, and this defect has been only imperfectly remedied by her editors. One is seldom in doubt as to what she is saying, but often puzzled by the syntax of her sentences, which abound in unrelated clauses. She does not appear to have re-read what she wrote. Several times in the course of the *Life* she remarks that she may have mentioned something before. It does not seem to have occurred to her that she could have turned back to see. She never verified her dates, and frequently lost the thread of her narrative when following a digression of consuming interest. A few liberties, therefore, have had to be taken in this translation. Sometimes punctuation has been made to conform with sense, in defiance of the best scholarly readings; and sometimes a bare 'this' or 'that' has had to be expanded, since the subject to which it refers has not in fact been mentioned for several pages.

Although a natural writer and a mistress of metaphor, proverb, and telling image, Teresa was not yet, in this first of her works, expert in literary construction. While setting out to describe both the inner and the external events of her life, she was chiefly concerned to tell of her conversion to the contemplative life, at the age of forty, and her subsequent progress in it. She was not content, therefore, to follow a purely auto-biographical thread for very long. For the first ten chapters she does so, though without dwelling in great detail on any worldly event, or giving more than a passing description of the people she met. Proper names are very few, most of her friends being referred to merely as 'a cousin of mine', or 'a certain learned Jesuit who was then my confessor', or merely, 'a sister in the convent where I was'. Nevertheless these almost anonymous characters are frequently called to life in a single line.

Teresa was no cold intellectual, but quickly became involved in the life and problems of anyone with whom she came into touch. We see her compelling a priest who was living in sin to throw away the amulet with which his mistress had 'enchanted' him, and to set about mending his ways. We learn too, later in the book, of the alarm with which various other priests viewed her when they began to hear her confessions. They were very much afraid that she might become attached to them in the worldly sense: a suspicion which she found quite absurd. Yet many passages in her works and letters testify to the warmth of her affections, and right at the end of her life she was not ashamed to confess her deep disappointment when an old friend failed to accompany her on a journey. 'I must confess to you, Father,' she wrote to him, 'that the flesh is weak, and it has felt this more than I should have wished – in fact a great deal.'

When Teresa reached that point in her autobiography at which the contemplative life became her true vocation – the moment that she thought of as her second conversion – she broke off her narrative, and for a dozen chapters enlarged on the differences between the successive stages of mental prayer. This section of the book is built up about her famous simile of the 'Waters', and it is not until she has fully worked it out that she returns to the story of her life, to tell of her meeting with some Jesuits who were able to confirm the validity of her spiritual experiences, which all her previous confessors had called into question. But soon she is digressing again on the subject of 'locutions' (supernatural words that fall upon the inner ear with the authenticity of actual speech); and for five more chapters she deals exclusively with the inner life, not passing on until Chapter 29 to the story of her first foundation, that of the convent of St Joseph's, Ávila, and to the reforms that she inaugurated in the constitution of her own Discalced (or barefoot) branch of the Carmelite Order.

In Teresa's last eight chapters, the balance between outer and inner events is at last achieved, and we leave her, at the end of her book, seemingly bent on a life of austere withdrawal from the world. In fact, Teresa's *Life* ends just when she has passed the watershed between her years of spiritual endeavour and those in which she combined the religious life with one of great public activity. In these later years she wrote two books as great as the one before us: *The Foundations*, which tells the tale of her journeys and of the sixteen houses that she founded after St Joseph's, and *The Interior Castle*, otherwise called *The Mansions*, an analysis of inner prayer and spiritual states which is probably her masterpiece. But for readers who do not unquestioningly accept either Roman Catholic dogma or those beliefs about the religious life to which she subscribed, the autobiography is the more interesting and approachable book. In it we see how a self-willed and hysterically unbalanced woman, who seemed on the way to becoming a worldly nun of the conventional sort, was entirely transformed by profound experiences. At first she seems to have viewed her vows as no more than an insurance against the complete loss of her soul. This she feared as, when younger, she had feared the loss of her reputation. But, for the rest, the impulse which had driven her as a girl to the religious life had almost completely died away. How she gained strength to combat her own waywardness, and gradually grew, almost unaided by her ignorant confessors, to understand and assess the spiritual experiences that befell her, is the central theme of her book. One sees her impelled by forces that she could not even pretend to control; and as she describes them, one comes to understand something of their nature. For Teresa never failed to remember as she wrote those who were but beginners on the spiritual path along which she had progressed at so giddy a rate.

Teresa is, therefore, the best of the mystical writers for those who do not accept or understand the relationship between God and man that is assumed by the mystics of all ages and countries. She is careful to explain everything that she can, and she dwells longer on the early steps than on the later. Some of her writings are addressed to the novices of her convents, but here the audience that she has in mind is made up of those many priests and laymen of her acquaintance whose outward dignities had far outgrown their spiritual stature. It is for this reason that her *Life* has worn so well. Her pupil, St John of the Cross, is a more brilliant and poetic writer, possibly also a person of profounder religious experience, but he has little to say to the beginner; he is always on the heights.

Teresa begins with the picture of herself as one without any true vocation at all. As a young woman, she has attempted to advance in prayer from mere petitions and the recitation of the Office to the stage of inner contemplation. She had tried to calm her busy mind and to make contact with some deeper reality. But, working without help from anyone who had trodden this path before, she had failed lamentably. Attacked by vomiting, heart-spasms, cramps, and partial paralysis, and wracked by pains that were probably functional, not organic, she had been compelled to give up her spiritual exercises, to stop praying, and even temporarily to leave her convent in search of a cure. One may suspect that in her unguided ascetic practices she had subjected herself to undue strains, and that in her attitude to prayer in general, she had been grasping for results, in the shape of visions, locutions, and other 'sweetnesses', instead of working, as she afterwards learned to do, without thought of rewards. Her illness seems, at any rate, more readily explicable on these lines than in any strictly medical terms.

Teresa seems all her life to have been overwhelmed with a sense of her own wickedness, which may have contributed to her sorry state. This habit of self-reproach, which our century has learnt to think of as pathological, acts as a constant refrain to her writings. In every chapter she harps on her unworthiness. When she confesses at the opening of the book to such childish frivolities as a liking for scents and pretty clothes, to the enjoyment of gossip and the habit of seeking garrulous company, she comes near to alienating the modern reader's sympathy. If such disproportionate importance is to be attached to these slight and common failings, how inhumanly bleak the opening steps on the path to God must be! Then, when the Saint expresses her surprise that she still feels a worldly attachment to her sister, the twentieth century reader is likely to be more surprised still. To him it may seem that the spiritual life cannot, at least to-day, be lived in isolation from the world, its obligations and affections, and that what it demands is not a change of circumstances but a change of heart or attitude.

Teresa, as has been noted, was a woman of strong affections. Her family played a great part in her life, from her father to whom, in his last years, she dared not confess her defection from the life of prayer down to her niece, the little Teresa, who became one of her nuns at the age of sixteen, who accompanied her on some of her most difficult journeys, and who acted at the last as her secretary. Teresa's fight to free herself from worldly ties was hard and far from successful.

Her references to heretics too, to the rascally Lutherans who were, as she saw it, close allies of the devil, leave one aghast. The narrowness of her outlook was in no way less than that of the Inquisitors who were at that time condemning Jews to the stake for preferring their own faith, which had also produced its mystics, to Christianity, to which their fathers had been forcibly converted. Against such bigotry neither Teresa nor John of the Cross raised the least protest; nor did they even suspect that in the very cities where they walked Mohammedan mystics, less narrow and exclusive in their beliefs than they, had flourished in the days of the Moorish emirates.

2

It is necessary to discount those facets of Teresa's thought that divide her from the modern world, and also from the less dogmatic mystics of the East, from Plato and Plotinus, from the Greek Church fathers. If she had seen things in their way, Teresa would have incurred accusations of heresy, like those that had been levelled against the great fourteenth-century mystic, Meister Eckhart. She pursued her path close beneath the shadow of her Church's dogma, and by continually dwelling on it unconsciously shaped the imagery of her visions and locutions to suit its teaching. Often she protested that if her experience taught her one thing and the Church another, she was on the side of authority.

Clearly the visionary's mind must mould the ineffable forms that touch his inner eyes and ears; without some translation into the language of the discursive mind and the common emotions, they could not be expressed at all. Teresa uses the conventions most natural to her, those of the Counter-Reformation. When Christ appears to her he takes the form of some picture that she knows; and the little devils that she sends flying with splashes of holy water are the ugly little negroes that she had seen carved on pew-ends or on the capitals of columns. Her psychological understanding, on the other hand, is entirely authentic. In her analysis of those thoughts and imaginations whose perpetual stirring is a hindrance to visions, and in her symbolic explanation in terms of the different Waters of the emotional union that can take place between some depth within and some depth without–which is for her the soul's union with God–she is absolutely true to her experience. What her confessors had led her to expect were visions that appeared before the physical eye and words that struck the actual ear. But what she met with was nothing like this, and she said so. Again, she had been warned against the activities of the imagination, and many of her experiences had been condemned as imaginary, or even as temptations of devilish origins. But in her moments of rapture she was able to see the actual workings of her imagination and of her common intellect, at first stilled by the impact of this new state, but later returning and attempting to disrupt it. Teresa was a very acute analyst of exalted states, from whom one can learn a great deal about these tracts of the mind to-day lumped together under the general name of the *unconscious*. She knew what was genuine and what was not, and this she said too.

The *unconscious*, in its narrowest connotation, makes occasional incursions into Teresa's thoughts. There is that vision of hell as a narrow muddy passage leading to a cupboard in a wall, which is pure Kafka. Teresa was haunted by these hideous visions, as well as racked, throughout her life, by persistent symptoms of the disease that had nearly killed her as a young woman. But far more constantly she was transported into states far above those experienced by ordinary men. In these she knew, as if she had been told by God's own voice, what she should do and say in any situation. The foundation of St Joseph's was carried through under this divine inspiration, as was the writing of large parts of the *Life* and of her other works. She did not herself know how to explain her loftiest experiences, but left it to God to explain them through her. There are several descriptions by her fellow nuns of moments when they saw her with glowing features, writing as if at a heavenly dictation. But not all the supernatural states that possessed Teresa were equally welcome to her. She herself tells how, in prayer, she would be lifted into the air, to her own consternation and to the alarm of those sisters who were praying beside her in the choir.

These mysterious levitations were matched after her death by the equally mysterious incorruptibility of her body. Both are well-known phenomena which occur in the histories of many saints and that can only be accounted for by some actual change in the physical structure that takes place at the same time as spiritual transformation. In Teresa's case the fragrance that surrounded her uncorrupted body led to most dis-graceful results. In the wild rush to acquire sacred relics, various of her limbs were torn from her corpse. Her old friend Father Gracián, who had only lately so disappointed her by failing to accompany her on a journey, inaugurated her dismemberment by cutting off one of her hands.

3

The events of Santa Teresa's life up to her fiftieth year are set out, though not with perfect accuracy, in the autobiography. A few facts and dates, therefore, are needed to make clear many points that she left imprecise. She was born in the neighbourhood of the little, walled Castilian town of Ávila, which had been a Christian stronghold in the Moorish wars, on 28 March 1515, and named Teresa Sánchez de Cepeda y Ahumada. She was of mixed Jewish and Christian blood, her grandfather Juan Sánchez of Toledo being a relapsed Jewish convert. She was one of a large family, the daughter of her father's second wife. Of her mother's early death, her sister's marriage, and her entry as a boarder, at the age of sixteen, into the school run by the local Augustinian sisters, we are told in the autobiography. She was probably twenty-one when she took the Carmelite habit, and for about twenty years after that engaged in a continuous 'strife and contention between converse with God and the society of the world'. Her resulting breakdown in health is fully described by herself. At twenty-five, she seems to have been a complete invalid, and it was not till she was forty that the principal symptoms of her malady disappeared. Some time during this interval she found, as she tells us, the work of Francisca de Osuna, a Spanish Franciscan who was her contemporary though twenty years her senior, on the practice of that first stage of the contemplative life, the prayer of quiet. But at the time of her father's death in 1543, she seems, at least temporarily, to have abandoned her efforts to achieve it. It was not till 1555, when she was already forty, that some new and sporadic attempts bore fruit. It was then that she first read St Augustine's *Confessions*, which threw light for her on her own experiences, and it was at this time that she began to meet the Jesuits who had just established a college at Ávila.

Teresa's arguments with her old confessors, this acquiring of new friends, her advance to the stage of 'intellectual vision', and the beginnings of her Reform movement, which fill the years from 1557 to 1562, are fully described in the autobiography, which also says something about the processes of its composition. It was, as has been said, completed in its final form by the end of 1565, and on its last pages she speaks of her life as passing as if in a dream. Her supernormal experiences were the reality, and outward events moved her not at all. Her dearest concern seems to have been the instruction of her thirteen nuns at St Joseph's, for whom she composed her second book, *The Way of Perfection*. At the same time, also, she began to write more fully of her early spiritual development in a series of 'Relations', intended, like the *Life*, to be read by her confessors.

In the year 1567 Teresa was impelled to continue with her work of reformation and to begin a series of new foundations, the last of which was to be made in the last months of her life. Far from retiring into a life of contemplation, she was violently projected into one of great activity. But just as she had positively known it to be God's will that St Joseph's should be founded and flourish despite every obstacle, so she was filled with the certainty that the growth of the Discalced Carmelite Order and its eventual separation from the Unreformed Order was a divinely ordained task. The difficulties that she met were even greater than those of her first foundation; her strength in combating them even more flint-like. The tale of this work, of the countless difficulties encountered and the repeated journeys involved is told in her *Book of Foundations* and further illustrated by the many letters that have been preserved from this period of her life. From that covered by the autobiography hardly any survive, but from 1573 onwards she was in constant correspondence with a number of ecclesiastics, with nuns of her Order, and with certain great men and ladies to whom she looked for help in the form of endowments and assistance in combating the attacks which she and her Order sustained. Most of these were at the hands of conservative churchmen, but on one occasion she found an even more difficult enemy in the shape of a famous benefactor. The Princess of Eboli, a rich woman of dubious morals who was reputed to be the King's mistress, wrecked one of Teresa's houses by taking up her residence there in a fit of hysterical grief at the death of her husband. Teresa and her nuns were forced to retire.

The writing of the *Foundations* was followed by that of *The Interior Castle*, an amplification of those chapters in the *Life* that describe the progress of the soul in terms of the various 'Waters'. This book, which develops another metaphor, that of the soul's seven 'Mansions', is more mature in its experience than the *Life*, and more uniform in its composition. It was written at great speed in 1577, as the outcome of a vision that came to Teresa on Trinity Eve of that year.

From 1568 onwards Teresa was greatly strengthened by the formation of a company of Discalced friars who accepted her reform, chief among whom was her friend and pupil Juan de Yepes (1542–91), known to us as St John of the Cross. He became spiritual director of St Joseph's in 1572, but was seized and thrown into prison by his Unreformed brothers a year later. He was subjected to great hardships, and remained in captivity for fourteen years. Teresa herself was on occasions forced to resort to the highest authority in the land, Philip II himself, to save herself from similar treatment. The Unreformed Carmelites fought hard with ecclesiastical backing to suppress the Discalced, but Rome and the Court, as well as several grandees, were on Teresa's side.

Teresa's dealings were throughout her life chiefly with the great, to whom she stood up as an equal. Despite her initial reluctance to take office or responsibility, once she did so she prided herself on her reputation as a sound organizer and a good business woman. When negotiating a site for one of her new foundations she was careful to guard against any possible interference from the landlord that might one day endanger the prioress's freedom of action; and in attracting and selecting novices with sufficient dowries to put her nunneries on a sound footing, she was careful not to incur any passengers in the spiritual sense. Every one of her nuns, she said, must be fit to be a prioress.

Teresa was not only a sound woman of business, but also a born intriguer; and one can still see the delight with which, during the persecution of her Reformed houses, she would coin fictitious names for her friends, in case her letters should fall into the hands of the Unreformed faction; whom she calls the 'grasshoppers', in contrast to her own Order, the 'butterflies'. But nowhere, even at the height of her troubles, does she show, in her letters or in the *Foundations*, any hint of malice or any real hatred of her rivals. True, when exposing some tale of spiritual malingering on the part of a nun, or some attempt to gain more than her share of her superior's attention, she will speak of her own malicious nature. But even when she is most ruthless in her criticism of her 'daughters', or in combating some hostile ecclesiastic, she never indulges in those personal spites and slanderings that are the current coin of worldly rivalries.

'One of the things that makes me happy here,' she wrote from her foundation at Seville, 'is that there is no suggestion of that nonsense about my supposed sanctity. That allows me to live and go about without fear that the ridiculous tower of their imagination will come tumbling down on top of me.' A year or two later she is congratulating herself on *just* beginning to be a true nun.

Nevertheless the world persisted in believing that Teresa was a saint, and in 1622, a bare forty-five years after her death, she was canonized. In 1814, when Spain, with the help of its English allies, was driving out its French conquerors, she was proclaimed the national saint of her country.

4

The *Life* was first published together with other works of Teresa's in 1588, under the editorship of the poet and religious writer Luis de León. Two translations into English were made by Roman Catholic exiles in the seventeenth century, and one in the nineteenth century by David Lewis. The most recent and most authoritative, which follows the authoritative Spanish texts, is that of the late E. Allison Peers, which forms the greater part of a volume of his *Complete Works of Santa Teresa*. But, hitherto, the book has not been available in England in a cheap or handy form. The best biographies of Santa Teresa are Allison Peers' short sketch *Mother of Carmel* (S.C.M. Press, 1945) and an ampler French work by Michelle Auclair which has been translated as *Saint Teresa of Avila* (Burns Oates, 1953). Allison Peers' two-volume edition of the *Letters* (Burns Oates, 1951), however, probably makes even more lively biographical reading.

May 1956   J. M. C.

T HE LIFE OF THE HOLY MOTHER TERESA
    of Jesus and some of the favours granted to her by God, written
by herself at the command of her confessor, to whom she submits and
directs it, in the following words:

Having been commanded and left at full liberty to describe my way
of prayer and the favours which the Lord has granted me, I wish that I
had been allowed to describe also, clearly and in full detail, my grave
sins and the wickedness of my life. This would have been a great comfort to me, but I may not do so. In fact, I have been put under severe
restrictions in the matter. So I beg anyone who reads this account to
bear in mind, for the love of the Lord, how wicked my life has been –
so wicked, indeed that among all the Saints who have turned to God I
can find none whose history affords me any comfort. For I see that, once
the Lord called them, they never fell back into sin. I, however, not only
fell back and became worse, but seem deliberately to have sought ways
of resisting the favours which His Majesty granted me. For I knew that
I was obliged to serve Him, and realized that, of myself, I could not
pay the least part of the debt I owed Him.

May He be blessed for ever who waited for me so long. I pray Him
with all my heart for the grace to write this account that my confessor
demands of me both truthfully and with complete clarity. The Lord,
too, I know, has long desired that it should be written, but I have never
been bold enough to begin. May it be to His glory and praise; and may
it lead my confessors to know me better, and so help me in my weakness
that I may be able to render some part of the service that I owe to the
Lord. May all things praise Him for ever. Amen.

CHAPTER I

How the Lord began to rouse her soul in childhood to a love of virtue,
and what a help it is in this respect to have good parents

IF I had not been so wicked, the possession of devout and God-fearing parents, together with the favour of God's grace, would have been enough to make me good. My father was fond of reading holy books, and had some in Spanish so that his children might read them too. These, and the pains my mother took in teaching us to pray and educating us in devotion to Our Lady and certain Saints, began to rouse me at the age, I think, of six or seven. It was a help to me that I never saw my parents inclined to anything but virtue, and many virtues they had. My father was most charitable to the poor, and most compassionate to the sick, also to his servants; so much so that he could never be persuaded to keep slaves. He felt such pity for them that when a slave-girl of his brother's was, on one occasion, staying in his house, he treated her like one of his own children. He said that he could not bear the pain of seeing her not free. He was an extremely truthful man, and was never heard to swear or speak slander. He was also most rigid in his chastity.

My mother too was a woman of many virtues, who endured a life of great sickness, and was extremely modest. Although she possessed remarkable beauty, she never showed the least signs of setting any store by it. Although she died at thirty-three, she already dressed like a woman advanced in years. She was very calm, and of great understanding. Throughout her life she endured severe sufferings, and she died in a most Christian manner.

We were three sisters and nine brothers, and all, by God's mercy, took after our parents in virtue, except myself, though I was my father's favourite. And before I began to sin against God I think he had some reason to cherish me particularly. Indeed, it saddens me to remember the good propensities with which the Lord endowed me, and what bad use I managed to make of them. For my brothers and sisters never stood in the way of my serving God.

I had one brother almost of my own age,[1] whom I loved best, though I was very fond of them all and they of me. We used to read the lives of

1. Rodrigo, who was four years her senior.

the Saints together, and when I read of the martyrdoms which they suffered for the love of God, I used to think that they had bought their entry into God's presence very cheaply. Then I fervently longed to die like them, not out of any conscious love for Him, but in order to attain as quickly as they had those joys which, as I read, are laid up in Heaven. I used to discuss with my brother ways and means of becoming martyrs, and we agreed to go together to the land of the Moors, begging our way for the love of God, so that we might be beheaded there. I believe that our Lord had given us courage enough even at that tender age, if only we could have seen a way. But our having parents seemed to us a very great hindrance.

We were astonished when we were told that pain and bliss will last for ever; and very often we would discuss this saying. We took great pleasure in repeating over and over again: 'For ever, for ever and ever'. Through this constant repetition it pleased the Lord that the way of truth should be impressed upon my mind even in my earliest childhood.

As soon as I saw that it was impossible to go anywhere where I should be put to death for God's sake, we decided to become hermits; and we used to try very hard to build hermits' cells in an orchard belonging to the house. We used to pile up heaps of small stones, but they immediately tumbled down again, and so we found no way of achieving our desires. But even now it puts me into a state of devotion to see how early God gave me what I subsequently lost through my own fault. I gave alms, to the small extent of my powers. I contrived to be alone, in order to say my prayers, which were many. I was especially fond of telling my beads, a favourite practice of my mother's in which we naturally imitated her. When I was with other girls I especially enjoyed playing at nunneries, and pretending to be nuns; and I think I wanted to be one, though not so much as I wanted the other things I have mentioned.

I remember that when my mother died I was a little under twelve; and when I began to realize my loss, I went in my distress to an image of Our Lady and, weeping bitterly, begged her to be my mother. Though I did this in my simplicity, I believe that I benefited by it. For whenever I have turned to the supreme Virgin I have always been conscious of her aid, and in the end she brought me back to herself. It distresses me now to see that I did not persist in the good desires with which I began, and also to reflect on the reasons.

O my Lord, since You seem determined that I shall be saved – and may it be Your Majesty's pleasure that I am – and since You seem resolved to grant me as many graces as You have done, might You not have found it good – not for my gain but for Your own honour – that this habitation in which You have had to dwell for so long, should have been less greatly defiled? It distresses me, Lord, even to say this, since I know that all the blame has been mine. I do not think that You left anything undone to make me Yours entirely, even from my youth.

Nor could I complain of my parents, even if I felt inclined to do so. For I saw nothing in them that was not entirely good and devoted to my welfare. But as I grew older and began to be aware of the natural graces with which the Lord had endowed me, – and people said that they were many – instead of giving Him thanks for them, I began to use them all, as I shall now relate, to offend against Him.

CHAPTER 2

*How she came gradually to lose these virtues, and of the importance of
associating in childhood with good people*

WHAT I am about to describe is something which, I believe, began
to do me great harm. I sometimes think how wrong it is of
parents not to contrive that their children shall always and in every way
see only what is good. For though my mother was, as I have said, extremely good herself, when I came to the age of reason I did not imitate
her goodness as much as I might have done – indeed, I hardly did so at
all – and evil things did me a great deal of harm. She was very fond of
books of chivalry, and this amusement did not have the bad effect on her
that it came to have on me, because she never neglected her duties for
it. But we were always making time for reading, and she let us, perhaps
in order to distract her mind from her great sufferings, or perhaps
merely for the sake of amusing her children and keeping them from
pursuing other wickednesses. This habit of ours so annoyed my father
that we had to take care he never saw us with our books. But I began
to become addicted to this reading, and this little fault, which I had
observed in my mother, began to chill my desires and to lead me astray
in other respects as well. It did not seem wicked to me to waste many
hours of the day and the night on this vain occupation, even though I
had to keep it secret from my father; and I was so enthralled by it that
I do not believe I was ever happy if I had not a new book.

I began to wear finery, and to wish to charm by my appearance. I
took great care of my hands and my hair, using perfumes and all the
vanities I could obtain – and I obtained plenty of them, for I was very
persistent. I had no bad intentions, for I should never have wished anyone to sin against God because of me. This excessive care for my appearance, together with other practices which I did not think wicked,
lasted for many years, and now I see how wrong they must have been.
I had some cousins, who were the only people allowed to enter my
father's house. He was very careful about this, and would to God he
had been careful about them too. For I now see the danger of conversation, at an age when the virtues should be beginning to grow, with
those who do not recognize the vanity of the world, but encourage
one to give oneself up to it. They were about my own age, or a little

older. We always went about together, and they were very fond of me. I kept conversing with them about everything that pleased them, and I heard their accounts of their affections and follies, which were anything but edifying. What was worse, my soul became exposed to what has been the cause of all its troubles.

If parents were to ask me for advice, I would tell them to take great care what people their children consort with at this age. For great harm comes of bad company, since we are inclined by nature to follow the worse rather than the better. So it was with me. I had a sister many years older than I, from whose modesty and goodness – of which she had plenty – I learnt nothing, whereas from a relative who often visited us I learnt every kind of evil. Her conversation was so frivolous that my mother had tried her hardest to prevent her coming to the house. She seems to have realized what harm this person might do me. But there were so many pretexts for these visits that my mother was powerless. I loved the company of this person. I often talked and gossiped with her, for she helped me to get all the amusements I was so fond of, and even introduced me to some others. She also told me about her friends and own pastimes. Until I knew her, and I was then a little more than fourteen – I mean until we became friends and she took me into her confidence – I do not believe that I had ever turned away from God in mortal sin, or lost my fear of Him. But I was much more afraid for my good name, and this last fear gave me strength enough never entirely to forfeit it. Indeed I do not think that I should have wavered in this resolution for anything in the world, or that there was anyone in the world for whom I felt such love that I could have been persuaded to surrender it. So since my natural inclination led me to defend everything that seemed to touch my good name, I might have had strength enough not to smirch the honour of God. But I did not see that I was losing my honour in quite a different way. In my vain anxiety to protect it I went to great extremes. Yet I took none of the steps necessary for its preservation. All that really concerned me was that I should not altogether ruin my good name.

My father and sister were most upset by this friendship, and very often took me to task. But as they could not prevent this person from coming to the house their efforts were of no avail, for I was clever at doing what was wrong. I am sometimes astonished at the harm which a single bad companion can do, and if I had no experience in the matter I should never believe it. This is particularly so when one is young, for then the evil effects are worst. I wish that parents would take warning by me, and consider this very carefully. As a result of my intercourse with this person, I was so changed that I lost nearly all my soul's natural disposition to virtue, so influenced was I by her and by another who was given to the same kind of amusements.

From this I have learned what a great advantage is to be derived from good company; and I am quite certain that if at that age I had been friendly with good people, I should have persisted in virtue. For if when I was so young I had found anyone to teach me the fear of God, my soul would have grown strong enough not to fall. Afterwards, when I lost this fear altogether, only the concern for my honour remained, and was a torment to me in all that I did. When I thought that no one need ever know, I risked many things which were both dishonourable and sins against God.

I believe that my conversations with her harmed me from the start. But the fault must have been mine rather than hers. For afterwards my own wickedness was enough, abetted by the servants about me, whom I found disposed to help in any wrongdoing. Perhaps, if any of them had given me good advice I might have availed myself of it. But self-interest blinded them as passion blinded me. And yet I was never inclined to much evil, since I naturally loathed anything immodest, and preferred to spend my time in good company. However, when the occasion offered danger was at hand, and I exposed my father and brothers to it. From all this God delivered me, however, even though it was against my will. Thanks to Him I was not entirely lost, but my escape was not so secret as to prevent my damaging my reputation and arousing my father's suspicions.

I could not have been pursuing these vanities for more than three months when they took me to a convent[1] in the city where I lived, in which girls like myself were educated, though there were none there as depraved as I. The reason for this move was, however, so disguised that it was known only to one or two of my relatives and myself. They waited for a moment when it would arouse no surprise; and this came after my sister's wedding,[2] when it would not have been right for me to stay at home without a mother.

So great was my father's love for me and so complete my dissimula-

1. An Augustinian convent, just outside the walls of Ávila.
2. Doña Maria, an elder half-sister, married Don Martín de Guzman y Barríentos.

tion that he could not believe me to be so wicked, and so I was never in disgrace with him. It had been going on for such a short time that although something had leaked out nothing could be said with certainty; as I was so afraid for my reputation, I had taken every care to be secret. But I did not see that I could conceal nothing from Him who sees all things. O my God, what evil is done in the world by forgetfulness of this, and in the belief that anything done against You can be concealed! I am certain that great evils could be avoided if we could understand that our business is not to be on our guard against men but against displeasing You.

For the first week I suffered greatly, but more from the suspicion that my frivolities were known than from my being in a convent. For I was now weary of wrong-doing, and had never ceased to be much afraid of God even when I sinned against Him; and I had always contrived to make a speedy confession. At first I was very restless, but in a week, or rather less, I felt much happier than in my father's house. All the sisters were pleased with me, for the Lord gave me the grace of pleasing wherever I might be. So I was made much of, and though I was then bitterly averse to taking the habit, yet I was delighted to see nuns who were so good. For they were all very good in that convent, most pure and observant and modest in their behaviour.

In spite of this, the devil did not cease to tempt me, and my friends outside tried to disturb me by sending me messages. But since this was not allowed, they soon stopped. Then my soul began to get used once more to the good habits of my childhood, and I saw what a mercy God does to those whom He puts in the company of good people. His Majesty seems to have been seeking and seeking how He could bring me back to Himself. Bless you, Lord, for having suffered so much from me! Amen.

There was one thing that might, I think, have provided me with some excuse, if I had not had so many faults; and that was that this friend with whom I was intimate was a person who would, I thought, greatly improve upon marriage. When I consulted the priest who confessed me and some other persons, they told me that in many respects I was not offending God. There was a nun who slept with us seculars, and through her, it seems, the Lord chose to give me the beginnings of light, as I shall now relate.

29

CHAPTER 3

*How good company reawakened her desires, and how God began to
shed some light for her on the illusions under which she laboured*

As I began to enjoy this nun's good and holy conversation, I was
gladdened by the eloquent way in which she spoke of God, for she
was a very sensible and saintly woman. I think that there was never an
occasion when I did not delight to listen to her. She began by telling me
how she had come to be a nun, merely through reading the words of the
Gospel: 'Many be called but few chosen'.[1] She spoke to me of the
reward which the Lord gives to those who forsake everything for Him.
Her good company began to dispel the habits which bad company had
formed in me, to bring back to my mind the desire for eternal things,
and somewhat to rid me of my antipathy towards taking the veil,
which had been very great indeed. If I saw anyone weep as she prayed,
or show any other sign of a good state, I envied her extremely. For my
heart was so hard in this respect that even if I had read the whole
Passion through I should not have shed a tear; and this was a grief
to me.

I stayed in this nunnery for a year and a half, and was much the better
for it. I began to recite frequent prayers, and to ask everyone to pray to
God for me, that He might put me in that place where I might serve
Him. But I was still most anxious not to be a nun, for God had not yet
been pleased to give me this desire, though I was afraid of marriage also.
However, at the end of my stay there I was more inclined to take the
veil, though not in that house, on account of certain devotional practices which prevailed there. I observed these during the latter part of my
stay, and they seemed to me altogether excessive. Some of the younger
sisters encouraged me in this feeling; if all the nuns had been of the same
mind it would have been greatly to my profit. But I had also a close
friend[2] in another convent, and this made me decide that, if I was to be
a nun, it should be nowhere but in the house where she was. I was more
intent on the gratification of my senses and my vanity than on the good
of my soul. These good thoughts of entering religion came to me every

1. Matthew xx, 16.
2. Doña Juana Suárez, a nun of the Convent of the Incarnation, where
Santa Teresa afterwards professed.

now and then, and quickly departed. I could not make up my mind to act on them.

Although I was not careless of my own good during this time, the Lord was much more anxious than I to place me in that state which would be best for me. He sent me a serious illness, which compelled me to return to my father's house, and when I was better they took me to stay with my sister, who lived in a country village. She was extremely fond of me, and if she had had her way I should never have left her. Her husband was very fond of me too – or, at least, he showed me every kindness. This also I owe to the Lord, for I have received kindnesses everywhere – and all the service that I have done Him in return is to be what I am!

One of my father's brothers[1] lived on the way there, a sensible and most excellent man, then a widower, whom the Lord was also preparing for Himself. In his old age he gave up all his possessions and became a friar; and he made such an end that I believe he now dwells in the presence of God. This uncle insisted on my staying with him for some days. It was his practice to read good books in Spanish, and his everyday conversation was of God and the vanity of this world. He made me read these books to him, and though I did not much like them I pretended to. For I have always been most scrupulous in pleasing others, even when complaisance may have been painful to me; so much so that what would have been a virtue in others has been a great failing in me, for I have behaved most unwisely on occasions. O God, in how many ways did Your Majesty set about preparing me for the state in which He wished me to serve Him! Thus, without my willing it, the Lord compelled me to do violence to myself. Blessed be He for ever! Amen.

Although I remained only a few days with my uncle, yet thanks to the impression which the words of God, both heard and read, made upon my heart, and thanks to his good conversation, I began to understand the truth which I had heard as a child, that all is nothing, and that the world is vanity which quickly passes away. I began to fear that, if I had died of that illness, I should have gone to hell; and although I could not, even then, make up my mind to take the habit, I saw that the religious state was the best and safest; and so, gradually, I decided to make myself enter it.

I fought this battle for three months, urging this argument against

1. Don Pedro, who lived at Hortegosa, on the road to Castellanos.

myself: that the trials and hardships of the religious life could not be greater than those of purgatory; that I had thoroughly earned the pains of hell; that it would be a trifle to spend such time as I might live as though I were in purgatory, and that afterwards I should go straight to Heaven, which was my desire. In this intention of taking the habit I was more influenced by servile fear, I believe, than by love. The devil put it to me that because I had been so pampered, I should not be capable of enduring the rigours of the convent. I defended myself by citing the trials endured by Christ, and argued that it would be a small thing if I were to suffer a few for Him. I must have thought too that He would help me to bear them, but I have no memory of this last consideration. During that time I endured considerable temptations.

I had now become subject to severe fainting fits attended by fever, for I had always had very poor health. But I got fresh life from my continued fondness for good books. I would read the Epistles of Saint Jerome, which gave me such courage that I resolved to speak to my father of my resolve, which was almost like taking the habit. For I set such store by my word that I should never, I believe, on any account have turned back, once I had announced my intention. My father, however, was so fond of me that I was quite unable to obtain his consent; nor were the entreaties of others, whom I asked to speak to him, of the least avail. The most that I could get from him was that I could do as I liked after his death. I now began to distrust myself and my own weakness, and to fear that I might turn back. This delay seemed to me dangerous, and so I achieved my aims in another way, as I shall now relate.

CHAPTER 4

How the Lord helped her to force herself to take the habit, and of the
many illnesses which His Majesty began to send her

DURING the time that I was harbouring these resolutions, I persuaded one of my brothers, by talking to him of the vanity of
the world, to become a friar;[1] and we arranged together to go very
early one morning to the convent where that friend of mine was, of
whom I was so fond, though now, in my final determination, I would
have gone to any other where I thought I could best serve God, or
which my father might choose. For I set most store now by the salvation of my soul, and thought nothing of my comfort. I remember – and
I think that this is true – that when I left my father's house I felt such
dreadful distress that the pain of death itself cannot be worse. Every
bone in my body seemed to be wrenched asunder. For as I had no love
for God to subdue my love for my father and relatives, the whole action
did me such violence that, if the Lord had not helped me, my resolution
would not have been enough to push me forward. But here He gave me
courage to fight myself, and so I carried it through.

When I took the habit[2] the Lord immediately showed me how He
favours those who do violence to themselves in order to serve Him. No
one saw what I endured, or thought that I acted out of anything but
pure desire. At the moment of my entrance into this new state I felt a
joy so great that it has never failed me even to this day; and God converted the dryness of my soul into a very great tenderness. All the details
of the religious life delighted me. In fact sometimes when I used to
sweep the house at hours that I had once spent on my indulgence and
adornment, the memory that I was now free from these things gave me
a fresh joy, which surprised me, for I could not understand where it
came from.

When I remember this freedom, there is no task, however hard, that
I would hesitate to undertake if it were put before me. For now I know
from plentiful experience that if I resolutely persist in a purpose from
the beginning, and it is done for God's sake only, His Majesty rewards

1. Her younger brother Antonio, who became a Dominican.
2. At the Convent of the Incarnation, outside the walls of Ávila, on 3 Nov-
ember 1536, when she was twenty-one.

me even in this life in ways which only one who has known their joys can understand. In such cases, even before we begin, it is His will that the soul, for the increase of its merits, shall be afraid. Then the greater the fear, the greater and the sweeter the subsequent reward will be if we succeed. This I know from experience, as I have said, on many very serious occasions; and so if ever I were to be asked for an opinion, I would recommend anyone to whom a good inspiration repeatedly comes, never to neglect it out of fear. If he turns nakedly to God alone, he need not be afraid of failure, since God is all-powerful. May He be blessed for ever! Amen.

O my supreme Good! O my Rest! The graces that You had granted me till then should have been enough, seeing that Your compassion and greatness had brought me along so many devious ways to so secure a state, and to a house where there were so many servants of God from whom I might have learnt how to advance in Your service. When I remember the manner of my profession, the great resolution and joy with which I made it, and my betrothal to You, I do not know how to go on. I cannot speak of this without tears. Indeed they should be of blood and my heart should break, and that would be a slight repentance for all the offences I have committed against You since then. It seems to me now that I had good reason for not desiring this great honour, since I was to make very poor use of it. But You, my Lord, were prepared for me to misuse Your grace for almost twenty years, and to accept the injury so that I might become better. It seems, O God, as if I had promised to break all the promises I had made You, though this was not my intention at the time. When I look back on these actions of mine I do not know what my intentions were. But what they clearly reveal, O my Spouse, is the difference between You and myself. My joy at having been the means whereby the multitude of Your mercies has been made known certainly moderates my sorrow for my great sins. In whom, Lord, can those mercies shine out as they do in me, who thus obscured the great graces that You began to work in me by my evil deeds? Alas, O my Creator, if I try to offer an excuse, I have none. No one is to blame but I. If I had repaid You any of the love that You were beginning to show me, I could have since bestowed it on no one but You, and with that all would have been made well. But since I did not deserve it, and had no such good fortune, may Your mercy avail me now, O Lord!

The change in my life and diet affected my health; and even though I was very happy, 'that was not enough. My fainting fits began to become more frequent, and I suffered from such pains in the heart that everyone who saw them was alarmed. I had also many other ailments. I spent my first year, therefore, in a very bad state of health, though I do not think I offended God much during that time. As my condition was so serious that I was usually semi-conscious and sometimes lost consciousness altogether, my father took great pains to find some remedy; and as the local doctors could offer none, he arranged for me to be taken to a town[1] that had a great reputation for the curing of other diseases, and where they said that mine could be cured too. The friend whom I spoke of as being in the house, and who was one of the elder nuns, was able to go with me, since we were under no vow of enclosure. I stayed in that town for almost a year, and for three months of it suffered the greatest tortures from the remedies they applied to me, which were so drastic that I do not know how I endured them. In fact, though I did endure them, they were too much for my constitution, as I shall relate. My cure was to start at the beginning of summer, and I had left the convent as winter set in. The intervening time I spent with that sister of whom I have spoken,[2] in her house in the country, waiting for the month of April. For she lived only a short distance from that town, and I did not want to go away and come back again.

On my way I visited that uncle of mine whom I have mentioned,[3] whose house was on the road, and he gave me a book, called *The Third Alphabet*,[4] which contains lessons in the prayer of recollection. Although in my first year I had read good books – indeed I would not touch any others, since I knew what harm they had done me – I did not know how to practise prayer or how to recollect myself. So I was delighted with this book, and decided to follow its instructions with all my strength. Since the Lord had already given me the gift of tears and I liked reading, I began to spend time in solitude, to confess frequently, and to start on the way of prayer, with this book as my guide. For I found no other guide – no confessor I mean, – who understood me, though I sought one for the next twenty years. This did me great harm, for I very often fell back and might have been utterly lost, and a guide would at least have helped me to avoid the frequent risks I ran of offending God.

In these early days His Majesty began to grant me such great favours that, at the end of my time there, which amounted to some nine months

1. Becedas.   2. Doña María.   3. Don Pedro.
4. By the Franciscan, Francisco de Osuna, published at Burgos in 1537.

of solitude, although I was not so free of sin against God as the book demanded, nevertheless I passed that over. Utter scrupulousness seemed to me almost impossible. I guarded against committing any mortal sin – and would to God I had always done so – but I paid little attention to venial sins, and that was what undid me. Still the Lord began to be so gracious to me on this path as to raise me sometimes to the prayer of quiet, and occasionally to that of union, though I did not understand what either of these was, or how highly I should have valued them. If I had understood this, I think it would have been a great blessing to me. It is true that my experience of union lasted only for a short time; I do not know whether it was even for the length of an *Ave Maria*. But it left such an effect behind that, although I was not then twenty,[1] I seemed to feel the world far below me, and I remember pitying those who followed its ways even on their lawful pursuits. I tried as hard as I could to bring the presence of Jesus Christ, our Lord and our Good, into my heart; and this was my method of prayer. If I thought of any incident in His life, I represented it to myself within me, though what still gave me most pleasure was the reading of good books, which was my only recreation. For the Lord did not give me a talent for intellectual meditation or for making use of the imagination. My imagination is so sluggish that however hard I tried to think of or picture Our Lord's human presence – and I tried very hard – I never succeeded.

Now although, if they persevere, men may arrive more quickly at contemplation along this road where they cannot work with the intellect, it is a very laborious and painful one. For if the will is left without employment, and love has no present object to occupy it, the soul remains without support or activity, solitude and dryness give great pain, and stray thoughts attack most fiercely. People who are made like this need a greater purity of consciousness than those who can work with the intellect. If a man can reflect on the nature of the world, on his debt to God, on Our Lord's great sufferings, on his own small service in return, and on what He gives to those who love Him, he gets material with which to defend himself against stray thoughts, also against perils and occasions for sin. But anyone who cannot make use of this method runs a far greater risk, and should frequently resort to reading, since he can get help in no other way. Indeed inability to get this help is so very painful that if the master directing him forbids him to read, and thus help himself towards recollection, he will still need to make some small

1. This must be a mistake: she must have been twenty-three at the time.

use of books as a substitute for mental prayer, which he is unable to practise. But if the director insists on his spending great periods at prayer without the aid of reading, he will not be able to persist for long. His health would suffer if he were to do so, for this is a most painful process.

It seems to me now that it was by God's providence that I did not find anyone to teach me. For I believe it would have been impossible for me to persevere for the eighteen years during which I suffered this trial and these great aridities, through not being able, as I have said, to meditate. All that time, except immediately after taking Communion, I never ventured to start praying without a book. My soul was as much afraid to engage in prayer without one, as if it had to fight against a host. With this protection, which was like a companion and a shield on which to take the blows of my many thoughts, I found comfort, for I was not generally in aridity. But always when I was without a book, my soul would at once become disturbed, and my thoughts wandered. As I read, I began to call them together again and, as it were, laid a bait for my soul. Very often I had to do no more than open a book. Sometimes I read a little, sometimes much, according to the favour which the Lord showed me.

It seemed to me, in these beginnings that I am describing, that if I had books and could be alone, there was no danger that could deprive me of this great blessing. I believe that, with God's favour, this would have been the case, if I had had a master or someone who could have warned me to flee temptations at the beginning, or who could have helped me out of them when I entered a little way in. If the devil had attacked me openly then, I do not think I should have fallen into any grievous sin. But he was so subtle and I was so weak that all my resolutions were of little use. Nevertheless those days in which I had served God were of great profit to me; they helped me to bear the terrible infirmities that came to me with all the patience that I had received from Him.

I have often reflected with amazement on God's great goodness, and my soul has rejoiced in the thought of His magnificence and His mercy. May He be blessed for all this, for as I clearly see, He has never failed to reward me, even in this life, for any good desire. Poor and imperfect as my works have been, this Lord of mine has improved and perfected them, and has increased their value. As for my wickednesses and sins, He has immediately hidden them away. He has even allowed the eyes of those who have seen them to be blind to them, and has expunged them from their memory. He gilds my faults and makes some virtue shine that He himself has given me, almost compelling me to possess it.

I must now return to what I have been commanded. But, indeed, if I had to relate in detail the way in which the Lord dealt with me in those early days, I should need a better understanding than my own, with which to appreciate what I owe Him for this, also my own ingratitude and wickedness; all of which I have forgotten. May He be blessed for ever who has endured so much from me! Amen.

CHAPTER 5

She continues to speak of the great infirmities that she suffered, of the patience which the Lord gave her, and of how she derived good out of evil, as will be seen from one incident which happened in the town where she went to be cured

I FORGOT to say that in the year of my novitiate I suffered long periods of disturbance about things which were of little importance in themselves. I was very often blamed when I was not at fault. This much distressed me, and I bore it very imperfectly, though in my great joy at being a nun I could put up with everything. When they saw me seeking solitude and sometimes weeping for my sins, they thought that I was discontented and said so.

I had a fondness for all religious observances, but I could not bear anything that seemed to make me look small. I delighted in being well thought of, and was particular about all that I did; and all this seemed to me a virtue, though that will not serve me for an excuse, for I knew how to get my own pleasure out of everything, and so my wrong-doing cannot be excused by ignorance. The imperfect constitution of the convent does, however, offer some excuse. But, in my wickedness, I followed what I saw was wrong and neglected what was good.

There was then a nun in the house who was afflicted with a most serious and painful disease. She suffered from open sores on her stomach, which were caused by obstructions, and through which she discharged all that she ate. She very soon died of this. Now I saw that all the sisters were frightened by her disease, but for my part I only envied her her patience, and prayed God to send me any sickness He pleased provided He sent me as much patience with it. I do not think I was afraid of any affliction, for so set was I on gaining my eternal good that I was resolved to gain it in any way whatever. This amazes me, since I had not yet, I think, that love of God which I seem to have had ever since I began to pray. What I had was a light by which everything transitory seemed of small account, and the blessings that could be gained by despising the things of this world seemed of great value since these blessings are eternal. Well, His Majesty heard my prayer, and within two years I too was ill, though my illness was quite unlike that nun's. Yet I do not think that the complaint from which I suffered for the next three years was any less painful or hard to bear. Of this I will not speak.

When the time came that I was waiting for in the town that I mentioned – I was at my sister's awaiting my treatment – they took me off with the greatest care for my comfort – my father, that is, my sister and the nun who was my friend and had left the convent with me, because she was so fond of me. Now the devil began to disturb my soul, though God turned this trial into a great blessing. There lived in the place where I had gone for my treatment a priest of very good birth and understanding, who had also some learning, though only a little. I began to confess with him, for I have always been attracted by learning, though half-educated confessors have done my soul great harm, and I have never found any with as much of it as I should have liked. Indeed, I have discovered by experience that so long as they are virtuous and lead holy lives, it is better that they should have no learning than a little. For then they do not trust themselves – and I am not likely to trust them – but refer to those who are really learned. A really learned man has never led me astray; and these others cannot have done so willingly; it was only that they knew no better. I supposed them to possess knowledge and that my whole obligation was simply to accept what they said. This I willingly did because their instructions were lax and gave me considerable liberty. If they had been strict I should, in my wickedness, have looked for other confessors. What was in reality a venial sin, they told me was none at all, and what was most grave and mortal they called only venial. This did me so much harm that it is not surprising if I speak of it here in order to warn others against a very great evil. I clearly see that in God's eyes I had no excuse; the fact that what I did was in itself not good should have been enough to make me refrain from it. I believe that God permitted these confessors to deceive themselves and to deceive me on account of my sins. I myself deceived many of my sisters by passing on to them what had been told me.

I continued in this blindness, I believe, for more than seventeen years, until a Dominican father,[1] a man of great learning, partially undeceived me; and Fathers of the Company of Jesus afterwards made me very much afraid, by stressing the wickedness of these unsound principles, as I shall later relate.

I began, then, to confess to the priest I have spoken of, and he became extremely fond of me. I had then little to confess, compared with what

1. Father Vicente Barrón, who was also her father's confessor.

I had afterwards, nor had I had much since I became a nun. There was
nothing wrong in his affection for me, but being excessive it ceased to
be good. He clearly understood from me that nothing would induce
me to commit any grave offence against God, and he gave me the same
assurance for himself. So we had many conversations. Because I was
full of love for God at this time, what gave me the greatest pleasure was
to talk about Him; and this abashed my confessor, since I was so young.
Then out of the great affection he had for me, he began to tell me of his
wretched condition. This was no small matter, since for almost seven
years he had been in a state of peril owing to his affection for and relations with a woman of that town. Nevertheless he had continued to say
Mass. The fact that he had lost his honour and good name was quite
well known, but nobody dared to remonstrate with him. I felt great
pity for him, because I was very fond of him; and I was so worldly and
blind as to think it a virtue to be grateful and loyal to anyone who liked
me. Cursed be all loyalty that goes so far as to impinge on one's loyalty
to God! It is a folly that is customary in the world, and that I cannot
understand. For all the good that people do to us we owe to God, and
yet we count it virtuous not to break a friendship like this one, even
though it means going against Him. How blind the world is! Let me, O
Lord, be entirely ungrateful to the whole world, so long as I do not
lack one whit of gratitude to You. But, for my sins, I have been just the
opposite.

I managed to find out more about my confessor's circumstances
from members of his household. I learned more about his wretched
state, and saw that the poor man was not entirely to blame. For the
miserable woman had laid spells on him by means of a copper image,
which she had begged him, for love of her, to wear round his neck, and
no one had had enough influence on him to make him take it off. I do
not altogether believe this story about the spell. But I will tell what I
saw as a warning to men to be on their guard against women who
attempt tricks of this sort. Let them be sure that once a woman – who
is even more bound than a man to lead a chaste life – has lost her shame
before God, she cannot be trusted in any way at all. What is more, to
gain the gratification of her desires and of an affection inspired in her by
the devil, a woman will hesitate at nothing.

Although I have been so wicked myself, I have never fallen into any
such sin, nor have I ever tried to do wrong in this way, nor, even if I
could, would I have wanted to force anyone's affection, for the Lord

has guarded me from this. But if He had abandoned me, I should have sinned in this way as I have done in others. There is nothing in myself that can be relied on.

When I knew these circumstances I began to show him greater love. My intentions were good, but the act was not. However good the deed, one must never do the least wrong in performing it. Usually I used to talk to him about God, and this must have done him good, though I believe that his affection for me did more. For, to please me, he finally gave me the copper image, which I immediately got someone to throw into the river. Once this was gone, he became like one awaking from a long sleep, and began to remember all that he had done in all those years. He was amazed at himself, and grieved at his wretched state; and now he began to loathe that woman. Our Lady must have helped him greatly, for he most piously observed the feast of her Conception, and used to celebrate it with the greatest solemnity. In the end he entirely gave up seeing the woman, and could never thank God enough for having granted him light.

Exactly a year from the first day I saw him, he died. All this time he had been most active in the service of God. As for the great affection that he felt for me, I never thought that there was anything wrong in it, though it might have been of a purer nature. Moreover there were occasions when, if he had not kept himself in the near presence of God he might have committed very grievous sins. As I have said, I would not at that time have done anything that I knew to be a mortal sin, and I think that his knowing me to be so resolved increased his love for me. I believe that all men must feel more affection for women when they see them inclined to virtue; and even for their worldly purposes women must have more influence on men when they are good, as I shall explain later. I am sure that this friend is on the way to salvation. He made a good death, completely delivered from that temptation. It seems to have been the Lord's will that he should be saved in this way.

I was three months in that place, suffering great torments. The treatment was more severe than my constitution could stand. So strong were the medicines that after two months I was almost dead, and the pains in my heart, of which I had come to be cured, were so much more intense that I sometimes felt as if sharp teeth were being plunged into it. I was in such agony that they feared I might go mad. I had lost a great deal of strength, for I felt such a loathing for food that all I could take was a little liquid; and I had a continuous fever. I was reduced by the daily purges that I had been given for almost a month, and so shrivelled that my nerves began to contract, giving me such unbearable pain that I could get no rest by night or day, and fell into a state of great misery.

Seeing that I had gained nothing here, my father took me back again. Then I was again seen by the doctors, who all gave me up, saying that on top of this disease I had also consumption. This did not worry me much. What distressed me was the pain, which was everywhere from my head to my feet. For pains in the nerves, as the physicians say, are unbearable, and all my nerves were contracting. If I had not brought this on by my own guilt, it would have been a cruel torture indeed.

I cannot have remained in this tortured state for more than three months; it seemed impossible that anyone could bear so many ills together. I am amazed at myself now, and think of the patience which His Majesty gave me as a great mercy, for it clearly came from the Lord. It was a great help to my patience that I had read the story of Job in the *Morals* of St Gregory, which the Lord seems to have used to prepare me for this suffering, also that I had begun the practice of prayer. As a result, I was able to bear all this with considerable resignation. All my conversation was with God. I continually kept in mind and repeated these words of Job: 'What? shall we receive good at the hand of God, and shall we not receive evil?'[1] This seemed to give me strength.

In August the feast of Our Lady came round, and ever since April I had been in pain, though the three last months were the worst. I hastened to confess, for I have always been addicted to frequent confession. They thought that I was prompted by the fear of death, and in order that I should not be upset my father would not let me go. Such is the excess of fleshly love! For though my father was so Christian and so wise – he was very wise, and was not acting out of ignorance – this might have done me great harm.

That night I had an attack which left me insensible for almost four days. They gave me the Sacrament of Extreme Unction, and in every minute of every hour thought that I was dying. They never stopped reciting the Creed to me, as though I could have heard what was said. At times they were so sure that I was dead that afterwards I actually found some wax on my eyelids. My father was extremely distressed at not having allowed me to confess. Many cries and prayers went up to God. Blessed be He that He deigned to hear them.

For a day and a half a grave was left open in my convent, waiting for

1. Job ii, 10.

43

my body, and the rites for the dead were performed at a friary of our Order a short distance away. But it pleased the Lord that I should come round. I immediately asked to confess, and took Communion with many tears. But I do not think my tears came only from pain and sorrow at having offended God, which might have been enough to excuse me, if I had not the additional excuse of having been misled by those priests who had told me that certain things were not mortal sins which certainly were, as I have since seen.

Though my sufferings were so intolerable that I was left with little consciousness, I believe that I made a complete confession of all the ways in which I had offended God. For His Majesty has granted me this grace, among many others, that never since I first took Communion have I failed to confess anything that I thought was a sin, even a venial one. But I certainly believe that my salvation would have been in peril if I had died then, partly because my confessors had so little knowledge, and partly because I was so very wicked, also for many other reasons. Indeed, when I come to this point and realize how my Lord seems to have raised me from the dead, I am so filled with wonder that I am almost trembling.

It would be well, I believe, O my soul, if you were to examine the danger from which the Lord freed you. Then if you did not cease to offend Him out of love you would do so out of fear, since He might have slain you on a thousand other occasions in a more perilous state still. I do not think I am exaggerating much when I say 'a thousand', though he who told me to be moderate in recounting my sins may rebuke me. But I have glossed them over enough. I beg him, for the love of God, not to suppress any of my sins, since they only serve to reveal more clearly God's magnificence and His long-suffering towards the soul. May He be blessed for ever, and may it please His Majesty to destroy me rather than let me cease to love Him!

CHAPTER 6

Of her great debt to the Lord for making her resigned to her great trials,
of how she took St Joseph, the glorious, as her mediator and advocate,
and of the great profit that she derived from this

AFTER my four days of insensibility I was in such a state that only
the Lord knows the unbearable torments I suffered. My tongue
was bitten to pieces, and my throat was so choked from having eaten
no food and from my great weakness, that I could not even swallow
water. My bones seemed to be wrenched out of their sockets, and there
was a great confusion in my head. As a result of all those days of torture
I was all twisted into a knot, and unless someone moved them for me,
could no more move arm, foot, hand, or head than if I had been dead.
All that I could move, I think, was one finger of my right hand. It was
impossible for anyone to see me, for I was in such pain all over that I
could not bear it. They used to move me in a sheet, one taking one end
and one the other; and this state of things lasted till Palm Sunday. My
sole relief was that so long as I was not touched my pains often ceased,
and then when I had had a little rest I considered myself well. I was
afraid that my patience would fail, and so I was extremely pleased when
I found myself free from these sharp and continuous pains, even though
the cold fits of an intermittent fever from which I still suffered remained
almost unendurably severe. I continued to have a great distaste for food.

I was then in such a hurry to return to the convent that I had myself
carried there as I was. So instead of the corpse they had expected, the
nuns received a living soul, though the body was worse than dead and
most distressing to look at. My extreme weakness is beyond description; I was nothing but bones. As I have said, I remained in this state for
more than eight months, and my paralysis, although it grew less, continued for almost three years. When I began to crawl on hands and
knees, I praised God. I spent all this time in great resignation and, except
at the beginning, in great joy. For all this was trifling compared to the
pains and torments with which it had started. I was quite resigned to
God's will, even though He should leave me in this state for ever. My
sole anxiety, I think, was to get well in order to pray in solitude, as I
had learnt to. There was no possibility of this in the infirmary. I made
very frequent confessions, and spoke much about God, in such a way

as to edify all the sisters, who were amazed at the patience which the Lord had given me. For, unless it had come from His Majesty's hand, it appeared impossible that anyone could bear so much with so great a joy.

It was a great thing that He had given me the grace of prayer, as He had done, since this made me understand what it meant to love Him. In that short time I felt these virtues renewed within me, though in no great strength, since they were not sufficient to sustain me in righteousness. I would not speak the slightest evil of anyone, and it was my practice to avoid all gossip. I kept it always in mind that I must not allow others to say, or to say myself, anything about another that I would not like said about me. I kept this rule most rigidly on all possible occasions, though not so perfectly that I did not break it now and then when difficult situations occurred. But on the whole I kept it; and this so impressed the sisters who were with me and talked to me that they adopted the habit too. It came to be understood that where I was it was safe to turn your back; and it was the same with my friends and relations, and those who learnt from me. Still, I have certainly to account to God for having given them a bad example in other respects. May it please His Majesty to pardon me, for I have been the cause of much wrong-doing, though with no such wickedness in my intentions as appeared in the resulting acts.

I still desired solitude, and still loved to discourse and speak of God. If I found anyone with whom I could do so, it gave me greater joy and satisfaction than all the politeness – or, to be correct, coarseness – of worldly conversation. I took Communion and confessed more frequently still, and this out of a real desire. I greatly loved to read good books, and was most repentant for having offended God. I remember that very often I did not dare to pray, because I was afraid of the great distress that I should feel for having offended Him; it was like a heavy punishment. This fear so grew on me later that I do not know what torment I can compare it to. This torment did not increase or diminish with any fear of mine, but would come when I remembered the favours which the Lord was granting me in prayer, and how much I owed Him, and how badly I was repaying Him. I could not bear it; and I would get very angry with myself for all those tears I shed on account of my faults, when I saw how little I improved, and how neither my resolutions nor the efforts I made were enough to prevent my falling again, when I allowed an opportunity to occur. My tears seemed to me a fraud, and my guilt appeared even greater afterwards, since I saw how good the Lord had been in allowing me to shed them, and in giving me such great compunction. I would contrive to go to confession as soon after my fault as I could and, as I thought, did all that I could to return to grace. The whole trouble lay in my not cutting off the occasions for sin at the root, and in my confessors for giving me so little help. If they had told me the risks I was running, and that I must abstain from these conversations, things would most certainly have been remedied, since I could not on any account have borne, even for one day, to go in mortal sin with the knowledge that I was doing so. All these signs of the fear of God came to me through prayer, and the greatest of these was that I went about enveloped in love, for the thought of punishment no longer occurred to me. All the time that I was so ill, my conscience remained very much awake against mortal sins.

O my God, how I longed for the health to serve You better, and this was the cause of all my undoing! When I saw myself so paralysed and still so young, and how the physicians of the world had dealt with me, I decided to invoke those of heaven to heal me. For though I bore my illness most joyfully, I still wanted to get well. But sometimes I reflected that I might regain my health and yet be lost, and that it would be better to stay as I was. But I always thought that I should serve God much better if I recovered. This is our mistake, never to resign ourselves absolutely to what the Lord does, though He knows best what suits us.

I began by having Masses said, and prayers that had been approved. For I was never a lover of those other kinds of devotion to which some people – especially women – resort, together with ceremonies that I could never bear but which greatly move them. I have since been told that these practices are unseemly and superstitious. I took as my lord and advocate the glorious St Joseph, commending myself earnestly to him, and I clearly saw that out of this trouble, as out of other and greater troubles involving my honour and the salvation of my soul, this my lord and father delivered me, doing me greater benefits than I knew how to ask for. I do not remember to this day ever having asked him for anything that he did not grant me. I am amazed at the great mercies which the Lord has done me through this blessed saint, and from what perils, both of body and soul, he has delivered me. The Lord seems to have given other saints grace to help in some troubles, but I know by experience that this glorious saint helps in all. For His Majesty wishes to teach us that, as He was Himself subject to him on earth – for having the title of father, though only his guardian, St Joseph could command him – so in heaven the Lord does what he asks. This has also been the experience of some other persons whom I have told to commend themselves to him; and there are many more who have lately come to revere him, through having newly discovered that this is true.

I managed to observe his feast with the greatest possible solemnity. But, though my intentions were good, I would celebrate it with more vanity than spirituality, being anxious for splendour and effect. For I had this fault that if the Lord gave me grace to do anything good, my way of doing it was always full of imperfections and defects; and as for wrongdoing and meticulousness and vanity, I had great skill and diligence in them. May the Lord forgive me! I wish that I could persuade everyone to venerate this glorious saint, for I have great experience of the blessings that he obtains from God. I have never known anyone who was truly devoted to him and offered him particular service who did not visibly increase in virtue, for he gives very real help to those souls who commend themselves to him. For some years now I have always made some request of him on each of his festival days, and it has always been granted. If my petition is wrong in any way, he corrects it for my greater good.

If I were a person who had authority to write, I would enlarge on this statement, and most minutely describe the benefits which this glorious saint has done to me and other persons. But in order not to do more than I have been commanded, I shall have to write much more briefly than I would wish about some things, and at unnecessarily great length about others, and so appear to be lacking in discretion. I only beg for the love of God that anyone who does not believe me shall try for himself. Then he will learn by experience what great good comes of recommending oneself to that glorious patriarch, and paying him service. Persons who practise prayer, in particular, should always be his devotees. I do not know how anyone can think of the Queen of the Angels, during the time when she suffered so much with the infant Jesus, without giving thanks to St Joseph for the help he then gave them. If anyone cannot find a master to teach him prayer, he should take this glorious saint for master, and he will not go astray on the road. May it please the Lord that I have not done wrong in venturing to speak of him. For though I publicly profess my devotion to him, in serving him and imitating him I have always failed. But he was true to his nature when he cured my paralysis, making it possible for me to rise and walk; and I was true to mine in making but poor use of this benefit.

Who could have said that I should fall so soon after receiving so many gifts from God; after His Majesty had begun to give me virtues, which themselves roused me to serve Him; after having been so near to death and in such great peril of losing my soul; after He had raised me up, in soul and body, so that everyone who saw me was amazed to find me alive? What a perilous life this is, O my Lord, that we must lead! Here as I write this, it seems that, with Your favour and Your mercy, I might say with St Paul, though I am not perfect like him: 'Nevertheless I live; yet not I, but Christ liveth in me'.[1] For some years now, as it seems to me, You have led me by the hand, and I find in myself desires and resolutions – in some ways and to some extent tested by experience during that time – to do nothing, however trifling, that is contrary to Your will, though I must commit many offences against Your Majesty without knowing it. It seems to me too that nothing can be presented to me that I would not undertake with great resolution for love of You. In some things You have Yourself helped me to succeed, I do not love the world or the things of the world, and nothing seems to give me pleasure unless it comes from You; everything else is to me like a heavy cross. Yet I may be deceived, and it may be that my desires are not as I have said. But You know, O Lord, that to the best of my belief I am not lying, since I am afraid, and with good reason, that You may abandon me again. I know now how little my strength and small virtue can achieve if You are not always granting me Your grace and helping me not to forsake You. May it please Your Majesty that I be not forsaken by You even now, when I imagine myself to be in this state.

I do not know how we can wish to live, seeing that all things are so uncertain. Once, my Lord, it seemed to me impossible that I should forsake You utterly. But now that I have forsaken You so often I cannot help being afraid. Whenever You withdrew only a little way from me, I immediately fell to the ground. May You be blessed for ever since, although I have forsaken You, You have never so utterly forsaken me as not to raise me up again by continually giving me Your hand. Very often, Lord, I did not want it, nor did I want to hear how repeatedly You called me again, as I shall now relate.

1. Galatians ii, 20.

49

CHAPTER 7

*How she began to lose the graces the Lord had given her, and of the evil
life she began to lead. A description of the dangers arising from the
lack of strict enclosure in convents*

So I began, by way of amusement after amusement, of vanity after
vanity, and of one occasion for sin after another, to expose myself
to very great dangers, and to let my soul become so distracted by many
vanities that I was ashamed to turn back to God and approach Him in
such intimate friendship as that of prayer. What is more, as my sins increased I began to lose my joy and pleasure in virtuous things. I saw
very clearly, my Lord, that this departed from me because I departed
from You. Now the devil began to practise a most terrible deception on
me, under the disguise of humility. Seeing myself to be so utterly lost, I
began to be afraid to pray. It seemed better to me to live like the
majority, since in my wickedness I was one of the worst; to pray only so
much as I was bound to, and that vocally; and not to practise mental
prayer or commune with God, since I deserved to keep company with
the devils, and was deceiving those about me by presenting an outward
appearance of goodness. This was no fault of the convent where I was,
for I skilfully managed to keep the sisters' good opinion, though I did
not do this deliberately by a pretence of piety. In the matter of ostenta-
tion and hypocrisy – glory be to God – I never remember knowingly
having offended Him. If I saw the first stirrings of such a thing in me, it
so distressed me that the devil departed beaten and I would be the
better for it. So he has never tempted me much in this way. Perhaps,
however, if God had allowed him to try this temptation upon me as he
did others, I should have fallen here too; but till now His Majesty has
preserved me from this, may He be blessed for ever! On the contrary, I
was much distressed that they should think so well of me, since I knew
what I was like within.

This belief of theirs that I was not so wicked was the result of their
seeing me, although so young and so exposed to so many temptations,
frequently withdraw into solitude, and pray and read a great deal, and
often speak about God. They also observed that I liked to have His
picture in a great many places, that I asked for an oratory of my own,
and that I tried to furnish it with objects of devotion. They heard me

speak ill of no one, and noted other such things about me that gave me the appearance of virtue. Yet I was vain, and knew how to get credit for those qualities usually esteemed in the world. As a result they gave me as much liberty as is given to the oldest nuns, and even more; and they placed great confidence in me. I never took any liberties or did anything so illicit as to talk through slits or over walls or by night, for the Lord placed His hand upon me. It seemed to me – for there were many things that I used to ponder deeply and with great care – that it would be very wrong of me to compromise the honour of all those sisters, who were so good while I was so wicked. As if all the other things that I did had been good! But in truth, although I often acted wrongly, my faults were never as deliberate as these would have been.

For this reason I think that it did me great harm not to be in an enclosed convent. The freedom which those good sisters could quite innocently enjoy – their obligation being limited, since they had taken no vows of enclosure – would have taken me, who am wicked, straight to hell, had not the Lord, by His special mercies, using His own means and remedies, rescued me from this peril. A convent of unenclosed nuns seems to me a place of very great peril, and more like a road to hell for those bent on wickedness than a remedy for their weaknesses. But this must not be taken as referring to that convent of mine, since there are so many there who serve the Lord in absolute sincerity and great perfection that His Majesty, in His goodness, cannot fail to show them favour. Besides it is not one of those that are entirely open, and all observances are kept there. I am speaking of others that I know and have seen.

These houses make me particularly sad. Where the standards and amusements of the world are followed and a nun's obligations are so imperfectly understood, the Lord must call not once but many times on each of them individually, if they are to be saved. God grant that they may not all mistake sin for virtue, as I so often did! It is so difficult to make people see this that the Lord will need to take the matter right into His own hands. Parents to-day do not think of placing their daughters where they may tread the path of salvation, but let them run into greater danger than they would in the world. If they would take my advice, they would at least try to safeguard their good names. It would be better for them to make humble marriages for their girls than to put them in convents of this kind, unless they are most devoutly inclined. May God turn their virtues to good purpose, or else they will be better off at home. If they mean to be wicked there, they cannot hide their evil ways for long, but in a convent their goings-on will be hidden for a very long time, and in the end it will be the Lord who reveals them. These poor girls do harm not only to themselves but to everyone else, and often they are not to blame, since they merely follow the ways they are shown. Many of them are to be pitied; wishing to withdraw from the world, and thinking that they are going to serve the Lord and avoid the perils of the flesh, they find themselves in a place ten times as bad, without knowing what to do, or how to help themselves. Youth, sensuality, and the devil invite and incline them to follow certain ways which are essentially worldly; and they see such conduct counted as, so to speak, all right. They seem to me, in a way, like those unhappy heretics, who wilfully blind themselves and argue that the path they follow is good, believing it to be so, yet without real belief in it because they have something inside them that tells them it is wrong.

O, what terrible harm, what terrible harm befalls religious people – I am speaking now as much of men as of women – where the rules of religion are not properly kept, where two ways are open, one of virtue and observance, and the other of irreligion, and where both are almost equally trodden! No, I am wrong, they are not equally trodden, since for our sins the less perfect is the more frequented, and as it is the broader it is the more favoured. The way of true religion is so little used that friars or nuns who begin truly to follow their calling have more to fear from members of their own communities than from all the devils. They have to be more cautious and exercise greater dissimulation when speaking of the friendship that they wish to have with God, than on the subject of those other friendships or desires that the devil ordains shall flourish in religious houses. I do not know why we are surprised that there are so many evils in the Church, when these, who should be the models from whom all derive virtue, so nullify the work wrought on the religious Orders by the spirits of the saints of old. May His divine Majesty be pleased to find a remedy for this, as He sees needful. Amen.

So, when I began to indulge in these conversations, seeing that they were customary, it did not seem to me that they would bring the harm and distraction to my soul that I afterwards found such behaviour to entail. As the receiving of visitors is such a common practice in many convents, I did not think that it would hurt me any more than it hurt the others, who were, as I saw, good women. I did not realize that they were much better than I, and that what was a danger to me was not so dangerous to others. Yet I have no doubt that there was always some harm in it, if only because it was a waste of time.

Once when I was with one person, at the very beginning of our acquaintance, the Lord was pleased to show me that such friendships were not good for me, and to warn me and give me light in my great blindness. Christ appeared before me, looking most severe, and giving me to understand that there was something about this that displeased Him. I saw Him with the eyes of my soul more clearly than I could ever have seen Him with the eyes of the body, and the vision made such an impression on me that, although it was more than twenty-six years ago, I seem to see His presence even now. I was greatly astonished and disturbed, and I never wanted to see that person again.

I was much harmed at that time by not knowing that one can see things with other eyes than those of the body. It was the devil who encouraged me in my ignorance, and made me think any other form of sight impossible. He made me believe that I had imagined it, that it might be his own work, and other things of that sort. The thought remained with me, nevertheless, that it was of God and not of the imagination. But as the vision was not to my liking, I made myself lie to myself. Then, as I dared not discuss the matter with anyone and great pressure was put on me once more, as I was assured too that there was no harm in my seeing such a person, and that by doing so I should not injure my reputation, but rather enhance it, I resumed these conversations and even later got to know other people in the same way. I spent many years in this pestilent pastime which, when I was engaged in it, never seemed as bad as it was, though I clearly saw at times that it was evil. But no one caused me the same distraction as the person I am speaking of, for I was very fond of her.

On another occasion when I was with this person, we saw coming towards us – and other persons who were there saw this also – something like a great toad, but moving much more swiftly than toads move. I do not understand how such a creature could have emerged from the place in question in broad daylight. None had ever done so before, and the occurrence had such an effect on me that I do not think it was a natural one. What is more I have never forgotten it. O mighty God, with what care and compassion did You warn me in every way, and what little advantage did I take of Your warnings!

There was a nun in that house, an elderly relative of mine and a great servant of God, who was most strict in her observances. She also gave me warnings from time to time. Yet not only did I not listen to her, but I took offence, for I thought that she was shocked for no reason. This I mention in order to illustrate my wickedness and God's great goodness, and to show how richly I deserved hell for my great ingratitude. Moreover should it be the Lord's will and pleasure that some nun may read this book one day, I would wish her to take warning by me. I implore all nuns, for the love of our Lord, to avoid such pastimes as these. May it please His Majesty that I may now set right some of the many whom I have led astray. I used to tell them that there was nothing wrong in this practice, and assure them that they were in no danger. This I did in blindness, for I would not have deceived them deliberately. But, as I have said, through the bad example that I gave I was the cause of much evil, though I never thought that I was doing any harm.

In those early days, when I was still ill and did not know how to help myself, I felt a very great desire to be of use to others. This is a very usual temptation in beginners; in my case, however, it led to good results. I was so fond of my father that I wanted him to receive the benefit that I seemed to be deriving from the practice of prayer. I thought that there could be no greater good in this life, and so by roundabout ways and as best I could, I began to prevail on him to pray, and gave him books on the subject. Since he was, as I have said, a very good man, this practice took a hold on him, so much so that in five or six years, as far as I remember, he had made such progress that I used to praise God for it. This encouraged me greatly. He had very great trials of various kinds, and bore them all with the greatest resignation. He often came to see me, for it comforted him to speak of divine matters.

Now that I had become so distracted and no longer prayed, I could not bear him to think, as I saw he did, that I was still as I had been. So I undeceived him, since I had been a year or more without praying, thinking that to refrain was an act of greater humility. This, as I shall explain later, was the greatest temptation that I fell into, and almost caused my ruin. For while I practised prayer, if I offended God one day I recollected myself on the days that followed, and withdrew further from opportunities of sin. When that blessed man came to visit me, it was very hard to see him under the false impression that I was communing with God as before. I told him, therefore, that I no longer prayed, but did not tell him the reason. I put forward my infirmities as an excuse. For though I had recovered from the worst of them I have suffered from indispositions and sometimes from grave ones, ever since. Lately my complaints have not been so troublesome, but they still bother me in many ways. In particular, for the last twenty years I have suffered from morning sickness, and cannot take any food until past midday – sometimes not until much later. Now that I take Communion more frequently, I have to bring it on at night before I go to bed, with feathers or in some other way; and this is much more disturbing. But if I do not, I feel much worse. I think I am never quite free, either, from aches and pains, which are sometimes very severe, especially around the heart, though the fainting-fits, which were then so continuous, are now very rare, and I have been free for the last eight years from the paralysis and from those attacks of fever that I used to have so often. But I take my complaints so lightly now that often I rejoice in them, believing that the Lord is in some way served by them.

My father believed me when I gave him that excuse, since he never told a lie himself; and, considering the relations between us, I ought never to have told one. The better to convince him – for I clearly saw that I had no excuse – I told him that it was as much as I could do to attend the services in choir; not that this would have been sufficient reason for giving up something which demanded no physical effort, but only love and constant habit. Our Lord always gives us the opportunity if we want it. I say always, for though one is sometimes prevented by chance and sickness from enjoying spells of solitude, there are always other times when we have the necessary health; and in sickness itself, or amidst casual happenings, so long as the soul is a loving one it is always possible to pray by offering up the distraction itself and remembering Him for whom we are suffering it. At the same time we must resign ourselves to it and to the countless other things that may happen to us. It is here that love comes in; for we are not certain to pray when we are alone, nor necessarily unable to do so when we are not.

With a little care we may find great blessings at times when the Lord sends us trials that deprive us of our hours for prayer, and I had found them myself when my conscience was clear. But, having the good opinion of me that he had, and loving me as he did, my father believed what I told him, and in fact was sorry for me. As he had attained such heights of prayer himself, he used not to stay with me very long, but went away once he had seen me, for staying, he said, was a waste of time. As I was wasting mine on other vanities, I did not take much notice of this remark.

My father was not the only person whom I prevailed upon to practise prayer, though I was walking in vanity myself. There were certain nuns as well, whom I saw to be much given to vocal prayer, and whom I taught how to make a meditation. I helped them and gave them books. For, as I have said, ever since I started prayer I have always felt the desire that others should serve God. Now that I no longer served the Lord as I knew how to, I thought that the knowledge His Majesty had given me ought not to be lost, and wanted others to serve Him through me. I say this to show how blind I was to let myself be lost while trying to save others.

At this time my father was struck down by the illness of which he died. It lasted several days. I went to look after him, myself more sick in soul than he in body, owing to my many vanities. But during all this wasted time that I am speaking of, I was never, so far as I was aware, in mortal sin. If I had known myself to be, I should on no account have continued in it. I was greatly distressed by his illness; and I think that I repaid him to some degree for what he had suffered during mine. Distressed as I was, I forced myself to be active; and though in losing him I was losing all the good and comfort of my life – for he was all that to me – and I was so determined not to show him my grief that I behaved to the end as if I felt none at all. But I felt as if my soul were being torn from my body when I saw his life depart, for I was very fond of him.

The Lord must be praised for the death that he died. Not only did he welcome death, but he gave us worthy advice after receiving Extreme Unction. He urged us to recommend his soul to God, to pray God to have mercy on him, and always to serve Him, remembering that all things come to an end. He told us with tears how deeply grieved he was not to have served Him better, for he would have liked to be a friar – a friar of the very strictest Order. I most certainly believe that a fortnight before his death the Lord had made him realize that it was approaching; for up to that time, ill though he was, he did not think that he would die. But afterwards, although he got much better and his doctors told him so, he took no notice of them, but busied himself with the ordering of his soul.

His chief distress was an acute pain in the back, which never left him; sometimes it was so severe as to be a torture. I said to him that since he used to think so devoutly of our Lord carrying the Cross on His back, he must suppose that His Majesty now wished him to feel something of the pain that He had then endured. This so comforted him that I do not believe I heard him complain again. He remained for three days almost unconscious. But on the day he died the Lord restored him his consciousness so completely that we were amazed, and he stayed conscious until, half-way through the Creed, which he was repeating with us, he suddenly expired. He lay there, looking like an angel; and it seemed to me that he was an angel, as they say, both in his soul and his disposition. For he was a very good man.

I do not know why I have said this except to make my wretched life appear more wicked. After witnessing such a death and realizing what his life had been, I ought to have made some effort to resemble him, by myself growing better. His confessor, a very learned Dominican,[1] said that he had no doubt of my father's having gone straight to heaven; he had been his confessor for some years, and praised the purity of his conscience.

This Dominican father, who was a good and god-fearing man, was a great help to me. I confessed to him, and he seriously undertook the task of setting my soul right and showing me the bad state I was in. He made me take Communion once a fortnight, and gradually, as I began to talk to him, I told him about my prayers. He charged me not to give them up, since he thought they could not possibly do me anything but good. So I began to resume them though I did not avoid occasions of sin; and I never abandoned them again. I led a very wretched life, for as I prayed I gained a clearer knowledge of my faults. On one side God called me, and on the other I followed the world. All divine things gave me great pleasure; yet those of the world held me prisoner. I seem to have wanted to reconcile two opposites as completely hostile, one to another, as the spiritual life and the joys, pleasures, and pastimes of the senses. I found great difficulty in praying, for the spirit was not the master but the slave; and so I could not shut myself inside myself – which was my whole method of procedure in prayer – without shutting a thousand vanities in with me. I spent many years in this way, and now I am astonished that anyone could have suffered so much without giving up the one or the other. I know very well that by this time it was no longer in my power to abandon prayer, for He who desired me in order to do me greater mercies, held me in His hand.

O my Lord, if only I could tell of the situations from which God delivered me, and how I plunged into them again and again; and of the dangers I incurred of utterly losing my good name, from all of which

1. Father Vicente Barrón.

He delivered me! I continued to show by my deeds what sort of person I was, and the Lord went on covering up the evil, and revealing some little virtue, if I had any, making it look great in people's eyes, so that they always thought much of me. Though my follies were sometimes crystal clear, they would not believe in them since they saw things in me which they considered good. This was because the Knower of all things saw it to be necessary, in order that I should receive some credence when I afterwards spoke of matters concerning His service. His supreme generosity did not look on my great sins, but on the desires that I so often felt to serve Him, and on my grief that I had not the strength in me to carry them out.

O Lord of my soul, how can I extol the mercies You showed me in those years? Indeed, at the very times when I most offended You, You quickly prepared me by a very great repentance, to taste Your gifts and graces. Truly, my King, You used the most refined and painful punishment that I could possibly have borne, since You well knew what would give me the greatest pain. You chastised my sins with great favours. I do not think that I am speaking foolishly, though I might well become quite distraught now that I recall my ingratitude and my wickedness. In the condition I was in, it was more painful when I had fallen into a grave fault, to receive mercies than to be punished. A single fault, I am sure, troubled, shamed, and distressed me more than many illnesses and severe trials put together. For these I knew that I deserved, and they seemed to be a partial payment for my sins, though all my sufferings were but small and my sins were great. But to find myself receiving fresh graces when I had shown so little gratitude for those already received, is a kind of torture that is terrible to me, and to everyone, I believe, who has any knowledge or love of God. By considering the state of true virtue, we can deduce our own distance from it. Hence my tears and anger when I observed my feelings, and saw myself just about to fall once more, although my resolutions and desires were then – I speak of that particular time – quite strong.

It is a dreadful thing for a soul to be alone among such perils, and I think that if I had had anyone with whom I could have spoken of all this, it would have helped me not to fall again, perhaps out of mere shame, though I felt no shame before God. For this reason I would advise those who practise prayer, especially at first, to cultivate the friendship and company of others who are working in the same way. This is a most important thing, because we can help one another by our prayers, and all the more so because it may bring us even greater benefits. Since people find comfort in the conversation and mutual sympathy of ordinary friendship, even when it is not of the best sort, and enjoy talking of their worldly pleasures, I do not know why those who are beginning truly to love and serve God should not be allowed to discuss their joys and trials with others, and those who practise prayer have plenty of both. If the friendship which they desire to have with His Majesty is sincere, there need be no fear of vainglory. When the first promptings of it assail them, they will come off victorious. I believe that anyone who will bear this thought in mind when discussing the subject will profit both himself and his hearers and will emerge more enlightened both in his own understanding and by the enlighten-ment of his friends.

Anyone who feels vainglory when engaged in such a discussion will feel it also when he hears Mass and is moved to devotion in the presence of others, and when he performs other acts which must be done, or he is no true Christian, and from which he cannot possibly refrain out of fear of vainglory. This is a most important consideration for souls who are not fortified in virtue, since they have so many enemies and friends to incite them to sin. Indeed I cannot sufficiently insist on its importance. Such scruples as mine are, I believe, an invention of the devil, who finds them very valuable. He uses them to persuade men who truly desire to love and please God to conceal their intentions, while he incites others to make open show of their evil purposes. This state of things is now so usual that people seem to glory in it, and offences committed in this way against God are freely proclaimed.

I do not know if what I write is foolish. If it is, your Reverence must strike it out. But if it is not, I entreat you to help me in my simplicity and add a great deal to this, for people are so lukewarm in all that pertains to God that those who serve Him must back one another up if they are to progress. It is considered a good thing to pursue the vanities and comforts of the world, and few look on them with disapproval. So if anyone begins to devote himself to God there are so many that speak ill of him that he must find companions for his protection, until such time as they are all strong enough not to be depressed by suffering. If he does not, he will find himself in great difficulties.

I think that this must have been the reason why some of the saints departed into the desert. It is a kind of humility for a man not to trust himself, but to believe that God will help him in his dealings with those whom he meets. Charity increases by being diffused, and from this there come countless blessings. I should not dare to speak of this subject if I did not know from plentiful experience how important it is. In truth, I am the weakest and wickedest of mortals. But I believe that one who humbles himself, though strong, and who trusts not in himself but in someone who has had experience in these matters, will lose nothing. Of myself I may say that if the Lord had not revealed this truth to me, and given me constant opportunities of speaking with persons who practise prayer, I should have gone on rising and falling again until I tumbled into Hell. I had plenty of friends to help me fall. But when it came to picking myself up I found myself completely alone. Indeed, I wonder now that I did not remain where I fell. Praise be to God for His mercy, for only He held out His hand. May He be blessed for ever! Amen.

CHAPTER 8

Of the great profit that she derived from not entirely abandoning prayer, for fear that she might lose her soul. She describes the excellence of prayer as a help towards winning back what is lost, and exhorts everyone to practise it. She tells what great gains it brings and how very beneficial it is even for those who may later give it up, to devote some time to anything as good

It is not without reason that I have dwelt so long on this period of my life. I plainly see that it will give no one any pleasure to read about anyone so wicked, and I would wish my readers to hold me in abhorrence as a soul so obstinate and ungrateful to One who conferred such mercies on it. I wish also that I had permission to tell how often I failed God through not having leaned on the strong pillar of prayer.

I spent nearly twenty years on this stormy sea, falling and evermore rising again, but to little purpose as afterwards I would fall once more. My life was so far from perfection that I took hardly any notice of venial sins and, though I feared mortal sins, I was not sufficiently afraid to keep myself out of temptations. I must say that this was one of the most painful ways of life that can be imagined. I derived no joy from God and no pleasure from the world. When I was among the pleasures of the world, I was saddened by the memory of what I owed to God, and my worldly affections disturbed me when I was with God. A battle like this is so painful that I do not know how I managed to endure it for a month, still less for so many years. Nevertheless, I can plainly see the great mercy which the Lord did me, in still giving me the courage to pray, while thus consorting with the world. I say 'courage' because I do not know anything for which greater courage is needed than for plotting against the King, knowing that He knows it and yet never withdrawing from His presence. For though we are always in the presence of God, it seems to me that those who practise prayer are present in a special way, for they see that He is watching them, while the rest may be in God's presence for several days without remembering that He can see them.

It is true that in these years there were many months, and I believe once a year on end, in which I kept myself from offending God, and gave myself much to prayer. During that time I took various careful precautions against sinning – and I mention this because what I am writing must tell the whole truth. But since I have little memory of those good days, they must have been few and the bad ones numerous. Yet not many days passed without great periods of prayer except when I was very ill or very busy. When I was ill, I was nearer to God, and I contrived that the nuns who were around me should be so too. I prayed the Lord for this, and often spoke with Him. So, omitting the year of which I have been speaking, of the twenty-eight years since I started to pray I have spent more than eighteen in this strife and contention between converse with God and the society of the world. As for the rest, which remain to be described, the battle has not been light, though its causes have been different. But since I have, as I think, been in God's service, and have come to know the vanity of the world, all has gone smoothly, as I shall tell later.

My reason for relating all this at such length is, as I have already said, to show God's mercy and my ingratitude, also that men may understand what a great blessing God confers on a soul in disposing it to serious prayer, although it is not as prepared for it as it should be. Yet if it perseveres through sins and temptations and the countless varieties of snares laid by the devil, I am certain that the Lord will bring it in the end to the port of salvation, just as – so far as can be seen at present – He has brought me. May it please His Majesty that I may never be lost again!

The great blessings possessed by those who practise prayer – and by this I mean mental prayer – have been described by many saintly and good men. Glory be to God for this! If it were not so, though I have little humility, I am not presumptuous enough to speak on this subject. I can say what I know from experience, namely that however sinful a man may be, he should not abandon prayer once he has begun it. It is the means by which all may be repaired again, and without it amendment would be much more difficult. Let him not be persuaded by the devil, as I was, to give it up out of humility. Let him believe rather that his words are true who says that if we will truly repent and resolve not to offend Him, He will return to his former friendship with us[1] and grant us favours once more, sometimes even more generously than before, if only our repentance deserves it. As for the man who has not begun to pray, I beg him for the love of our Lord not to forego this great blessing.

1. A reference to Ezekiel xviii, 21.

Here there is no place for fear, only for desire. Even if a man does not make progress or strive for perfection, so that he may deserve the gifts and delights lavished by God on those who do, yet he will gradually attain knowledge of the road that leads to Heaven; and if he perseveres I place my hope for him in the mercy of God, since no one ever took His Majesty for his friend without receiving a reward. Mental prayer is, as I see it, simply a friendly intercourse and frequent solitary conversation with Him who, as we know, loves us. Now if love is to be true and friendship lasting, certain conditions are necessary. On the Lord's side, as we know, these cannot fail, but our nature is wicked, sensual, and ungrateful. Therefore, you cannot succeed in loving Him as He loves you, since it is not in your nature to do so. But when you see how important it is to you to have His friendship, and how much He loves you, you must rise above the pain of being so much in the company of One who is so different from you.

O my God, how infinitely good You are! It is in this relationship that I seem to see You and myself. O joy of the angels, when I think of it, I long to dissolve in love for You! How true it is that You suffer those who will not suffer You to be with them! What a good friend You are, O my Lord, to comfort and endure them, and wait for them to rise to Your condition, and yet in the meantime to be patient of the state they are in! You take into account, O Lord, the times they loved You, and for one moment of penitence forget all their offences against You. This I have clearly seen in my own case, and I cannot see, O my Creator, why the whole world does not strive to draw near to You in this bond of friendship. The wicked, whose nature is unlike Yours, should come to You so that You may make them good. They should allow You to be with them for some two hours each day even though they may not be with You, but are engaged in a thousand revolving thoughts and distractions, as I used to be. But by making this effort against themselves, and desiring to be in such good company – for at the beginning, and sometimes later on, they can do no more – you compel the evil spirits, Lord, to cease their attacks, and every day the devil has less strength against them, till finally you give them the victory. So, O Life of all lives, You slay none of those who trust in You, and want You for their friend, but preserve the life of the body in greater health, and give life to the soul.

I do not understand the fears of those who are afraid to begin mental prayer. I do not know what frightens them. It is to the devil's profit to instil fear into us, so that he may do us real harm. By making me afraid he prevents my thinking how I offended God and how much I owe Him, of the existence of hell and of glory and of the great trials and sorrows that He endured for me. This was the whole extent of my meditation, for so long as I was subject to these dangers. It was on this that I dwelt whenever I could, and very often over a period of some years I was more occupied with the wish that the time I had assigned myself for prayer would end, and with listening whenever the clock struck, than with other and better thoughts. Very often I would have undertaken any sharp penance that might have been laid upon me more willingly than the act of recollection preparatory to prayer. Indeed, the violence with which the devil assailed me was so irresistible, or my bad habits were so strong, that I never got so far as to pray; and the depression I felt on entering the oratory was so strong that I had to avail myself of all my courage to force myself in. As for courage, they say that mine is far from slight, and it is well known that God has given me more than a woman's share of it, though I have made poor use of it.

In the end the Lord came to my help, and after I had forced myself to pray I found greater peace and joy than at some other times when I have prayed because I wanted to.

If the Lord bore for so long, then, with so wicked a creature as I – and this was clearly the way in which all my ills were remedied – why should anyone be afraid, however wicked he may be? However bad his condition, he will not remain in it for as many years as I did after receiving so many favours from the Lord. Seeing that He bore so long with me only because I desired and sought some place and time for Him to be with me, how could anyone despair? This desire came to me very often without my willing it, merely because I had forced myself to seek it, or the Lord Himself had forced me to do so. If prayer is so beneficial and so necessary, therefore, to those who do not serve Him but offend Him, and if no one can find any possible harm in it that would not be greater without it, why should men who serve God and wish to do so give it up? I can see no reason, unless it is that they wish to add more trials to those that they must endure in this life, and to close the door on God in order to prevent His giving them the joy of prayer. I am truly sorry for them, since they are serving God at great cost to themselves. For the Lord Himself pays the costs of those who practise prayer; in return for a little effort on their part He gives them such consolations as will enable them to bear all their trials.

Since there will be much to tell of these joys which the Lord gives to those who persevere in prayer, I will say no more here, only that prayer is the door to those very great favours that He has conferred upon me. Once it is closed, I do not know how He can do so. Though He may wish to take His delight in a soul and to give it delight, He has no means of entrance. Unless He finds it solitary and pure and deeply desirous to receive His favours, He can do nothing. If we put many obstacles in His way and make no effort to remove them, how can He come to us? Nevertheless we wish God to grant us great favours!

In order to reveal His pity and to show what a great benefit I drew from not having abandoned prayer and reading, I will here describe the assaults that the devil delivers on a soul in order to gain it, and the compassion with which the Lord endeavours to win it back. It is important that my readers should understand this, and so guard themselves against the dangers for which I did not myself watch out. I implore them, above all, for the love of Our Lord and for the great love with which He is continually seeking to win us back to Him, to guard against the occasions for sin. For once caught, we have nothing to rely on when so many enemies assail us, and our own weaknesses are so great that we cannot defend ourselves.

I wish that I could describe the captivity which my soul suffered in those days. I fully realized that I was a prisoner, but did not know how; nor could I entirely believe that what my confessors made so little of was as wicked as I felt it to be in my soul. One of them, to whom I had gone with a scruple, told me that even if I were raised to high contemplation, such happenings and conversations were not unfitting. This was towards the end, when, by the grace of God, I was withdrawing more and more from great dangers, although not altogether avoiding the situations from which they arose. When my confessors saw my good resolutions and my constancy at prayer, they thought that I was doing a great deal. But in my soul I knew that I was not fulfilling my obligation towards Him to whom I owed so much. I am sorry now for my soul's great suffering, and for the little help it received from anyone but God, also for the opportunities to wander off in pursuit of its pastimes and pleasures, which were offered to it by those confessors who said that they were legitimate.

Sermons too were a torment to me, and no small one, since I was very fond of them. If I heard anyone preach earnestly and well, I felt a particular affection for him rise in me unbidden; I do not know how this came about. A sermon rarely seemed so bad to me that I did not listen to it with pleasure, even though others who heard it said that the preaching was poor. But if it were good, it brought me a most special refreshment. To speak of God or hear Him spoken of hardly ever wearied me, once I had begun to pray. In one way I drew great comfort from sermons, but in another they distressed me because they made me see that I was far from being what I should have been.

I prayed the Lord to help me. But, as it seems to me now, I must have erred in not placing my complete trust in His Majesty and completely mistrusting myself. I sought for help, and made efforts. But I could not have understood that nothing is of much use unless we abandon all reliance on ourselves, and place it in God. I wished to live, and clearly saw that I was not living but wrestling with the shadow of death. There was no one to give me life. For He who might have done so was right in not coming to my aid, seeing that He had brought me back to Himself so many times, and each time I had forsaken Him.

CHAPTER 9

*Of the means by which God began to rouse her soul, to give it light
in its great darkness, and to strengthen her virtues, so that she should
not offend Him*

My soul had now become weary. But the wretched habits it had contracted did not let it rest, though it wished to. It happened one day, however, that as I went into the oratory I saw an image which they had procured for a certain festival that was observed in the house, and which they had placed there. It was of Christ terribly wounded and it was so moving that when I looked at it the very sight of Him shook me, for it clearly showed what He suffered for us. So strongly did I feel what a poor return I had made for those wounds, that my heart seemed to break, and I threw myself on the ground before Him in a great flood of tears, imploring Him to give me strength once and for all not to offend Him again.

I had a very deep veneration for the glorious Magdalen, and very often thought of her conversion, especially when I was taking Communion. As I then knew for certain that the Lord was within me, I would place myself at His feet, thinking that my tears would not be rejected. I did not know what I was saying, but He did great things for me in allowing them to flow, seeing that I so quickly forgot my grief again. But then I used to recommend myself to that glorious saint so that she might win me pardon.

But on this last occasion, before the image I have spoken of, I seem to have done better, because I had quite lost my trust in myself and put all my confidence in God. I think I said to Him then that I would not rise up until He granted me my prayer. I certainly believe that this benefited me, for from that time I have begun greatly to improve. This was my method of praying: – Since I could not meditate intellectually, I would try to call up the picture of Christ within me, and I found myself the better, as I believe, for dwelling on those moments in His life when He was most lonely. It seemed to me that when He was alone and afflicted he must, like anyone in trouble, admit me. I had many of these simple thoughts, and I was particularly fond of the prayer in the Garden, where I could accompany Him in His Agony. I thought of the sweat and affliction that He endured there. I only wished that I could have

67

wiped away that painful sweat. But I remember that, in my prayer, I never dared make up my mind to do so, for then my sins appeared before me in all their gravity. I would stay with Him there as long as my thoughts allowed me. But I had many tormenting thoughts.

For many years, almost every night before I went to sleep, as I commended myself to God in order to sleep well, I would always dwell for a while on this scene of the prayer in the Garden; and this even before I became a nun, since I had been told pardon for many sins was to be gained in this way. I am sure that my soul gained greatly from it, because I began to adopt the habit of prayer without knowing what it was; and it became so usual with me that I could no more have omitted it than the practice of crossing myself before going to sleep.

But to return to what I was saying about the torture that my thoughts inflicted on me. This method of prayer without intellectual meditation brings the soul either great profit or great loss – I mean by the wandering of the attention. If it benefits it benefits greatly, since it is moved by love. But to attain this state is very costly except to those whom the Lord wishes to bring very quickly to the prayer of quiet – and I know of some. For those who tread this path a book is useful as a means of prompt recollection. I also found it helpful to look at fields, water, or flowers. These reminded me of the Creator. I mean that they woke me, and brought me to a recollected state, and served me as a book. They reminded me also of my ingratitude and my sins. My mind was so stupid that I could never call up heavenly or exalted thoughts on any occasion until the Lord had presented them to me in another way.

I had so little aptitude for picturing things in my mind that, if I did not actually see a thing, I could make no use at all of my imagination in the way that others do who can induce recollection by calling up mental images. Of Christ as a Man I could think, but never in such a way as to call up His picture in my mind. Although I read of His beauty and looked at images of Him, I was like a person who is blind or in the dark. He may be talking to someone and feel that he is with him because he knows for certain this man is there – I mean he understands and believes him to be there – but he cannot see him. It was like this with me when I thought of Our Lord. This is why I was so fond of pictures. I pity those who are so wretched as to have lost this fondness, through their own fault. It is very clear that they do not love the Lord, because if they did they would enjoy looking at His picture in the same way as worldly men enjoy gazing on portraits of those whom they love.

At this time I was given St Augustine's *Confessions*, seemingly by the ordainment of the Lord. I did not ask for it myself, nor had I ever seen it. I am most devoted to St Augustine, because the convent in which I lived before taking my vows was of his Order, and also because he had been a sinner. I derived great comfort from those saints who have sinned and yet whom the Lord has drawn to Himself. I thought that I could obtain help from them, and that as the Lord had pardoned them he might pardon me. But one thing that I have already mentioned disturbed me. The Lord had called them only once and they had not sinned again, but my relapses were so many that it distressed me. Yet when I remembered the love He bore me I took fresh courage, for I never doubted His mercy, though I very often doubted myself.

O my Lord, I am amazed that my soul was so stubborn when I received such help from You! It frightens me to think how little I could do by myself and of those attachments that hindered my resolution to give myself entirely to God. When I began to read the *Confessions* I seemed to see myself portrayed there, and I began to commend myself frequently to that glorious saint. When I came to the tale of his conversion, and read how he heard the voice in the garden,[1] it seemed exactly as if the Lord had spoken to me. So I felt in my heart. For some time I was dissolved in tears, in great inward affliction and distress. How a soul suffers, O my Lord, by losing its liberty! Once it was mistress of itself, and now what torments it endures! I am amazed to-day that I was ever able to live under such torture. Praise be to God, who gave me life to escape from so absolute a death.

I believe that my soul gained great strength from His Divine Majesty, and that He must have heard my lamentations and taken pity on all my tears. A desire to spend more time with Him began to grow in me. I longed to remove from my sight all opportunities for sin; and once they had gone I returned immediately to love of His Majesty. I clearly understood that I loved Him – or at least I thought that I did. But I did not understand as I should have done, what the love of God really is. I do not think that I had yet prepared myself to seek His service when His Majesty began to grant me favours once more. He seems deliberately to have contrived to make me accept what others labour with great efforts to acquire – I mean the joys and comforts that He gave me in these latter years. I never presumed to beg for these gifts or for sweetness in devotion. I only demanded the grace not to

1. *Confessions*, Book VIII, chap. 12.

offend Him again, and pardon for my great sins. When I saw how great they were, I never ventured deliberately to desire joys or comforts. He showed me sufficient compassion, I think – and truly He was most merciful to me – in allowing me to approach Him and drawing me into His presence. I saw that except by His agency I should not have come there.

Only once in my life do I remember asking Him for consolation, and that was when I was very dry. But when I observed what I was doing, I was so upset that my very distress at finding myself so lacking in humility gave me just what I had ventured to ask for. I knew quite well that it was lawful for me to pray for it. But it seemed to me to be lawful only for those who are ready and who have tried with all their strength to attain true devotion by not offending God, and by a resolute disposition to do what is right. These tears of mine seemed to me womanish and feeble, since they did not gain me what I desired. All the same, I believe that they helped me, because, as I say, especially after these two occasions when they caused me great compunction and distress of heart, I began to give myself more constantly to prayer, and to be less taken up with those things that did me harm. Nevertheless, I did not abandon them altogether. But God, as I say, helped to turn me from them. As His Majesty was only waiting for some preparation on my part, the spiritual graces went on growing in me in a way that I shall describe. But it is not usual for Our Lord to give them to those whose conscience is as clouded as mine was.

CHAPTER 10

She begins to explain the favours which God gave her in prayer, tell-
ing the extent to which we can help ourselves, and how important it
is that we shall understand the favours God is granting us. She begs
those to whom this book is to be sent to keep the rest of it secret, since
they have ordered her to describe in detail the favours that she has
received from God

I USED at times, as I have said, to experience the very fleeting beginnings of something which I am now going to describe. When I
made that inward picture in which I threw myself at Christ's feet, and
sometimes also when I was reading, there would come to me un-
expectedly such a feeling of the presence of God as made it impossible
for me to doubt that He was within me, or that I was totally engulfed
in Him. This was no kind of vision; I believe it is called *mystical theology.*
The soul is then so suspended that it seems entirely outside itself. The will
loves; the memory is, I think, almost lost, and the mind, I believe,
though it is not lost, does not reason – I mean that it does not work, but
stands as if amazed at the many things it understands. For God wills it to
realize that it understands nothing at all of what His Majesty places
before it.

Before that I had experienced a continual tenderness in devotion,
which is partially attainable, I believe, by our own efforts; it is a gift
not wholly of the senses, nor yet of the spirit, but entirely God-given. It
seems to me, however, that we can greatly help ourselves to obtain it
by considering our lowliness and our ingratitude to God, by thinking
how much He has done for us, of His Passion with its grievous pains and
of His life of sorrow, also by rejoicing in the sight of His works, in His
greatness, and in His love for us. There are many other things, too,
which anyone who seriously wants to make progress will often stumble
upon, even though he may not be watching out for them. If in addition there is a little love, the soul is comforted, the heart is softened, and
tears come. Sometimes we seem to force ourselves to weep, but at other
times the Lord seems to draw tears from us, so that we cannot resist Him.
His Majesty seems to reward us for our little efforts with the very great
gift of comfort, which a soul receives when it finds itself weeping for so

great a Lord. This does not surprise me, for it has ample reason to be comforted. Here it takes pleasure, here it finds joy.

The comparison which occurs to me seems a good one. These joys of prayer must be like those that are enjoyed in Heaven. For as souls in Heaven receive from the Lord no deeper vision than they have earned by their merits on earth, and as they realize how small these merits are, each saint is content with the place assigned to him, there being the very greatest difference in Heaven between one joy and another – an even greater difference than that between one spiritual joy and another on earth, though this is itself very great. Indeed, when a soul is at its beginnings and the Lord grants it this favour, it is almost as if there were nothing else for it to desire; it feels fully rewarded for all the service it has done Him. It has ample reason for thinking like this, since a single one of those tears which – as I have said – we can almost obtain for ourselves – though nothing whatever can be done without God – cannot, in my opinion, be purchased with all the labour in the world, so great is the gain which it brings us. And what greater gain can we have than some evidence that we are pleasing God? Let anyone, therefore, who has come so far give Him great praise, and acknowledge how much he is in His debt. For now it seems that God will take him into His house, and has chosen him for His kingdom, if he does not turn back.

Let him take no notice of certain kinds of humility which I intend to discuss. Some think it humble not to recognize that the Lord is bestowing gifts on them. Let us understand the situation very clearly, that God is bestowing them without any merit of ours. Let us be grateful to His Majesty for them. For if we do not know what we receive, we shall never wake into love. It is most certain that, so long as we at the same time recognize our poverty, the richer we see ourselves to be, the greater will be our progress and the truer our humility. Another mistake is for the soul to be afraid, and to think itself incapable of receiving great blessings. Then when the Lord begins to grant them it begins to frighten itself with the dread of vainglory. Let us believe that He who gives us the blessings will also give us grace to detect the devil when he begins to tempt us in this way, and make us strong enough to resist him. This will come to us if we walk in simplicity before God, endeavouring to please Him alone, and not men.

It is a plain fact that we love a person most when we frequently remember the kind actions he has done us. If it is lawful, therefore, and indeed meritorious, always to remember that we owe our being to God, and that He created us out of nothing and preserves us, also all the other benefits of His death and Passion, which He suffered for each one of us living to-day long before He created us, why should it be wrong for me to know and realize and frequently consider that, though I used to speak of vanities, the Lord has now granted me the wish to speak only of Him?

Here is a jewel which, when we remember that it has been given to us and that we possess it, forcibly invites us to love. All these benefits come of prayer founded on humility. How will it be then when we find ourselves possessed of other jewels more precious, such as contempt for the world and even for ourselves, which some servants of God have already received? Such souls must clearly look on themselves as more in God's debt and under still greater obligation to serve Him. They will understand that nothing of this comes from ourselves, and acknowledge the Lord's generosity. For on a soul as wretched and poor and undeserving as mine, for whom the first of these jewels would have been enough and more, He was pleased to confer greater riches than I could desire.

We must draw fresh strength with which to serve Him and manage not to be ungrateful, for the Lord's gifts are made on one condition, that if we do not make good use of His treasures and of the estate to which He raises us, He will take them away again, and we shall be left poorer than before. Then His Majesty will give those jewels to one who will display them, and profit himself and others by their use. For how can a man make good use of them and spend them liberally if he does not know that he is rich? Taking our nature into account, it is, I believe, impossible for anyone to have the courage for great exploits if he does not know that he is favoured by God. So miserable are we, and so attracted to the things of this world, that unless a man realizes that he holds some earnest of the joys above, he will hardly succeed in abhorring and thoroughly detaching himself from the things of this world. It is by such pledges that the Lord gives us that strength which we have lost through our sins.

A man will hardly wish to be universally disapproved of and abhorred, nor will he seek all those other great virtues possessed by the perfect, if he has no pledge of the love God bears him, and no living faith. Our nature is so dead that we go after what we see in front of us; and so it is these very favours that arouse and strengthen our faith. It may well be that I who am so wicked measure others by myself, and that others need no more than the truths of the faith to enable them to perform works of great perfection. But I, being a poor wretch, have need of everything.

Others must speak for themselves. I merely relate what happened to me, as I have been commanded. If the recipient of this does not approve of it, he will tear it up, and he will know better than I what is wrong with it. But I implore him, for the Lord's sake, to let what I have so far said about my wretched life and my sins be published. I give permission for this, here and now, to him and to all my confessors, of whom he is one. They may publish this now in my lifetime, if they like, so that I may no longer deceive the world, which thinks there is some good in me. I am speaking in all sincerity when I say that, in so far as I understand myself at present, this will give me great comfort.

This permission does not apply to what I am going to say from now on. If the rest is shown to anyone I do not wish him to be told whose experience it describes, or who wrote it. That is why I mention neither myself nor anyone else by name and have done my best to write in such a way as not to be recognized. I beg your Reverence, for the love of God, to preserve my secrecy. Persons as learned and serious as my confessors have enough authority to confirm any good thing that the Lord may grant me the grace to say, in which case it will be His, not mine. For I am not learned nor have I led a good life, and I have neither a scholar or anyone else to guide me. Only those who have commanded me to write this[1] know that I am doing so, and they are not here at present. I have almost to steal the time for writing, and that with difficulty, because it hinders me from spinning, and I am living in a poor house where there is a great deal to do. If the Lord had given me greater skill and a better memory, I might have profited by what I have heard and read. But I have very little of either. So if anything I have said is right, it is because the Lord has willed it for some good purpose of His own; anything that is wrong will be mine, and your Reverence will strike it out.

In neither case will it be of any advantage to publish my name. Nothing good I may have done ought, of course, to be talked about during my lifetime, and after my death there will be no point in mentioning it since that would only bring discredit on the good thing itself, and no

1. Father Domingo Báñez and Father García de Toledo. (Note by Father Gracián).

one would believe it when it was related of one so base and wicked as I. So, as I think that you and the others who are to see this book will do what I am asking you for the love of God, I am writing quite freely. Otherwise I should have great scruples about writing anything except an account of my sins, though about this work I have none. For the rest, the mere thought that I am a woman is enough to make my wings droop. How much more then the thought that I am not only a woman but wicked!

So for everything beyond the simple story of my life your Reverence must take the responsibility, since you have pressed me so hard to give some account of the favours that the Lord confers on me in prayer, so long as my tale is consistent with the truths of our holy Catholic Church. If it is not, your Reverence must burn it immediately, and I agree to its destruction. I will set down my experience, so that, if it conforms to Christian belief, it may be of some use to your Reverence. But if it does not, you will deliver my soul from its delusion so that the devil may have no gain where I think that it is I that am gaining. For the Lord well knows – as I shall tell later – that I have always watched for anyone who could give me light.

However clearly I may wish to explain this matter of prayer, it will be very obscure to anyone who has not the experience. I shall describe certain impediments, which I believe prevent men from advancing on this path, also certain other sources of danger about which the Lord has taught me by experience. More recently, I have also discussed the subject with men of great learning and persons who have led spiritual lives for many years; and they have seen that in the twenty-seven years during which I have practised prayer, ill though I have trodden the road and often though I have stumbled, His Majesty has granted me experiences for which others need thirty-seven, or even forty-seven, although they may have progressed in penitence and constant virtue. Blessed be He for all things, and may He, for His name's sake, make use of me. My Lord knows that all I desire is that he may be praised and magnified a little when men see how on a foul and stinking dunghill he has planted a garden of such sweet flowers. May it please His Majesty that I may not by my own fault root them up again, and be once again what I was. I entreat your Reverence, for the love of the Lord, to beg this of Him for me, for you have a clearer knowledge of what I am than you have allowed me to set down.

CHAPTER II

She explains why we cannot attain the perfect love of God in a short time, beginning with a comparison which sets out the four stages of prayer. Here she says something about the first, which is very profitable for beginners and for those who receive no consolations in prayer

Now to speak of those who are beginning to be the servants of love – for this, I think, is what we become when we decide to follow along the way of prayer Him who loved us so greatly. It is so high an honour that even the thought of it brings a strange joy. Servile fear vanishes immediately, if we act as we should in this first stage. O Lord of my soul and my Good, why do you not wish a soul immediately to ascend into the joy of possessing this perfect love, once it has resolved to love You and does all that is in its power by abandoning everything, the better to employ itself to this end? But I am wrong. I should have said, and my complaint should have been: Why do we not – for the fault is wholly ours – wish to enjoy this great honour immediately? For the perfect possession of this true love of God brings all blessings with it. We are so niggardly and so slow to give ourselves entirely to God that we do not prepare ourselves to secure that precious thing, which His Majesty does not wish us to enjoy if we have not paid a high price first.

I clearly see that there is nothing in the world with which we could buy so great a blessing. But if we did what we could by not clinging to anything here, and turned all our thoughts and conversations towards Heaven, I certainly believe that this blessing would be very quickly given to us, provided that we were to prepare ourselves thoroughly and quickly, as some saints have done. But we think we are giving ourselves entirely, when we are only offering God the revenue or fruits of our land, while still keeping the stock and ownership in our own hands.

We resolve to be poor, and that is a great merit. But very often we resume our precautions and take care not to be short of necessities, also of superfluities, and even to collect friends who will supply us. In this way we take greater pains and, perhaps, expose ourselves to greater danger in our anxiety not to go short than we did before, when we had possession of our estates. Presumably we also gave up all thought of our own importance when we became nuns, or when we began to lead a spiritual life and to pursue perfection. Yet the moment our self-importance is wounded we forget that we have given ourselves to God. We want to snatch it up and tear it out of His very hands, as they say, even after we have, to all appearances, made Him lord over our will. And it is the same with everything else.

That is a fine way of seeking God's love! We expect it by the handful, as they say, and yet we want to keep our affections for ourselves! We make no attempt to carry our desires into effect, and fail to raise them above the earth, and yet we want great spiritual comforts. This is not good, for the two aims are, as I see it, irreconcilable. So, since we do not manage wholly to give ourselves up, we never receive the whole of this treasure. May it please the Lord to give it us drop by drop, even though receiving it may cost us all the labours in the world.

The Lord shows great mercy to a man when He gives him the grace and courage to strive resolutely with all his strength for this blessing; for God will not deny Himself to one who perseveres. Little by little He will strengthen that soul, so that it may emerge with the victory. I said 'courage', because the devil puts forward so many obstacles in the beginning, to prevent a man from setting out on that road. The devil knows the harm that this will do him, through the loss not only of that soul but of many others. For if a beginner tries hard, with God's help, to gain the summit of perfection, I think he will never reach heaven alone, but will take many others with him. God will prize him as a good captain and give him his company; and the devil will put such perils and difficulties in his way that he will need not merely a little courage but a great deal, also much help from God, if he is not to turn back.

To speak then of the early experiences of those who are determined to pursue this blessing and succeed in this enterprise – I will continue later with what I had begun to say about *mystical theology*, as I believe it is called – it is in those early stages that the labour is hardest, for it is they who labour and the Lord who gives the increase; whereas in the further stages of prayer the chief thing is joy. Nevertheless, at the beginning, the middle, and the end, all bear their crosses, though not all crosses are alike. For all who follow Christ must tread the road that He trod, unless they want to be lost. But how blessed are their labours that even in this life are so superabundantly rewarded!

Here I shall have to make use of a comparison though, being a woman and writing only what I have been commanded to write, I should like to avoid it. But this spiritual language is so difficult to use for those like myself who have no learning, that I must find some other means of expression. It may be that my comparisons will not very often be effective, in which case your Reverence will be amused at my stupidity. It strikes me that I have read or heard this one before. But as I have a bad memory I do not know where it occurred or what it illustrated. But for the present it will serve my purpose.

A beginner must look on himself as one setting out to make a garden for his Lord's pleasure, on most unfruitful soil which abounds in weeds. His Majesty roots up the weeds and will put in good plants instead. Let us reckon that this is already done when a soul decides to practise prayer and has begun to do so. We have then, as good gardeners, with God's help to make these plants grow, and to water them carefully so that they do not die, but produce flowers, which give out a good smell, to delight this Lord of ours. Then He will often come to take His pleasure in this garden and enjoy these virtues.

Now let us see how this garden is to be watered, so that we may understand what we have to do, and what labour it will cost us, also whether the gain will outweigh the effort, or how long it will take. It seems to me that the garden may be watered in four different ways. Either the water must be drawn from a well, which is very laborious; or by a water-wheel and buckets, worked by a windlass – I have sometimes drawn it in this way, which is less laborious than the other, and brings up more water – or from a stream or spring, which waters the ground much better, for the soil then retains more moisture and needs watering less often, which entails far less work for the gardener; or by heavy rain, when the Lord waters it Himself without any labour of ours; and this is an incomparably better method than all the rest.

Now to apply these four methods of watering, by which this garden is to be maintained and without which it will fail. This is my purpose, and will, I think, enable me to explain something about the four stages of prayer, to which the Lord has, in His kindness, sometimes raised my soul. May he graciously grant that I may speak in such a way as to be of use to one[1] of the persons who commanded me to write this, whom the Lord has advanced in four months far beyond the point that I have reached in seventeen years. He prepared himself better than I, and therefore, without any labour on his part, his garden is watered by all these four means; although it only receives the last water drop by drop. But, as things are going, with the Lord's help, his garden will soon be

1. Father Pedro Ibañez (Note by Father Gracián).

submerged. If my way of explaining all this seems crazy to him, he is welcome to laugh at me.

We may say that beginners in prayer are those who draw the water up out of the well; which is a great labour, as I have said. For they find it very tiring to keep the senses recollected, when they are used to a life of distraction. Beginners have to accustom themselves to pay no attention to what they see or hear, and to put this exercise into practice during their hours of prayer, when they must remain in solitude, thinking whilst they are alone of their past life. Although all must do this many times, the advanced as well as the beginners, all need not do so equally, as I shall explain later. At first they are distressed because they are not sure that they regret their sins. Yet clearly they do, since they have now sincerely resolved to serve God. They should endeavour to meditate on the life of Christ, and thus the intellect will grow tired. Up to this point we can advance ourselves, though with God's help of course, for without it, as everyone knows, we cannot think one good thought.

This is what I mean by beginning to draw water from the well – and God grant there may be water in it! But at least this does not depend on us, who have only to draw it up and do what we can to water the flowers. But God is so good that when for reasons known to His Majesty – and perhaps for our greater profit – He wishes the well to be dry, we, like good gardeners, must do what we can ourselves. Meanwhile He preserves the flowers without water, and in this way He makes our virtues grow. Here by water I mean tears, or if there be none, a tenderness and inward feeling of devotion. But what shall a man do here who finds that for many days on end he feels nothing but dryness, dislike, distaste and so little desire to go and draw water that he would give it up altogether if he did not remember that he is pleasing and serving the Lord of the garden; if he did not want all his service to be in vain, and if he did not also hope to gain something for all the labour of lowering the bucket so often into the well and bringing it up empty? It will often happen that he cannot so much as raise his arms to the task, or think a single good thought. For by this drawing of water I mean, of course, working with the understanding.

Well, what, I repeat, shall the gardener do now? He shall be glad and take comfort, and consider it the greatest favour that he is working in the garden of so mighty an Emperor. He knows that He is pleasing his Master in this, and his purpose must be to please Him and not himself. Let him praise Him greatly, for having placed such trust in him, and for seeing that though he receives no payment he is carefully carrying out the task assigned to him. Let him help the Master also to bear His Cross, and think how He carried it all through His life. Let him not seek his kingdom here, nor ever abandon prayer, and let him resolve never to let Christ fall beneath His Cross, even though this dryness may last all his life. The time will come when he will receive his whole reward at once. Let him not be afraid that his labour is in vain. He is serving a good Master, who is watching him. Let him pay no attention to evil thoughts, but remember that the devil put them into the mind of Saint Jerome[1] also, in the desert.

These labours bring their reward. I endured them for many years, and when I drew one drop of water from this blessed well I thought of it as a mercy from God. I know that they are very great labours, and that more courage is needed for them than for most worldly trials. But I have clearly seen that God does not fail to reward them highly, even in this life. A single one of those hours in which He has allowed me to taste of His sweetness has seemed to me afterwards a certain recompense for all the afflictions I bore during my long perseverance in prayer.

I believe that it is our Lord's pleasure to send these torments and many other temptations, which often occur at the beginning and sometimes later also, in order to test His lovers, and to discover whether they can drink of the cup and help Him to bear His Cross, before He entrusts them with great treasures. I believe that it is for our good that His Majesty chooses to lead us in this way, so that we may thoroughly realize our own worthlessness. For the favours that follow are so exalted that before granting them to us He would have us first know by experience our own wretched state, in order that ours may not be the fate of Lucifer.

Is there anything that You do, O Lord, that is not for the greater good of that soul which You know to be already Yours, and which places itself in Your power to follow You wherever You go, even to death on the Cross, and which is determined to help You carry that Cross and not to leave You alone with it? No one who discerns this resolution in himself has anything to fear. You spiritual persons have no reason to be distressed. Once you have reached so high a state as this, in which you wish to converse alone with God, and abandon all worldly amusements, the greater part of the work is done. Praise the Lord for it,

1. A reference to the twenty-second epistle of St Jerome, in which he describes the visions of luxury that came to him in the desert.

and trust in His kindness, for He has never failed His friends. Blindfold the eyes of the mind, which asks why He gives devotion to this person after a few days, and none to you after so many years. Let us believe that it is all for our greater good. Let His Majesty guide us where He will. We are not our own now, but His. He shows us a great favour when He grants us a desire to dig in His garden, and to be so near its Lord. For He is certainly near us. If it be His will that these plants and flowers shall grow, some of them with water drawn from this well and some without it, what is that to me? Do as You will, O Lord, and let me not offend You. If You have, of Your kindness alone, given me any virtues, do not let them perish. I wish to suffer, Lord, because You suffered. Fulfil Your will in me in every way, and may it please Your Majesty that a thing of such high price as Your love shall never be given to people who serve You only for what You give them.

It is of especial note – and I say this because I know it from experience – that the soul which begins resolutely to tread this path of mental prayer, and can manage not greatly to care about consolations and tenderness in devotion, neither rejoicing when the Lord gives them nor being discouraged when He withholds them, has already gone a large part of the way. Though it may often stumble, it need have no fear of falling back, for its building has been begun on firm foundations. The love of the Lord does not consist in tears or in these consolations and tendernesses which we so much desire and in which we find comfort, but in our serving Him in justice, fortitude, and humility. Anything else seems to me rather an act of receiving than of giving on our part.

As for a poor woman like myself, a weak and irresolute creature, it seems right that the Lord should lead me on with favours, as He now does, in order that I may bear certain afflictions with which He has been pleased to burden me. But when I hear servants of God, men of weight, learning, and understanding, worrying so much because He is not giving them devotion, it makes me sick to listen to them. I do not say that they should not accept it if God grants it to them, and value it too, for then His Majesty will see that it was good for them, but they should not be distressed when they do not receive it. They should realize that since the Lord does not give it to them they do not need it. They should exercise control over themselves and go right ahead. Let them take it from me that all this fuss is a mistake, as I have myself seen and proved. It is an imperfection in them; they are not advancing in freedom of spirit but hanging back through weakness.

I do not say this so much for beginners – though I do stress it, since it is most important for them to start with this freedom and resolution – but for others. For there must be many who have made a beginning and never succeeded in reaching the end. It is, I believe, mainly due to their not having embraced the Cross from the first, that they are now distressed and think they are making no progress. When their understanding ceases to work it is more than they can bear, though perhaps even then their will is putting on weight and gaining new strength without their knowing it. We must realize that the Lord pays no heed to these things, and that though they seem faults to us they are not so. His Majesty knows our wretchedness and the lowliness of our nature better than we do ourselves. He knows that all the time these souls are longing to think of Him and love Him for ever. This is the resolution that He wants; the other afflictions that we bring upon ourselves only serve to disturb the soul which, if it is incapable of profiting from one hour's prayer, will be disabled by them for four. Very often – I have very great experience of this and know that it is true, for I have made careful observations and afterwards discussed them with spiritual persons – this arises from physical indisposition, for our condition is so wretched that this poor imprisoned soul shares in the miseries of the body. Seasonal changes and the alterations of the humours very often prevent it, for no fault of its own, from doing what it will and make it suffer in all kinds of ways. The more one tries to compel it at these times, the worse it gets and the longer the trouble lasts. Let us use discretion to see when this is the cause; the poor soul must not be smothered. People in this state must understand that they are ill and change their hours of prayer, and very often these changes will have to be continued for some days. They must endure this banishment as best they can. It is very unfortunate for a soul that loves God to find itself in this state of misery and unable to do what it will because of its evil guest, the body.

I spoke of discretion because sometimes the devil is the cause. It is never right, therefore, invariably either to abandon prayer when the mind is much distracted and perturbed, or to torture the soul into doing what is beyond its power. There are other, exterior acts, such as works of charity or reading, although at times the soul will be unable to perform even these. Let it then serve the body, for the love of God, so that on many other occasions the body may serve the soul. Let it take some pious recreation, preferably a really religious conversation or a walk in the country, as the confessor may advise. In all these things it is important to have had experience, for this shows us what is suitable for us, but let God be served in every way. His yoke is sweet, and it is of the utmost consequence that the soul shall not be dragged, as they say, but gently led, so that it may make the greater progress.

I repeat my advice, then, and I do not mind how many times I do so. It is most important, I say, that no one should be distressed or afflicted because of aridities or disturbances or distractions in his thoughts. If he wishes to gain freedom of spirit and not always to be troubled, let him begin by not being afraid of the Cross. Then he will see how Our Lord will help him to carry it, and will advance joyfully and gain profit from everything. It is clear now that if the well yields no water we can put none in. It is true too that we must not be careless, and fail to see when there is some there, for at such times it is God's wish by means of it to multiply our virtues.

CHAPTER 12

*More about the first state. She tells how far we can, with God's help,
progress by ourselves, and speaks of the danger of seeking supernatural
and extraordinary experiences until the Lord bestows them on us*

ALTHOUGH I digressed in the last chapter, and said a great deal
about other things that seemed to me necessary, my aim was to
explain how much we can advance by our own efforts, and how in this
first stage of devotion we can, to some extent, help ourselves. For when
we think and reflect on the Lord's sufferings for us, it moves us to compassion, and this sorrow, with the tears that rise from it, is sweet. To
think of the glory we hope for, of the love which the Lord bore us, and
of His Resurrection rouses a joy in us that is neither entirely spiritual nor
entirely worldly, but is a virtuous joy; and our sorrow also is most
meritorious. Of the same nature are all those things that cause a devotion, acquired in part by the understanding, though it can neither be
earned nor gained if God does not give it. It is best for a soul that He
has raised no higher than this not to attempt to rise by its own
efforts. Let this be carefully noted, for more will be lost than gained
by the endeavour. In this condition a soul can perform many acts to
confirm it in its resolution to serve God, and to awaken love in itself;
and do other things also to help the growth of its virtues, as is explained
in a book entitled *The Art of Serving God*,[1] which is very good and suitable for persons in this condition, since their understanding is active.

The soul can also picture itself as in the presence of Christ, and
accustom itself to feel deep love for His blessed humanity. It can have
Him always with it, and talk to Him, and ask Him for what it needs and
complain to Him of its troubles and rejoice with Him in its pleasures,
and yet never allow them to make it forgetful of Him. For this it has no
need of set prayers, but can use such words as express its desires and its
needs. This is an excellent and very speedy way of advancement. Anyone who strives to carry this precious Companion with him, and who
makes good use of His company, really learning to love the Lord to
whom we owe so much, is in my opinion making real progress.

We should not worry, therefore, as I have said before, if we are not

1. By the Franciscan, Alonso de Madrid, a work first published in Seville in
1521 and several times reprinted.

conscious of our devotion. We should instead thank the Lord for allowing us the wish to please Him, even though our works are poor. This practice of carrying Christ with us is profitable at all stages. It is a most certain method both of advancement in the first stage, and of quickly attaining the second; and in the later stages it is a safeguard against dangers occasioned by the devil.

This, then, is what we can do. Anyone who tries to pass on and raise his spirit to taste of pleasures that are denied him will, in my opinion, lose in a double sense.[1] For these pleasures are supernatural, and when his understanding is asleep, his soul is left desolate and very dry. Moreover as the whole edifice is founded on humility, the nearer we draw to God the more this virtue must be developed, and if it is not, all is lost. It seems a sort of pride in us too that makes us wish to rise higher when God is already doing more for us than we deserve by drawing us, in our condition, near to Him. It must not be supposed that I am now referring to the raising of the mind to consider the high things of Heaven and its glories, or of God and His great wisdom. I never did this myself, for, as I have said, I had not the ability for it. I was so aware of my wickedness that, even when it came to thinking of worldly things, God of His mercy allowed me to understand that it was no small presumption in me to do so. Having recognized this truth, I should have been very much more presumptuous if I had reflected on the subject of heaven. But other people will profit by this practice, especially if they are learned. For learning is, I think, an invaluable help in this exercise, particularly when it goes with humility. I observed this a few days ago in some learned men who have only just begun, but have made great progress. This makes me most anxious that more learned men shall become spiritual, and I shall return to this topic later on.

When I say that people must not rise if God does not raise them, I am speaking the language of spirituality. Anyone with experience will understand me. But if I have not made myself plain, I can say no more.

In the *mystical theology*, which I have begun to speak of, the understanding ceases to work because God suspends it, as I shall explain further, if I can and if God gives me the grace to do so. What we must not do is to presume or imagine that we can suspend it ourselves. We must not cease to work with it, or we shall find ourselves stupid and

1. That is, will lose the prayer of recollection and will fail to reach the prayer of quiet. He puts his mind to sleep, but meets only with dryness, because he is not ready for higher experience.

apathetic, and the result will be neither the one thing nor the other.[1] For when the Lord suspends it and makes it still, He gives it something to amaze it and keep it occupied, so that in the time of a single Credo it understands more than we could understand in many years with all our human efforts.

To occupy the powers of the mind and at the same time to imagine that we can keep them quiet is folly. I say once more, although this is not generally understood, that there is no great humility in this. It may not be sinful, but it certainly causes distress, for it is labour thrown away, and leaves the soul somewhat frustrated, like a man who has tried to take a leap and has been pulled back. It feels that it has used its strength, and yet has not achieved what it intended to. Anyone who will reflect on the matter will perceive from the smallness of the gain achieved this slight lack of humility of which I have spoken. For humility has this excellent quality, that no work which is done in a humble state leaves any distaste in the soul. I think that I have made this clear, though perhaps only to myself. May the Lord open the eyes of those who read this, and grant them experience. For however slight that experience is, they will immediately understand.

For many years I read a great deal, and understood nothing; and for a long while, although God taught me, I could never find words with which to explain His teaching to others; and this caused me no small distress. When His Majesty wishes, he teaches us everything in a moment in the most amazing way. One thing I can truly say; although I talked with many spiritual persons, who tried to make me understand what the Lord was teaching me so that I might be able to speak about it, I was so stupid that I derived not the slightest advantage from their explanations. However, as the Lord has always been my teacher – may He be blessed for ever, for it shames me to confess that this is true! – it may have been His will that I should have no one but Him to thank. So without my wishing or asking for it – for I have never been curious about these things, though such curiosity would have been a virtue in me, but only curious about vanities – God gave me absolutely clear understanding of this in a single moment, together with the power to express it to my confessors, who were amazed. But I was even more amazed, since I was more aware of my stupidity. This was only a short while ago, and now I do not seek to know anything that the Lord has not taught me, unless it be something that touches my conscience.

1. That is, neither the prayer of recollection nor the prayer of quiet.

I repeat my warning that it is most important not to raise the spirit if the Lord does not raise it for us; and if He does, we know it immediately. This straining is especially harmful to women, because the devil can delude them. I am quite certain, however, that the Lord will never allow anyone to be harmed who endeavours to approach Him with humility. On the contrary, such a person will derive great gain and advantage from the attack by which Satan intended to destroy him.

I have dwelt for so long on this way of prayer because it is the commonest with beginners and because the advice I offer is very important. I admit that it has been better expressed by others in other places, and that I have felt some shame and confusion in writing this, though not enough. Blessed be the Lord for it all, whose will and pleasure it is that a woman like myself should speak of things that are His, and of such a sublime nature.

CHAPTER 13

She continues to speak of this first stage, and gives advice concerning certain temptations that the devil sends at times. This chapter is very useful

I THINK it right to speak of certain temptations that I have observed, which occur at the beginning – I have experienced some of them myself – and to give some advice about some matters that seem to demand it. In the early stages, then, one should try to be cheerful and not strained; for there are people who think that devotion is ruined if they relax for a moment. It is well to feel distrust for oneself, and not to allow self-confidence to lead one into situations which habitually cause one to sin against God. This is a most necessary precaution until we become confirmed in virtue, since there are not many who are so perfect that they can be careless in situations dangerous to their own particular natures. Throughout our lives it is well for us to recognize the worthlessness of our nature if only in order to keep our humility. But there are many occasions – as I have said – when it is permissible to take some recreation, so that we may return to our prayer invigorated. Discretion is necessary in everything.

We must have great confidence, for it is most important not to limit our good desires but to believe that, with God's help, if we gradually increase our efforts, we shall reach, though perhaps not at once, that height which many saints have attained to, through His favour. If they had never resolutely desired this, and gradually put their desires into effect, they would never have come to their high state.

His Majesty is the friend and lover of courageous souls, so long as they proceed humbly and without trust in themselves. I have never seen any such person hanging back on the road, nor have I ever seen a cowardly soul, even with the protection of humility, make as much progress in many years as the courageous make in a few. It amazes me how much can be done on this road by spurring oneself on to great things. Even though the soul may not have the strength for them immediately, it soars into the air and reaches a great height. However, like a fledgling whose wings are still weak, it may soon grow weary and get no further.

At one time I used often to reflect on those words of St Paul: 'I can do all things through Christ which strengtheneth me'.[1] I well understood that through myself I could do nothing. This greatly helped me, and so did St Augustine's 'Give me what You ordain, and ordain what You will'.[2] I would often think how St Peter lost nothing by casting himself into the sea, although after he had done so he was afraid.[3] These first resolutions are of great importance, although at this early stage one must proceed very haltingly and depend on the discretion and advice of a director. But we must take care that he is not of the kind that teaches us to be like toads, content if our souls show themselves just capable of catching small lizards. Humility must always be present, to show us that this strength springs from no strength of ours.

But we need to understand what sort of humility this must be. I believe the devil is very successful in preventing those who practise prayer from advancing further by giving them false notions of humility. He persuades us that it is pride that gives us such great aims, and that makes us wish to imitate the saints and desire martyrdom. He tells us directly, or makes us think, that we poor sinners may admire but must not imitate the deeds of the saints. I would agree with him to the extent that we must consider which of their deeds we are to admire and which we can imitate, since it would be wrong if a weak and sickly person were to undertake great fasts and severe penances, or to go into a desert where he could not sleep or find anything to eat, or to attempt other like austerities. But we must reflect that, with God's help, we can strive to hold the world in profound contempt, to despise honours, and not to be attached to possessions. But we are so mean-spirited that we imagine the earth would slide from beneath our feet if for one moment we were slightly to turn our attention from the body and give it to the spirit. Since worldly anxieties disturb our prayer, we think that to have abundance of all that we require is a help to recollection. It distresses me that we have so little trust in God and so much self-love as to be troubled by such things. The fact is that when the spirit is making such small progress, a few trifles give us as much anxiety as great and important matters give to others. Yet in our minds we think of ourselves as spiritual!

Now this kind of life seems to me an attempt to reconcile soul and

---

1. Philippians iv, 13.
2. *Confessions*, Book x, chap. 29.
3. A reference to Matthew xiv, 29.

body, so that we may not lose our comfort in this world or the enjoyment of God in the next. We shall do all right if we walk in righteousness and cling to virtue, but we shall advance at a snail's pace. Freedom of spirit is not to be had in that way. It seems to me quite a good course of procedure for those in the married state, who have to live in accordance with their vocation. But I cannot recommend it for any other state, nor can I be persuaded that it is a good method. I tried it myself, and should have been practising it to this day if the Lord had not shown me a short cut.

So far as my desires went, they were always ambitious. But, as I have said, I tried to achieve prayer and live according to my own pleasure, both at the same time. I think that if there had been anyone to impel me to higher flights, he might have brought me to the point of putting my desires into effect. But, for our sins, men who are not excessively cautious in these matters are very few and far between; and that, I think, is the reason why beginners do not quickly achieve great perfection. For Our Lord never fails us, and it is no fault of His; it is we who are at fault and miserable.

We may also imitate the saints by striving after solitude and silence, and after many other virtues which will not kill these wretched bodies of ours, that are always asking to have everything arranged to suit them, and thus bring disorder to the soul. The devil also starts incapacitating our bodies, the moment he detects the slightest apprehension in us. That is enough for him; he immediately tries to persuade us that all this devotion will kill us or make us ill; and when we weep, he suggests that this will make us blind. I have been through all this, and so I know it. I know too that we can desire no better kind of sight or health than to lose both in such a cause. As my own health was so bad, I was always hampered and useless until I decided to take no notice of my body or of my state of health; and now I bother very little about either.

It pleased God to let me see this trick of the devil's. Then, whenever he suggested that I was making myself ill, I would answer 'It doesn't matter if I die!' and 'Rest! I don't need rest but the Cross', and so on. I clearly saw that although I am very sickly, in most cases my illnesses were temptations of Satan, or arose from my own weakness. Since I have given up caring so much for my ease and comfort, my health has been very much better. It is very important at the beginning, when we embark on prayer, not to be frightened by our own thoughts. You may take my word for this; I know it by experience. This recitation of my mistakes may be of some use to others, if they will take warning by it.

There is another very common temptation; and that is, when one begins to enjoy the calm and fruit of prayer, to wish everyone else to be very spiritual too. The wish is not wrong; but attempts to bring it about may not be good unless carried out with great discretion and in such a disguised way that one does not appear to be trying to teach. If a person is to do any good in such matters he must be very strong in the virtues, so as not to put temptations in the way of others. This I discovered for myself, and so I understand the danger. For when – as I said before – I persuaded others to practise prayer, on the one hand they heard me say so much about the great blessings that come of it and, on the other, they saw how poor I was in virtues although I prayed. Thus I led them into temptations and foolish conduct; and they had some excuse for this, since, as they afterwards told me, they failed to see how these two things could be compatible. For this reason they imagined that there was nothing wrong in certain habits that were definitely evil, for they saw me practise them myself at a time when they had a good opinion of me.

This is the devil's work; he seems to make use of the virtues in us to sanction, in so far as he can, his own evil purposes. However small our wickedness may be, he must gain a great deal by it, especially when it is practised in a religious House. How much more must he have profited then from my wickedness, seeing that it was very great! Thus in several years only three persons benefited by what I said to them; while in the three or four years since the Lord has strengthened me in virtue many have derived profit by me, as I shall relate hereafter. Such lapses bring us another great disadvantage also: the loss suffered by our own soul. For the utmost that we can attempt at the beginning is to look after the soul, and to reflect that there is nothing in the world but it and God; and this is a very useful thing to remember.

There is another temptation that we ought to be aware of and take precautions against. We all have a zeal for virtue and feel distressed when we see the sins and faults of others. The devil tells us that this distress is caused only by the desire that God may not be offended, and by our concern for His honour. So we immediately try to set matters right, and get so excited that we cannot pray. The greatest harm of all lies in our thinking that this is a virtue, and a sign of perfection and great zeal for God. I am not speaking of the distress occasioned by public offences that may become habitual in some congregation, nor by such crimes against the Church as those heresies by which we see so many souls are lost. Such distress is very proper, and consequently causes us no excitement. The security of a soul that applies itself to prayer lies in its ceasing to be anxious for anything or anybody, in its watching itself and pleasing God. This is very important. If I were to tell of the mistakes I have seen people make, through reliance on their own good intentions, I should never be done.

Let us endeavour always to look at the virtues and good qualities that we find in others, and to keep our own great sins before our eyes, so that we may see none of their failings. This is one way of working; and although we may not be able to manage it perfectly at once, we shall acquire one great virtue by it: we shall consider everyone else better than ourselves. Then, with God's grace – which is always necessary, since when we do not have it all efforts are useless – we shall begin to progress. At the same time we must beg Him to grant us this particular virtue, which He denies to no one who makes efforts himself.

This counsel should also be considered by those who are very active with their intellects, deriving many thoughts and ideas from a single subject. But as for those who cannot work in this way, – as I could not – all the advice that they need is to be patient until the Lord gives them both occupation and light. For they can do so little by themselves that their understanding is more of a hindrance than a help to them. To those who make use of their intellects I would say further that they ought not to spend their whole time in this way. Though it is most meritorious and they find prayer sweet, they fail to realize that they ought also to observe a kind of Sunday, when they should rest from their labours. They think that this would be a waste of time, but I consider this waste a very great gain. Let them picture themselves, as I have suggested, as in the presence of Christ, and without tiring their minds, let them talk and rejoice with Him. They should not weary themselves by composing speeches, but lay their needs before Him, and acknowledge how right He is not to allow us in His presence. There is a time for one thing and a time for another, so that the soul may not be wearied with always eating the same food. The meats are very tasty and nourishing, and once the palate has grown used to them they bring great sustenance to the life of the soul, together with many other benefits.

I will explain myself more fully, for everything to do with prayer is difficult, and very hard to understand unless one finds a director. Though I should like to be brief, and a mere indication would be enough for the clear understanding of him who commanded me to write on this subject, I am too stupid to express or convey in a few words something which it is so important to explain properly. Having gone through so much myself, I am sorry for those who begin with books alone. For it is strange what a difference there is between understanding a thing and subsequently knowing it by experience. But, to return to what I was saying, we set out to meditate on some incident in the Passion; let us say the binding of Our Lord to the pillar. The mind begins to work out the causes leading to the great pain and anguish which His Majesty must then have suffered in His desolation. If the intellect is an active one, or endowed with learning, it can derive much else from such a thought. This should be the beginning, the middle, and the end of prayer for us all. It is a most excellent and safe path for all, until such time as the Lord leads us to other supernatural ways.

I say 'all', yet there are many souls who make more progress by meditating on other subjects than the Holy Passion. For as there are many mansions in heaven, so there are many roads leading to them. Some people derive benefit from imagining themselves in hell, and others, who are distressed by thinking of hell, from imagining themselves in heaven. Some meditate on death. Others, if they are tender-hearted, become exhausted by always dwelling on the Passion, but derive great benefit from thinking of the power and greatness of God as revealed in His creatures, and of His love for us, which is expressed in all things. This last is an admirable method, so long as it is combined with frequent thoughts on the Passion and the life of Christ, the past and present source of all our good.

The beginner requires advice, so that he may see where his greatest benefit lies. To this end a director is most necessary. But he must be an experienced man, or he will make many mistakes, and may guide a soul without understanding its ways or allowing it to understand itself. For since the soul knows that it is most meritorious to obey a director, it dare not transgress the commands it receives. I have met souls so constrained and tormented by the inexperience of their masters that I have been really sorry for them. There was one who did not know how to act for herself; for directors who do not understand spirituality afflict their penitents in body and soul, and block their progress.

Another person who talked to me had been kept in bondage by her director for eight years; he would not allow her to leave the stage of self-examination, and yet the Lord had raised her to the prayer of quiet. Consequently she was suffering great trials. This self-examination must never be neglected, however; for there is no soul on this path who is such a giant that he does not often need to turn back and be a child at the breast again. This must never be forgotten. Indeed I shall repeat it many times, since it is most important. For there is no state of prayer so high that it is not necessary often to return to the beginning, and the questions of sin and self-knowledge are the bread which we must eat with even the most delicate dish on this road of prayer. Without this bread no one could be nourished, but it must be eaten in moderation. Once a soul finds itself exhausted and clearly understands that there is no good in it; once it feels itself ashamed before so great a King, and sees how little it pays towards the great debt it owes Him, what need is there to waste time on this? It will be better for us to go on to other dishes that the Lord puts before us, and that we should be wrong to neglect. His Majesty knows better than we what kind of food suits us.

Therefore it is very important that the director shall be prudent – I mean a man of sound understanding – and that he shall also be experienced. If he has learning as well, that is a great advantage. But if these three qualities cannot be found together, the two first are the more important, because we can always find learned men to consult when we have need of them. I mean that learned men are of little use to beginners, unless they also practise prayer. I do not mean that beginners should not have conversations with men of learning, for I would rather see spirituality based on truth than accompanied by prayer. Learning is a great thing, for it teaches us who know little, and gives us light. Then, when we come to the truths in Holy Scripture, we act as we should. God deliver us from foolish devotions!

I should like to explain myself further, for I seem to be getting involved in many subjects. I have always had this failing of not being able to explain anything except – as I have said – at the cost of a great number of words. A nun begins to practise prayer; and if her director is foolish, he takes the idea into his head that she ought to obey him rather than her superior. This he will do without any evil intention, but under the impression that it is the right thing. Indeed, if he is not a monk it will seem right to him. In the case of a married woman, he will tell her that she should be praying when she has work to do at home, even though this may annoy her husband. He cannot advise her how to arrange her time and work so that everything may be done in the proper religious way. Not being enlightened himself, he cannot enlighten others, however much he would like to.

Although learning may not seem necessary in a director, my opinion has always been and always will be that every Christian should endeavour to consult some learned person, if he can; and the greater his learning the better. Those who take the path of prayer have great need of learning; and the more spiritual they are, the greater the need.

Let us not deceive ourselves by saying that learned men who do not practise prayer cannot be suitable directors for those who do. I have consulted many such, and for some years now have sought them out most eagerly because of my increased need of them. I have always got on well with them; for even though some of them have no experience, they are not enemies of the spirit or ignorant of its nature, for they are familiar with the Holy Scripture, where the truth about it can always be found. I firmly believe that a person who practises prayer and consults learned men will never be carried away by any delusions of the devil, unless he be willingly deceived. I believe that the powers of evil are very much afraid of learned men who are humble and virtuous. They know that such people will find them out and defeat them.

I say this because some people hold that learned men cannot help us on the path of prayer unless they are also spiritual. I have just said that a spiritual director is necessary. But if he is not a learned man that is a serious drawback. Great help can be obtained by consulting a learned man who is virtuous, even if he is not spiritual. Such a person will be of great use to us. For God will instruct him what he shall teach, and may even make him spiritual in order that he may be of assistance to us. I do not say this without experience; it has happened to me in at least two cases. I repeat that anyone in religion who puts his soul in the hands of a single director, without making sure that he is a man of this kind, will be making a great mistake, since he also owes obedience to his own Superior. His director may be lacking in all the three qualities I spoke of,[1] and that will be no light cross for the penitent to bear, without his also voluntarily subjecting his understanding to a man whose understanding is poor. I, at least, have never been able to bring myself to do this, nor do I think it right.

If the beginner is a person living in the world, let him praise God that

1. Learning, humility, and virtue.

he is free to choose whom he will obey, and let him be sure not to give up his justifiable freedom. Let him rather remain without a director until he finds the right one, whom the Lord will provide if his life is founded in humility, and if he has the desire to succeed. I praise God – and we women and unlearned folk must render Him infinite thanks – that there are persons who have laboured so hard to reach the truth, of which we ignorant people know nothing.

I am often astonished that learned men, and monks in particular, will give me the benefit of what they have worked so hard to acquire, and at no more cost to me than the mere asking. To think that there may be people who will not take advantage of this! God forbid that this should be! I see these learned men bearing the very great trials of the religious life with its penances, its poor food, and its yoke of obedience – really, it sometimes makes me quite ashamed to think of it! They get scant sleep, and nothing but trials and crosses. Yet I think it would be very wrong for anyone to forego the benefits of such a life through his own fault. Then, possibly, some of us who are exempt from these trials, who have the food dropped into our mouths – as they say – and live at our ease, sometimes think that, because we practise prayer a little more than they, we have a right to consider ourselves superior to them!

Bless You, O Lord, who have made me so incapable and so useless! But I bless You much more for having awakened so many who may awaken us. We should pray most regularly for those who give us light. What would become of us without them amid these mighty storms that now beset the Church? If some of them have been wicked, the good will shine with greater brightness. May it please God to hold them in His hand and help them to help us. Amen.

I have wandered far from the purpose with which I began. But everything is of use to beginners who are setting out on this high journey, and will help to keep their feet on the right road. To return, however, to what I said about meditating on Christ at the pillar – it is good to reflect for a while and think of the pains He suffered, and of why He suffered them, and of who it was that suffered them, and of the love with which He suffered them. Yet we should not always weary ourselves by pursuing such thoughts, but rather stay there beside Him, with all our thoughts stilled. We should occupy ourselves, if we can, by gazing at Him who is gazing at us, and should keep Him company, and talk with Him, and pray to Him, and humble ourselves and delight in Him, and remind ourselves that we do not deserve to be there. Anyone who can do this, though he may be at the very beginning of prayer, will make great progress; and this form of prayer is very beneficial – at least my soul has found it so. I do not know if I have made myself clear, but your Reverence will know that. May the Lord allow me always to please Him for ever. Amen.

CHAPTER 14

She begins to explain the second stage of prayer, in which the Lord
already grants the soul more special consolations. These she describes
in order to show that they are supernatural, and this is a
most noteworthy chapter

HAVING spoken of the effort and physical labour entailed in watering the garden, and what efforts it costs to raise the water from
the well, let us now turn to the second method of drawing it which the
Owner of the plot has ordained. By means of a device with a windlass,
the gardener draws more water with less labour, and so is able to take
some rest instead of being continuously at work. I apply this description
to the prayer of quiet, which I am now going to describe.

Now the soul begins to be recollected, and here it comes into touch
with the supernatural, to which it could not possibly attain by its own
efforts. True, sometimes it seems to have grown weary through turning
the wheel, and toiling with its mind, and filling the buckets. But in this
state the level of the water is higher, and so much less labour is required
than for drawing it from a well. I mean that the water is closer because
grace reveals itself more clearly to the soul. This entails a gathering of
the faculties within oneself so as to derive a greater savour from that
pleasure. But they are not lost or asleep. The will alone is occupied in
such a way that it is unconsciously taken captive. It simply consents to
be God's prisoner, since it well knows how to surrender to One whom
it loves. O Jesus, my Lord, how precious Your love is to us then! It
binds our own love so closely to it as to leave us no liberty to love anything but you!

The other two faculties – the memory and the imagination – help the
will to make itself more and more capable of enjoying this great blessing, though, on the other hand, it sometimes happens that they are a
great hindrance to it, even when the will is in union. But then it should
never pay attention to them but stay in its joy and quiet. For if it tried
to make them recollected, both it and they might lose the way. Then
they behave like doves who are not satisfied with the food given to
them by the owner of the dovecot, without their working for it, and
go out to seek nourishment in other places, but find so little that they
come back. So these two faculties come and go, hoping that the will can

give them some part of what it is enjoying. If it be the Lord's pleasure, it throws them some food and they stop; if not, they resume their search. One must reflect that these activities benefit the will; without them, the memory and the imagination might do it serious harm by trying to give it a picture of what it is enjoying. The will must be careful in its dealings with them, as I shall explain.

Everything that happens now brings very great consolation, and costs so little labour that, even if prayer is continued for some time, it brings no weariness. The intellect now works very gently and draws up a great deal more water than it drew from the well. The tears that God sends now are shed with joy; although we are conscious of them, they are not of our getting.

This water of great blessings and favours which the Lord now gives us makes the virtues grow incomparably more than they did in the previous state of prayer. Our soul is already rising from its wretched state, and receives some little intimation of the joys of heaven. It is this, I believe, that increases the growth of the virtues, and brings them closer to God – that true Virtue, from which all virtues spring. For His Majesty begins to communicate Himself to the soul, and would have it feel how He is communicating Himself.

On arriving at this state, the soul begins to lose the desire for earthly things – and no wonder! It clearly sees that not even one moment of this joy is to be obtained here on earth, and that there are no riches, estates, honours, or delights that can give it such satisfaction even for the twinkling of an eye. For this is the true joy, the content that can be seen to satisfy. Those of us who are on earth, it seems to me, rarely understand where this satisfaction lies. It is always up and down. First we have it, then it leaves us, and we find that it has all gone and that we cannot get it back, since we have no idea how to do so. Even if we wear ourselves to shreds with penance and prayer and other austerities, it is of little use unless the Lord is pleased to grant us that joy again. God, in his greatness, will have the soul realize that He is so near to it that it need not send messengers, but may speak to Him itself. Nor need it cry aloud, since He is now so close that it has only to move its lips and He will understand.

It seems absurd to say this, since we know that God always understands us and is always with us. This is so, and there is no doubt about it. But now our Emperor and Lord wants us to understand that He understands us, and to realize the effect of His presence. He would have us know by means of the great inward and outward satisfaction that He gives it, and by the difference – which I have already mentioned – between this joy and delight and those of the world, that He is about to begin a special work in the soul. He seems to be filling up a void in it, which was scooped out by our sins.

This satisfaction lodges in the innermost part of the soul, which does not know whence nor how it came. Often it does not even know what to do or wish or ask for. It seems to find everything at once, and yet not to know what it has found. I do not know how to explain this. Many things demand learning, and learning would indeed be very useful here, to explain what is meant by general or particular aids, since there are many who do not know this. With learning one could show how the Lord now wishes the soul to see this particular aid with the naked eye – as they say. It would be useful to explain many other matters too, about which mistakes are made. But as this is to be read by persons who will know if there is any error in it, I will go on without worrying. I know that I need not be anxious from the point of view either of learning or of spirituality, since it is going into the hands of men who will understand what I write, and remove anything that is wrong.

I should like to explain this because it is a fundamental point, and because when the Lord begins to grant these favours the soul itself does not understand them or know what it ought to do. If God leads it, as He led me, along the path of fear and there is no one who understands it, it is a grievous trial. But it will be very glad to read an account of itself and to see that it is travelling on the right road. It will be a great advantage for it to know what it should do in order to make progress in any one of these states. I have suffered greatly and lost much time through not knowing what to do, and so feel great pity for those souls who find themselves alone when they reach this state. Even though I had read many spiritual books in which these matters are discussed, they are not very explicit. If the soul has not a great deal of experience, it will have as much as it can do to understand its state, however much they say.

I very much wish the Lord would help me to describe the effects of these things on the soul, now that they begin to be supernatural, so that men may know by the results whether they are from the spirit of God. I mean that I would have them know in so far as anything can be known here below, for it is always well to proceed with fear and caution. Even if they are from God, the devil can at times transform himself into an angel of light,[1] and if the soul is not very experienced, it will not realize this. To realize this, indeed, it must have so much experience that it must have attained to the very summit of prayer.

The little time I have does not help me to explain myself. Therefore His Majesty must undertake this Himself. For I have my work to do in the community and much other business, since I live in a house that has only recently been founded,[2] as will be explained hereafter. So I can never settle down to my writing, and must work a little at a time. I wish I had leisure, for when the Lord gives inspiration things go easily and better. Then it is like doing a piece of embroidery with the pattern before one. But if the spirit is lacking, there is no more agreement between the words than in so much gibberish, as one might say, even though one may have spent many years in prayer. Therefore it seems to me a very great advantage to be in the state of prayer when I am writing. Then I realize that it is not I that speak, nor is it I that am putting the words together with my own understanding. Afterwards I do not know how I have managed to speak at all. This has happened to me many times.

Now let us return to our garden or orchard, and see how the trees begin to grow heavy with blossom and afterwards with fruit, and how the carnations and other flowers begin to smell sweet. This comparison delights me, for often when I was a beginner – and may it please God that I have now truly begun to serve His Majesty – I mean 'begun' in relation to what I have to say later about my life – it used to give me great joy to think of my soul as a garden, and of the Lord walking in it. I would beg Him to increase the fragrance of those little flowers of virtue, which seemed as if they were beginning to bud, and to preserve them for His greater glory. I desired nothing for myself, and begged Him to prune any that He pleased, for I already knew that the plants would bloom the better for it. I speak of 'pruning' because there come times when the soul feels itself to be anything but a garden. Everything appears to be dry, and there is no water to keep things green. It seems indeed as if the soul has never had any virtue in it. Now it suffers great trials, for the Lord wishes the poor gardener to suppose that all his efforts to tend and water the garden have been in vain. Then is the

1. Reference to 2 Corinthians xi, 14.
2. St Joseph's, the foundation of which she will later describe.

proper time for weeding, and rooting out every worthless plant, however small it may be. We must realize that if God withholds the water of grace no work is enough. We must consider ourselves as nothing, or less than nothing. In this way great humility is gained, and then the flowers begin to grow again.

O my Lord and my Good, I cannot say this without tears and a great rejoicing in my soul that You should wish to be with us, and are with us, in the Sacrament! This we can implicitly believe, for it is so; and we can make this comparison in utter truth. If our sins do not prevent us we may rejoice in You as You rejoice in us, for You say that it is Your delight to be with the children of men.[1] O my Lord, what does this mean? Whenever I hear these words they always give me great comfort as they did when I was far astray.

Can there possibly be any soul, O Lord, that reaches the stage where You grant it such graces and favours, and understands that You rejoice to be with it, and yet falls back into sin after so many favours and such great demonstrations of the love You bear it? Of this love there can be no doubt, since its effects are visible. Yes, there is indeed such a soul; I have fallen back in this way not once but many times. May it please Your goodness, Lord, that I may be the only thankless one, the only one who has committed this great wrong, and behaved with such excessive ingratitude. Yet Your infinite goodness has produced some good even from that; the wickeder I have been, the more the glory of Your great mercies has shone out. What great reason I have to sing of them for ever!

I beseech You, O Lord, that it may so shine, and that I may sing of Your mercies for ever, since You have been pleased to grant them to me so liberally that all who see them are astonished. As for me, very often they draw me out of myself, that I may praise You better. For so long as I am in myself without You, Lord, and am like the cut flowers of the garden, I can do nothing, and this wretched soil is once more the dunghill that it was before. Do not allow this, O Lord, or suffer a soul that You have purchased with so many labours to be lost, a soul that you have so often ransomed anew, and have snatched from the teeth of the hideous dragon.

Forgive me, your Reverence, for wandering from my subject, and do not be surprised, for I am following my own purpose. The writing seems to take control of my soul; and it is very often quite hard to break

1. Proverbs viii, 31.

off my praise of God, when the great debt that I owe Him springs to my mind as I write. I do not think that this will displease you, Father, for I believe we can both sing the same song, though in a different way. But my debt to God is by far the greater, since He has forgiven me more, as your Reverence knows.

CHAPTER 15

Continuing the same subject, she gives certain advice on behaviour during the prayer of quiet. She tells how there are many souls that advance to this stage, but few who pass beyond it. The matters touched upon here are most essential and profitable

LET us now return to our subject. This quiet and recollection of the soul manifests itself largely in the peace and satisfaction, the very joy and repose of the faculties, and the most sweet delights that it brings with it. As the soul has never gone beyond this stage, it thinks that there is nothing left to desire, and would, like St Peter, gladly make its home here.[1] It dares not move or stir, for fear that this blessing may slip through its fingers; sometimes it is afraid even to breathe. The poor creature is not aware that, just as it could do nothing to acquire this blessing, so it is still less able to hold it any longer than the Lord wishes. I have already said that in this first recollection and stillness the powers of the soul are not suspended. But the soul is so replete with God that, although two of its faculties may be distracted, yet so long as recollection lasts, peace and quiet are not lost, since the will is in union with God. On the contrary the will gradually calls the intellect and the memory back again. Although it is not yet completely absorbed, it is so occupied, without knowing with what, that whatever efforts the distracted faculties may make they cannot rob it of its joy and contentment. In fact it effortlessly helps to keep this little spark of love for God from going out.

May it please His Majesty graciously to allow me to give a clear account of this, since there are many souls that come to this stage, and few that pass beyond it. I do not know whose fault this is, but it is certainly not God's. For when His Majesty shows a soul such a favour as to let it advance so far, I do not believe that He will fail to be more merciful still, unless there are faults on our side.

It is most important that the soul which reaches here shall realize the great dignity it has attained, and the great favours that the Lord has done it. It must see that it should not rightfully belong to the earth, since He of His goodness seems about to make it a citizen of heaven, if its faults do not prevent it. Alas for it if it turns back! I think it will go

1. A reference to Matthew xvii, 4.

downhill, as I was going if the Lord's mercy had not brought me back. This check must as a rule, I think, be due to grave faults. It would be impossible to give up so great a blessing except out of blindness caused by much evil.

Therefore, for the love of God, I implore those souls whom His Majesty has mercifully allowed to reach this state to know themselves, and with a humble and holy presumption to hold themselves in high esteem, so that they may not turn back to the fleshpots of Egypt. But if through weakness, wickedness, and their own mean and wretched natures, they fall as I did, let them always bear in mind the good that they have lost. Let them distrust themselves and walk in fear, as they have reason to do, for unless they turn back to prayer they will go from bad to worse. I call it a real fall when a man comes to loathe the path that has led him to much good. In talking to such souls I do not say that they will never offend God or fall into sin. Of course there are good reasons why anyone who has begun to be so blessed should guard himself carefully against falling; for we are miserable creatures. What I particularly urge is that they should not give up prayer. Prayer will teach them what they are doing, and then the Lord will grant them repentance and the strength to rise again. They must believe and go on believing that if they give up prayer, they will – as I hold – run into great danger. I am not sure whether I understand what I am saying, for, as I have said, I am judging from my own experience.

This prayer, then, is a little spark of true love for Him which the Lord begins to kindle in the soul. He wishes the soul to come to understand the nature of this love with its attendant joy. This quiet and recollection, and this little spark – so long as it proceeds from the spirit of God and is not a sweetness given by the devil or induced by ourselves – is not a thing that can be acquired, as anyone who has experience of it must immediately realize. But this nature of ours is so greedy for moments of sweetness that it seeks for them in every way. But soon it becomes very cold. For however much we try to kindle the fire in order to catch this sweetness, we seem merely to be pouring water on it and putting it out. Now this God-given spark, however tiny it may be, causes a great noise; and if we do not quench it through our own fault it begins to light the great fire, which – as I shall tell in due course – throws out flames of that mighty love of God, with which His Majesty endows the souls of the perfect.

This little spark is a sign or pledge that God gives to this soul to show that He is already choosing it for great things, if it will prepare itself to receive them. It is a great gift, far greater indeed than I can say. I am sorry for this, because – as I have said – I know many souls who reach here, and those who go further, as they should, are so few that I am ashamed to speak of it. I do not mean that they are really few, for there must be many of them, since God does not uphold us for no reason. I am speaking only of what I have seen. I should very much like to recommend such souls to take care not to hide their talents. For it would seem that God is pleased to choose them to be helpful to many others, especially in these days when strong friends of God are needed to support the weak. Those who recognize this grace in themselves should look upon themselves as His friends, if they wish to fulfil the obligations which even the world demands of faithful friendship. If they do not, let them walk in fear and trembling, I repeat, since they may be doing harm to themselves – and please God it be only to themselves!

All that the soul has to do at these times of quiet is merely to be calm and make no noise. By noise I mean working with the intellect to find great numbers of words and reflections with which to thank God for this blessing, and piling up its sins and faults to prove to itself that it does not deserve it. Then the commotion starts, the intellect works and the memory seethes. Indeed these faculties sometimes tire me out, for though I have very little memory I cannot keep it under control. The will must quietly and wisely understand that we cannot deal violently with God; and that our efforts are like great logs of wood indiscriminately piled on, which will only put out the spark. It must admit this and humbly ask: 'Lord, what can I do now? What has the slave to do with her Master, or earth with heaven?' Or let it speak any words of love that suggest themselves, in the firm and sure knowledge that what it says is the truth. But let it pay no attention to the intellect, which is merely being tiresome.

If the will wishes to inform the intellect of the nature of its joy, or strives to bring it into recollection, it will not succeed. It will often happen in this quiet and union of the will that the intellect will be in great disorder. But the will had better leave it alone and not run after it. It – I mean the will – should remain in the enjoyment of that grace, and recollected like the wise bee. For if no bees entered the hive and all flew about trying to bring one another in, there could not be much honey made.

The soul will lose a great deal if it is not careful about this, especially when the intellect is a lively one. Once it begins to compose speeches and draw up arguments, especially if these are clever, it will soon imagine that it is doing important work. All that the reason should do then is clearly to understand that there is no reason except His goodness why God should do us such great mercies. We must realize how near we are to Him, and beg His Majesty for grace, and pray to Him for the Church, and for those who have been commended to us, and for souls in purgatory – and this not with noisy words but with a feeling of desire to be heard. This is a prayer that comprises a great deal, and more is achieved by it than by much intellectual reflection. In order to kindle this love the will should stir up some reasons of its own which it will itself provide when it sees its own improved state. It should perform certain acts of love, too, for Him to whom it owes so much. But it must not, I repeat, allow any noise from the intellect, engaged in its search after profound reflections.

A few straws laid on with humility – and they will be less than straws if it is we who lay them on – are more effectual here, and will be of more use in kindling the fire than any number of faggots made of what seems to us the most learned argument, which will put it out in a moment.

This is good advice for those learned men at whose command I am now writing. For, by the goodness of God, all of them will reach this state. It may be that they will spend their time in applying passages from Scripture. But although they will not find it difficult to put their learning to good use, both before and after prayer, still in periods of prayer itself they will have, in my opinion, little need to make these applications since they will only serve to make the will lukewarm. At such times the understanding is so close to the light that it sees with great clarity, and even I, though I am what I am, seem to be quite different. Thus, ordinarily I hardly understand anything that I recite in Latin, particularly from the Psalms. Yet when in this state of quiet, I have sometimes not only understood the Latin as if it were Spanish, but have, to my delight, gone further and seen the meaning of the Spanish.

Let us leave out of account the occasions when these learned men have to preach or teach, and when they will do well to make use of their learning for the benefit of poor people like myself, who have little of it. Charity is a great thing, and so is a constant care for souls, so long as it is undertaken simply and for God's sake. But in these periods of quiet, the soul should repose in its calm, and learning should be put on one side. The time will come when they will use it in the Lord's service, and then they will appreciate it so highly, since it is of such service to His Majesty, that they would not be without it for any treasure in the world. For then it is a great help. But, believe me, in the sight of Infinite Wisdom, a little study of humility and a single humble act are of more value than all the knowledge in the world. Here there is no room for discussion, but only for a plain knowledge of what we are. We must just present ourselves simply before God. He would have the soul make itself foolish – as indeed it is in His sight – for it is only out of His Majesty's great humility that He suffers it to be near Him, we being what we are.

Now the intellect is also active and gives thanks in careful phrases. But the will, in its tranquillity, is like the Publican[1] and dares not lift up its eyes. Yet perhaps it makes a better thanksgiving than the intellect can with all its turns of rhetoric. In short, mental prayer must not be entirely abandoned, nor yet some words of vocal prayer, if we sometimes wish to use them and can. But if the state of quiet is deep, it is difficult and very painful to speak.

I believe that it is possible to tell whether this state comes from the spirit of God or whether, starting from devotion given us by God, we have attained it by our own endeavours. For if, as I have said before, we try of our own accord to pass on to this quiet of the will, it leads to nothing. Everything is quickly over, and the result is aridity. If it comes from the devil, I think an experienced soul will realize it. For it leaves disquiet behind it, and very little humility, and does not do much to prepare the soul for the effects which are produced when it comes from God. It brings neither light to the understanding nor strength to the will.

Here the devil can do little or no harm, if the soul directs to God the delight and calm that it then feels, and fixes its thoughts and desires on Him, as it has already been advised to. Indeed, the devil can gain nothing. On the contrary, by God's grace, the joy that he arouses in the soul will cost him dear. For this joy will help the soul, who will think it to be of God, and so will often come to its prayer with a desire for Him. If it is a humble soul, and not curious or eager for pleasures, even when they are spiritual pleasures, but a lover of the Cross, it will pay little attention to delights sent by the devil. But it will not be able to treat those that come from the spirit in the same way; these it will value highly. When

1. Luke xviii, 13.

the devil, who is one great lie, sends the soul any pleasure or delight and sees it humbled thereby – and in all that pertains to prayer and consolation, we must take great care to make ourselves humble – he will realize that he has lost the game and very often will not try again.

For this reason, among many others, I indicated, when discussing the first stage of prayer and the first water, that when souls begin to pray their initial task must be to detach themselves from every kind of pleasure, and enter on their prayer resolved only to help Christ carry His Cross. They must be like good soldiers, willing to serve their King without present pay because they are sure of their final reward. They must keep their eyes fixed on the true and everlasting kingdom which we are striving to attain.

It is a very important thing always to bear this Kingdom in mind, especially at the beginning. But soon it becomes so clear that, if we are to go on living, we need rather to forget it than to try always to be remembering that all things are transitory, that they are nothing, and that such rest as we are granted here must not be prized. This may seem to be a very low ideal, and so it is. Those who are advanced in perfection would consider it a reproach and would be ashamed of themselves if they thought that they were only giving up the things of this world because they are perishable. Even if they were everlasting they would gladly surrender them for God. Why, the greater their perfection and the more lasting the world's goods, the greater would be their joy in this surrender. Here, in persons so far advanced, love has already grown, and it is love that does the work. But for beginners this initial detachment is of the utmost importance, and they must not despise it. The blessings to be gained by it are great, and that is why I recommend it so strongly. Even those who have reached great heights of prayer will need it at certain times when God wishes to test them, and when His Majesty seems to have deserted them.

As I have already said – and I do not want it to be forgotten – in this life of ours the soul's growth is not like the body's, although we speak as if it is and it really does grow. A child that has grown up and whose body has formed does not shrink and become small again. But this may, by the Lord's will, happen to the soul, as I know by my own experience, which is my only means of knowledge. This must be in order to humble us for our own greater good, and to prevent our being careless during this exile of ours. For the higher we climb the more cause we have to be afraid, and the less reason we have to trust in ourselves.

There come times when even those whose entire will is so subordinated to the will of God that they would let themselves be tortured rather than be guilty of one imperfection, and die a thousand deaths rather than commit sins, find themselves beset by temptations and persecutions. Then they find it necessary, if they are to avoid offending God, to make use of the primary weapons of prayer, and to reflect once again that all things are transitory, that there is a heaven and a hell, and on other things of this sort.

But to return to what I was saying, the fundamental means of delivering ourselves from the snares and pleasures that the devil sends is to begin with the determination to desire no pleasures but to walk in the way of the Cross from the very first. For the Lord Himself showed us this way of perfection, when He said: 'Take up your Cross and follow me'.[1] He is our example, and those who follow His counsel, with the sole desire to please Him, have nothing to fear.

They will see by the improvement that they detect in themselves that this is not the devil's work. Even if they fall, they will be able to rise again at once: a sure sign of the presence of the Lord. But they will have other signs too, which I will now describe. When God's spirit is at work there is no need to cast around for ways of inducing humility and shame. For Our Lord Himself reveals them in a very different way from any that we could find by our own poor reflections, which are as nothing when compared to that true humility which springs from the light thus given us by the Lord. This brings on a shame that quite overwhelms us. The revelation that we have no good in us, which is a gift from God, is a well-known experience; and the more generous the favours we receive from Him, the better we realize it. It fills us with a great desire to press forward in prayer, and to let no trial that may arise deflect us from it; the soul is willing to suffer anything. A certain security, combined with humility and fear for our salvation, immediately expels servile fear from the soul, and puts in its place a fear of much stronger growth, which springs from faith. Then we see that an entirely disinterested love of God is arising in us, and we desire spells of solitude, the better to enjoy this new blessing.

Let me conclude, or I shall grow weary, by saying that this is the beginning of all good things. The flowers have now grown and are on the point of bursting into bloom, as the soul will very plainly see. Now it can never believe that the Lord is not with it, until it turns back to view

1. Matthew xvi, 24.

its own faults and imperfections. Then it fears for everything, and it is well that it should. There are souls, however, that benefit more from the certain belief that God is with them than from all the fears that may strike them. If a soul is naturally loving and grateful, the memory of a favour received makes it turn to God more than all the tortures of Hell that it can picture to itself. At least, that was certainly the case with me, wicked though I am.

As I shall describe the signs of a good spirit more fully later on, I shall say nothing of them here, since it has cost me great efforts to understand them clearly; and I believe that, with God's help, I shall say something to the point. For not only have I my own experience to go on which has taught me a great deal, but I have had the help of some most learned scholars and very holy persons, whom we have reason to trust in the matter. So souls who, by God's goodness, reach this point need not in future weary themselves to death in the way that I did.

CHAPTER 16

*She treats of the third stage of prayer, and continues to explain things
of a very lofty nature, telling what the soul that has come so far can do,
and what are the effects of such great favours from the Lord. This is a
subject most likely to uplift the spirit in God's praise, and to give great
comfort to those who have come so far*

LET us now go on to speak of the third water that feeds this garden,
which is flowing water from a stream or spring. This irrigates it
with far less trouble, though some effort is required to direct it into the
right channel. But now the Lord is pleased to help the gardener in such
a way as to be, as it were, the gardener Himself. For it is He who does
everything. The faculties of the soul are asleep, not entirely lost nor yet
entirely conscious of how they are working. The pleasure, sweetness,
and delight are incomparably more than in the previous state, for the
water of grace has risen to the soul's neck, and it is powerless, knowing
neither how to advance nor to retreat; what it wants is to enjoy its very
great glory. It is like a man with the funeral candle in his hand, on the
point of dying the death he desires. It takes unutterable delight in the
enjoyment of its agony, which seems to me like nothing else but an
almost complete death to all the things of this world, and a fulfilment
in God. I know of no other words with which to describe or explain it.
The soul does not know what to do; it cannot tell whether to speak or
be silent, whether to laugh or weep. It is a glorious bewilderment, a
heavenly madness, in which true wisdom is acquired, and to the soul a
fulfilment most full of delight.

It is, I believe, five or six years since the Lord first granted me
frequent and abundant experience of this sort of prayer; and I have
never understood it or been able to explain it. I decided therefore that
when I came to this place in my narrative I would say little or nothing
about it. I knew very well that it was not a complete union of all the
faculties, and yet it was clearly higher than the previous state of prayer.
But I confess that I could not decide or understand where the difference lay.

It was your Reverence's humility, I believe, in consenting to accept
help from a person as simple as I, that caused the Lord to grant me this
prayer to-day, after Communion. His Majesty did not allow me to pass

beyond it, but suggested these comparisons to me, teaching me how to explain this state, and what the soul must do when in it. I was indeed amazed, and understood it all in a flash. Very often I was, so to speak, bewildered and intoxicated with love, and yet could never understand how it was. I knew very well that this was God's work, but I could never understand the way in which He worked here. In effect the faculties are in almost complete union, yet not so absorbed that they do not act. I am greatly delighted that I have understood it at last. Blessed be the Lord, who has given me this gift!

The faculties retain only the power of occupying themselves wholly with God. None of them seems to dare even to stir, nor can we make any one of them move without great and deliberate efforts to fix the attention on some external thing, though I do not think that at such times we can entirely succeed in doing this. Many words are then spoken in praise of the Lord. But they are disorderly, unless the Lord Himself imposes order on them. The intellect, at any rate, is of no value here. The soul longs to pour out words of praise. But it is in a sweet unrest, and cannot contain itself. Already the flowers are opening, and beginning to give off scent.

In this state the soul would have everyone behold it and – to the glory of God – know of its bliss, and help it to praise Him. It would have them partake of its joy, which is greater than it can bear alone. This reminds me of the woman in the Gospel who wanted to call, or did call her neighbours together.[1] Such must, I think, have been the feelings of that wondrous David, the royal prophet, when he played on the harp and sang the praises of God. I have a very great veneration for that glorious king, as I wish everyone else had, especially those who are sinners, like myself.

O my God, what must a soul be like when it is in this state! It longs to be all one tongue with which to praise the Lord. It utters a thousand pious follies, in a continuous endeavour to please Him who thus possesses it. I know someone[2] who, although no poet, yet suddenly composed some stanzas, full of feeling, which well expressed her pain. They were not the work of her intellect. But for the deeper enjoyment of that blessing which gave her such sweet pain, she complained of it to God. She would gladly have had herself cut to pieces, body and soul, to show the joy that she felt in that pain. What torments could have been offered her then that she would not have borne with delight for her

1. A reference to Luke xv, 9.   2. This is Santa Teresa herself.

Lord? She clearly sees that when the martyrs endured their tortures, they did little or nothing of themselves. For the soul knows well that its strength arises from outside itself.

But how will it feel when it returns to the senses and has to live in the world, and when it must resume the world's cares and formalities? I do not think that I have exaggerated in any way, but have been rather sparing in my description of this sort of joy that the Lord graciously allows the soul to enjoy in this, its exile. May You be eternally blessed, O Lord, and may all things praise You for ever!

Since as I write this I am still under the power of that heavenly madness, the effect of Your goodness and mercy, O my King, and a favour that You grant me for no merits of my own, I implore You that all those with whom I converse may also become mad through Your love, or let me have to do with none. Ordain that I may have no part in the affairs of this world, or take me from it entirely. This servant of Yours, O Lord, can no longer suffer such trials as come when it sees itself without You. If she must live, she wants no rest in this life – so give her none. This soul longs to be free. Eating is killing it, sleep brings it anguish. It sees itself wasting the hours of this life in comforts, though nothing can comfort it now but You. It seems to be living unnaturally, since now its desire is to live not in itself but in You.

O my true Lord and Glory, the Cross that You have prepared for those who reach this stage is indeed light, yet at the same time it is most heavy! It is light because it is sweet, and heavy because there are times when the soul has no patience left to endure it. Yet it would never wish to be free from that Cross, unless in order to come to You. When it remembers that it has never served You at all, and that by living it may yet do so, it longs for a much heavier burden, and never to die until the end of the world. It values its repose as nothing, compared with doing You some slight service. It does not know what to desire, but well knows that it desires nothing but You.

O my son – for the Father[1] to whom this is directed and who commanded me to write it is so humble that he wishes to be so addressed – these passages in which I seem to have overrun all bounds must be for your eyes alone. For no reason is strong enough to keep me confined when my Lord takes me out of myself. Since my Communion this morning, I do not believe that it is I who have been speaking. All that passes seems a dream; I wish that everyone I meet were afflicted with

1. Pedro Ibáñez.

this same infirmity. I beseech you, Father, let us all be mad, for the love of Him who was called so for our sake.

You say, Father, that you are fond of me. I want you to prove it by so preparing yourself that God may grant you this same mercy. For I see very few who are not too worldly-wise to do what they should, and I may be more at fault in this respect than anyone else. But your Revrence must now allow this to be. You are my confessor, to whom I have entrusted my soul. Dispel my illusions then by telling the truth; for truths of this sort are very rarely told.

I wish that we five,[1] who now love each other in Christ, could make some such arrangement. Just as others[2] have, in recent times, been meeting together in secret to plot wickedness and heresies against His Majesty, so we might arrange to come together now and then in order to dispel one another's illusions, and to advise one another of ways in which we could improve ourselves and be more pleasing to God. For no one knows himself so well as those who observe him, provided they do so lovingly and with the wish to do him good. I say 'in secret' because this sort of language is no longer in use. Even preachers have the habit of so framing their sermons as to displease nobody. Their intentions are good and their activities splendid, but they do not persuade very many to amend their lives. Why is it that there are so few who are led by sermons to abstain from public sin? Do you know what I think? It is because preachers have too much worldly wisdom. They do not fling all restraint aside and burn with the great fire of God, as the Apostles did; and so their flames do not throw out much heat. I do not say that their fire could be as great as the Apostles', but I wish they had more than I see they have. Do you know, Father, what our chief care ought to be? To hold our life in abhorrence and despise reputation. So long as we speak the truth and uphold it to the glory of God, we should not care whether we lose or gain everything. For he who is truly bold in God's service bears loss and gain alike with equanimity. I do not say that I am one of these, but I should like to be.

O what a grand freedom it is, to look upon the need to live and behave according to the world's laws as a captivity! When this comes as a gift from the Lord, there is no slave who would not risk everything

1. Her confessor Father Ibáñez, Father Daza, Doña Guiomar de Ulloa, Don Francisco de Salido, and herself.

2. Reference to a heretical group at Valladolid, led by one of Charles V's chaplains, which was broken up in 1559.

to earn his ransom and return to his own country. Since this is the true road, there is no reason to linger on it. We shall never succeed in winning a treasure of this size until our life is ended. May the Lord give us His help to this end! Tear up what I have written, sir, if you think fit, and consider this as a letter to yourself. Forgive me also if I have been very bold.

CHAPTER 17

She continues to explain the third stage of prayer, and completes her
account of its effects. She tells of the hindrances caused in this state by
the imagination and the memory

SUFFICIENT has been said about this kind of prayer, and of what the
soul has to do, or rather of what God does within it. He now takes
on the gardener's work, and desires it to rest. The will has only to consent to these graces that it enjoys, and to submit to all that true Wisdom
wishes to do to it. For this, some courage is certainly necessary, since
the joy is so great that at times the soul seems on the very point of
completely leaving the body. What a blessed death that would be!

Now I think it is good – as your Reverence has already been told –
for the soul to abandon itself entirely to the arms of God. If He will talk
it to heaven, let it go; if to hell, no matter since it is going there with its
own highest Good. If its life is to end altogether, so let it be; if it is to
live a thousand years, it wills that also. Let His Majesty treat it as His
own; it no longer belongs to itself; it is entirely given to the Lord, and
must cast aside all care. I mean that in a state of prayer as sublime as this,
the soul realizes that the Lord is doing His work without any labouring
of the intellect, which is merely amazed, as it seems to me, at seeing
God play the part of the good gardener. For when God brings a soul to
this state He can do all this and much more, and this is the effect of His
action. He will not let it do any work itself, except to delight in the
fragrance that the flowers are beginning to give off.

In one of these visits, however brief it may be, the Gardener, being
as he is the Creator of the water, pours it out without stint; and what the
poor soul has not been able to collect in perhaps twenty years of ex-
hausting intellectual effort, the heavenly Gardener gives it in a moment.
Then the fruit grows and ripens, so that the soul may, by God's will
draw sustenance from its garden. But he does not allow it to share
the fruit with others, until it has grown so strong by eating it as not to
consume it all by merely nibbling at it. For in this way it gets no
nourishment, and pays nothing back to the Giver, and it would then
be maintaining others at its own cost, whilst itself, maybe, dying of
hunger. The meaning of this will be perfectly clear to those who

have the understanding, and they will know how to apply it more effectively than I can describe it, for I am getting tired.

The virtues, then, are now stronger than they were during the preceding prayer of quiet. The soul sees that it has changed, and is unconsciously beginning to do great things with the fragrance given off by the flowers. It is now the Lord's will that they shall open, so that the soul may see that it possesses virtues, even though it also knows very well that it cannot and never could acquire them in many years, whereas the celestial Gardener has given them to it in a flash. The soul's humility is now greater and more profound than it was before. It clearly sees that it has done absolutely nothing except consent to the Lord's granting it graces, and embraces them with its will.

This state of prayer seems to me a most definite union of the whole soul with God, complete but for the fact that His Majesty appears to allow the faculties to be conscious of and to enjoy the great work that He is doing. Sometimes – indeed very often – the will being in union, the soul is aware of it and sees that it is rejoicing in its captivity. There is the will, alone and abiding in great peace, while the understanding and the memory, on the other hand, are so free that they can attend to business or do works of charity. I tell you this, my Father, so that you may see that it can happen, and may recognize the experience when it comes to you: I myself was driven quite frantic by it, and that is why I speak of it here.

Although it may appear to be the same, this differs from the prayer of quiet, of which I have spoken. In that first state the soul does not wish to move or stir but delights in the blessed repose of a Mary, whereas in this second state it can be like Martha also. Thus it is, as it were, leading the active and the contemplative life at once, and can apply itself to works of charity, to its professional business and to reading as well. Yet in this state we are not wholly masters of ourselves, but are well aware that the better part of the soul is elsewhere. It is as if we were speaking to one person, while someone else were speaking to us, so that we cannot attend properly to either.

This state can be plainly apprehended, and gives great joy and satisfaction when experienced. It is a splendid preparation for the attainment of very great quiet, once a moment of solitude or freedom from business arrives. It is like the life of a man who has satisfied his appetite and has no need of food. He feels so comfortable in his stomach that he could not sit down to ordinary fare. Yet he is not so replete that he would not eat with relish if he were offered something really tempting to his palate. So the soul is dissatisfied with the world's pleasures and does not desire them, because it has within it something that satisfies it better. Greater joy in God, a longing to satisfy its desires and more deeply to enjoy its times with Him: these are what the soul seeks.

There is another kind of union which, though still not complete, is more nearly so than the one I have just described. It is less perfect, however, than what has been called that of the third water. Should the Lord bestow all these upon your Reverence – supposing that He has not done so already – you will be very glad to find them described in writing, and so understand their nature. For the gift of our Lord's favour is one favour; but to understand what the gift and the favour are is another; and to have the power to describe and explain them to others is yet a third. Though it may seem that only the first of these is necessary to save the soul from fear and bewilderment and to enable it to travel with greater courage along the Lord's path, treading all the things of this world underfoot, an understanding of this state is a great advantage. This great power of understanding, indeed, is one for which everyone who receives it has great reason to praise the Lord. But those who do not have it have cause to praise Him too, for having bestowed it on some few who are living and can help us profit by it.

Now the kind of union of which I shall now speak comes about like this – and this is especially true of me, to whom God has granted this favour very often. God catches up the will, and the intellect too, as it seems to me, since it does not reason but is occupied in the enjoyment of God, like a spectator who sees so many things that he does not know where to look. As he catches sight of one thing he loses another, and could not give a description of anything.

The memory necessarily remains free, together with the imagination; and when they are left alone, it is marvellous to see what havoc they make, and how they try to throw everything into disorder. Personally, I am wearied by these disorderly faculties and I loathe them; and often I pray God to rid me of them on these occasions if they must trouble me so. Sometimes I say to Him: O my God, when can my soul be entirely united in Your praise, instead of being distracted and unable to control itself? Now I understand the harm done to us by sin, which has so bound us that we cannot do as we desire, and occupy ourselves always with God.

I say that this experience happens to me at times. It has done so to-day, and that is why I have it so well in mind. Then I see my soul torn asunder in the effort to be wholly where the greater part of it is: which it finds to be an impossibility. The memory and the imagination make such war on it that it cannot prevail against them, and though the other faculties, being in abeyance, are powerless to do anything, even harm, they do the soul a good deal of damage merely by disturbing it. When I say 'powerless to do harm', therefore, I mean that they have no strength and cannot concentrate. As the intellect gives the soul no help whatever in dealing with the imagination, it stays nowhere but flits from one thing to another like nothing so much as one of those restless and tiresome little moths that fly by night. In just this way it flies from one extreme to another. This seems to me a very apt comparison. For though the intellect has not the power to do any harm, it is troublesome to those who notice it. I know of no remedy for this, for hitherto God has never shown me one. If He had, I would gladly make use of it, since I am, as I have said, frequently tormented in this way. This shows us our wretched state, and clearly illustrates the great power of God. For all this fatigue and harm is caused us by the faculty that remains free, while the others, which are with His Majesty, give us rest.

The last remedy that I have tried is the one that I described when discussing the prayer of quiet; that is to take no more notice of it than one would of a madman, but to let it continue with its theme, which only God can take from it. Then it is reduced to slavery, and we must bear patiently with it, as Jacob bore with Leah. For the Lord grants us sufficient grace if he allows us to enjoy Rachel.

I say that it is reduced to slavery, because ultimately it cannot drag the other faculties after it, however hard it tries. They, on the contrary, without any great effort, make it follow them. Sometimes God is pleased to take pity on it when He sees it so confused and disturbed because of its desire to be joined to the other faculties. Then His Majesty allows it to burn in the flame of that divine candle, in which the others have already been reduced to ashes, their whole nature lost in what appears to be the supernatural enjoyment of this great bliss.

In all these states of prayer that I have described whilst speaking of this last water, which comes from a spring, the soul's bliss and repose is so great that even the body shares in its joy and delight to a clearly perceptible extent, and the virtues are highly developed also, as I have said. It seems that the Lord has been pleased thus to reveal these states in which the soul may find itself, and to do so as clearly, I believe, as is possible here upon this earth.

Discuss this, my Father,. with any spiritual person who has reached this stage and has some learning. If he says that it is right, take it that God has said so, and be grateful to His Majesty for it. For, as I have said, in course of time you will be very glad to have understood its nature. Meanwhile, if His Majesty allows you to enjoy it but not to understand it, still, granted that first favour, you, with all your intellect and learning, will come to know what it is with the help of this writing. Praise be to God for all things for ever and ever. Amen.

CHAPTER 18

She treats of the fourth stage of prayer, and begins an excellent explanation of the great dignity to which the Lord raises the soul in this state. This is meant to spur those who practise prayer to make efforts to reach this exalted state, which it is possible to attain on earth, though not through our merits, but only by the goodness of God. This chapter must be read with great care, since the argument is most subtle, and contains some most noteworthy observations

MAY the Lord teach me words with which to convey some idea of the fourth water. I shall indeed need His help more now than ever before. In this state, the soul still feels that it is not altogether dead, as we may say, though it is entirely dead to the world. But, as I have said, it retains the sense to know that it is still here and to feel its solitude; and it makes use of outward manifestations to show its feelings, at least by signs. Throughout, in every stage of the prayer that I have described, the gardener performs some labour, though in these later stages the labour is accompanied by so much bliss and comfort to the soul that the soul would never willingly abandon it. So the labour is not felt as such, but as bliss.

Here there is no sense of anything but enjoyment, without any knowledge of what is being enjoyed. The soul realizes that it is enjoying some good thing that contains all good things together, but it cannot comprehend this good thing. All the senses are taken up with this joy so that none of them is free to act in any way, either outwardly or inwardly. Previously, as I have said, the senses were permitted to give some indication of the great joy they feel. But now the soul enjoys incomparably more, and yet has still less power to show it. For there is no power left in the body – and the soul possesses none – by which this joy can be communicated. At such a time anything of the sort would be a great embarrassment, a torment and a disturbance of its repose. If there is really a union of all the faculties, I say, then the soul cannot make it known, even if it wants to – while actually in union I mean. If it can, then it is not in union.

How what is called union takes place and what it is, I cannot tell. It is explained in *mystical theology*, but I cannot use the proper terms; I cannot understand what *mind* is, or how it differs from *soul* or *spirit*. They all

122

seem one to me, though the soul sometimes leaps out of itself like a burning fire that has become one whole flame and increases with great force. The flame leaps very high above the fire. Nevertheless it is not a different thing, but the same flame which is in the fire. You, sirs, with your learning will understand this. I cannot be more explicit.

What I want to explain is the soul's feelings when it is in this divine union. It is plain enough what union is; in union two separate things become one. O my Lord, how good You are! May You be blessed for ever, O my God, and may all things praise You for so loving us that we can truly speak of Your communication with souls, even here in our exile! Though the souls may be good souls, this is a great bounty and magnanimity on Your part. In a word, it is Your bounty, O Lord, since You give according to Your nature. O infinite Bounty, how magnificent are Your works! Even one whose understanding is not taken up with the things of this world realizes to his surprise that he cannot understand these truths. Why, then, do You give such sovereign favours to souls that have so offended against You? This is truly beyond my understanding, and when I come to reflect on it I can get no further. Is there any way of going on that is not a turning back? As for giving You thanks for these great favours, I do not know how to, though sometimes I find it a help to utter nonsense.

Often immediately after I have received these favours, or as God begins to bestow them on me – for when one is in this state, as I have said, one has no power to do anything – I said words like these:

'Lord, see what You are doing, and do not forget so soon the gravity of my sins. But since You forgive me, You must have forgotten them already. Yet so that there may be some limits to Your mercies, I pray You to remember them. O my Creator, do not pour so precious a liquid into so broken a vessel. For You have seen already how often I spill it. Do not lay up treasures like these where the longing for this life's consolations is not so dead as it should be, or they will be utterly wasted. How can you entrust this walled city and the keys of its citadel to a defender so cowardly that he will let the enemy in at the first assault? Do not let Your love be so great, O eternal King, as to risk such precious jewels. Men seem to have an excuse for undervaluing them, O Lord, when You put them in the hands of one so wretched, so vile, so weak and miserable, and worthless as I. For though I may make efforts not to lose them, with the help of Your grace – and being what I am, I need quite a little – I cannot use them to bring profit to anyone else. I am, in short, a woman, and not even a good one, but wicked. When talents are placed in earth as vile as this, they seem not only hidden but buried. You do not usually bestow great graces and mercies like these, O Lord, upon a soul that is unable to benefit many others. You know already, Lord, that I beg this of You with all my will and all my heart, and that I have done so many times, and that I count it a blessing to lose the greatest good that can be had on earth if You will bestow these favours on one who will make better use of this blessing for the increase of Your glory.'

I have had occasion to say this and other such things many times. But afterwards I have seen my foolishness and lack of humility. For the Lord well knows what is fitting, and that my soul would have no power to achieve salvation if His Majesty did not bestow it on me with His great mercies.

I propose also to describe the graces and effects that remain in the soul, and to say what it can do of itself, if anything, towards attaining this high state.

This raising of the spirit or union comes with heavenly love. For in my opinion union is not the same thing as the elevation which takes place in that union. To anyone who has not experienced the latter there may seem to be no difference. But, in my view, though they are both one, the Lord works differently in each, and a far greater increase in the soul's detachment from creatures comes with the flight of the spirit. I have clearly seen that this is a special grace though, as I say, it may be the same as the other, or appear to be so. But a small fire is just as much a fire as a big one, and yet one can see the difference between them. In a small fire it takes a long time for a little piece of iron to become red hot; but if the fire is big even a large piece of iron will very quickly appear to change its nature. So it is, I think, with these two manifestations of the Lord's mercy; and anyone who has experienced raptures will, I know, understand me perfectly. To one who has not, however, this must seem nonsense, and it may be so. For one like myself to speak of such a matter, making an attempt to explain something which cannot even begin to be described in words, may very well appear ridiculous.

But I believe that the Lord will help me here. For His Majesty knows that, while my first intention in writing is to obey, my chief aim is to lure souls towards this sublime blessing. I will not speak of anything that I do not know from plentiful experience. That is why, when I began to write about this fourth water, it seemed to me more impossible to say anything about it than to speak Greek – and indeed it is very difficult – so I broke off and went to Communion. Blessed be the Lord who is so merciful to the ignorant! What virtues there are in obedience, which can do everything! God enlightened my understanding, partly with words, and partly by showing me how to use them. For here, as in the previous stage of prayer, His Majesty seems willing to say what I myself can neither say nor understand.

What I am saying is the whole truth, and therefore whatever is good in it is His teaching, and whatever is evil comes, of course, from that sea of wickedness, myself. Consequently I say that if there are any – and there must be many – who, after attaining these states of prayer which the Lord of His mercy has granted to this miserable creature, imagine that they have lost their way and wish to consult me about these matters the Lord will help His servant to declare His truth.

I am now speaking of that rain that comes down abundantly from heaven to soak and saturate the whole garden. If the Lord never ceased to send it whenever it was needed, the gardener would certainly have leisure; and if there were no winter but always a temperate climate, there would never be a shortage of fruit and flowers, and the gardener would clearly be delighted. But this is impossible while we live, for we must always be looking out for one water when another fails. The heavenly rain very often comes down when the gardener least expects it. Yet it is true that at the beginning it almost always comes after long mental prayer. Then, as one stage succeeds another, the Lord takes up this small bird and puts it into the nest where it may be quiet. He has watched it fluttering for a long time, trying with its understanding and its will and all its strength to find God and please Him; and now He is pleased to give it its reward in this life. And what a reward! One moment of it is enough to repay all the trials it can ever have endured.

While seeking God in this way, the soul is conscious that it is fainting almost completely away in a kind of swoon, with a very great calm and joy. Its breath and all its bodily powers progressively fail it, so that it can hardly stir its hands without great effort. Its eyes close involuntarily, and if they remain open, they see almost nothing. If a person reads in this state he can scarcely make out a single letter; it is as much as he can do to recognize one. He sees that there are letters, but as the understanding offers no help, he cannot read them, even if he wants to. He hears but does not understand what he hears. In the same way, his senses serve no purpose except to prevent the soul from taking its pleasure; and so they tend to do him harm. It is the same with the tongue, for he cannot form a word, nor would he have the strength to pronounce one. The whole physical strength vanishes and the strength of the soul increases for the better enjoyment of its bliss. The outward joy that is now felt is great and most perceptible.

However long this prayer lasts, it does no harm. At least it has never done me any; however ill I might have been when the Lord granted me this grace, I never remember an occasion when I experienced any bad effects from it. On the contrary I was left feeling much better. But what harm can so great a blessing possibly do? The outward results are so evident that there can be no doubt some great thing has taken place. Nothing else could have robbed us of our bodily strength, yet have given us so much joy that it is returned to us increased.

The truth is that it passes so rapidly at the beginning – at least it did with me – that it cannot be recognized either by these external signs or by the failure of the senses. Everything is too quick. But it is plain from the superabundance of grace that the sun must have shone very brightly here, to leave the soul thus melted away. Let it be observed too that however long the soul may enjoy this suspension of the faculties, the actual time is, in my opinion, very short. Half an hour would be a very long period of rapture, longer, I think, than any I ever experienced. Actually, it is very difficult to judge the time, since the senses are in abeyance. But I do not think that it can ever be long before one of them recovers. It is the will that maintains the contact. But the other two faculties soon begin to trouble it once more. But, as the will is calm, they become suspended again, and they are quiet for a little longer. But eventually they spring into life again.

In this way some hours may be – and are - spent in prayer. For once the two faculties have begun to grow drunk on the taste of this wine, they are very ready to give themselves up again in order to enjoy some more. Then they keep company with the will, and the three rejoice together. But this state of complete absorption, without any working of the imagination – for I believe that it too is in complete abeyance – is, as I say, of brief duration, though the faculties do not recover so completely as not to be for some hours in a sort of disorder, God every now and then drawing them once more to Himself.

Let us now come to the soul's inward sensations in this condition. These should be spoken of by those who know them; for as they are beyond understanding, so are they beyond description. I was wondering when I decided to write this – after taking Communion and experiencing that state of prayer of which I am writing – how the soul is occupied at that time. Then the Lord said to me: 'It dissolves utterly, my daughter, to rest more and more in Me. It is no longer itself that lives; it is I. As it cannot comprehend what it understands, it understands by not understanding.'

Anyone who has experienced this will to some extent understand. It cannot be expressed more clearly, since all that happens is so obscure. I can only say that the soul conceives itself to be near God, and that it is left with such a conviction that it cannot possibly help believing. All the faculties are in abeyance, and so suspended, as I have said, that their operations cannot be followed. If the soul has previously been meditating on any subject, it vanishes from the memory at once, as completely as if it had never been thought of. If it has been reading, it is unable to remember it or dwell on the words; and it is the same with vocal prayer. So the restless little moth of the memory has its wings burned, and can flutter no more. The will must be fully occupied in loving, but does not understand how it loves. If it understands, it does not understand how it understands, or at least, cannot comprehend anything of what it understands. I do not think that it understands at all, because, as I have said, it does not understand itself. Nor can I myself understand this.

There was one thing that I was ignorant of at the beginning. I did not really know that God is present in all things; and when He seemed to me so near, I thought that it was impossible. Yet I could not cease believing that He was there, since I seemed almost certainly to have been conscious of His very presence. Unlearned persons told me that He was there only in His grace. But I could not believe this, because, as I have said, He seemed to be really present; and so I was still distressed. I was delivered from this doubt by a very learned man of the Order of the glorious patriarch St Dominic, who told me that the Lord is indeed present, and described His way of communicating with us. This was a great comfort to me. It is to be observed and understood that this water from heaven, this greatest of God's graces, always brings very great profit to the soul, as I shall now explain.

CHAPTER 19

Continuing the same subject, she begins to describe the effects upon the soul of this stage of prayer. She earnestly exhorts those who have attained it not to turn back, even if they should afterwards fall, nor ever to give up prayer. She describes the harm that they would suffer if they did so. All this is most noteworthy and will be of great comfort to the weak and to sinners

AFTER this prayer of union, the soul is left with a very great tenderness, so much so that it would gladly dissolve, not in grief but in tears of joy. Quite unawares, it finds itself bathed in them, and does not know how or when it wept. But it has great delight in seeing the force of the fire assuaged by water, which yet makes it burn the more. This may sound utter nonsense, but all the same it happens.

Occasionally, when the prayer has ended, I have been so beside myself as not to know if it has been a dream or if the bliss I have been feeling has been a reality. But when I have seen myself drenched with tears, which have flowed painlessly, yet so quickly and with such violence that they might have fallen from a cloud in heaven, I have realized that it was no dream. This was at the beginning, when the condition soon passed away.

The soul is left, however, with so much courage that if it were to be torn asunder at that moment for God's sake, it would be greatly comforted. This is a time of vows, of heroic resolutions, and of strenuous desires, when the soul begins to loathe the world, and develops a very clear realization of its own vanity. The benefits that it receives are more numerous and sublime than any from previous states of prayer; and its humility grows greater. It plainly sees that no efforts of its own could ever help it to gain or keep this immeasurable favour. It sees clearly how unworthy it is, for in a room that the sun enters freely no cobwebs can be hidden. It sees its own wretchedness, and self-conceit is so far away that it cannot believe it ever had any. Now it sees with its own eyes that of itself it can do little or nothing, and that it hardly even gave its consent to what happened to it. The doors seem to have been shut on its senses rather, against its own will, in order that it might more abundantly enjoy the Lord. Being alone with Him, what can it do but love Him? It neither hears nor sees except by violent efforts, but can take little credit for that. Then its past life stands before it, and God's great mercy is truthfully revealed. The understanding need no longer go out hunting, for its nourishment is already prepared. The soul sees for itself that it deserves to go to hell, and that its punishment is bliss. It dissolves in praise for God, as I would gladly do now. Blessed be You, O Lord, for taking from so dirty a pool as I am such clear water for Your own table. Praised be You, O Joy of the angels, for being pleased thus to raise so vile a worm.

The benefit of this remains for some time in the soul. Now that it clearly understands that the fruit are not its own, it can begin to share them with others, without lacking any itself. It begins to show signs that it is a soul which guards heavenly treasures, and that it desires to distribute them freely. It prays to God that it may not be rich alone, and begins to benefit its neighbours, almost unconsciously and without any deliberate purpose. They understand how things are, because the flowers now smell so sweet that they are eager to come near them. They realize that the soul has virtue in it and, seeing how delicious the fruit are, long to share in the feast.

If the ground is well dug over by trials, persecutions, detractions, and infirmities – few can reach this point without them – and if it is well broken up by extreme detachment from self-interest, it will soak up so much water that it will hardly ever be parched again. But if it is ground that is still uncleared and choked with thorns, as I was at first; if it is still not free from occasions for sin, and not as grateful as it should be after such great mercies, then the earth will dry up again. If the gardener becomes careless, and if the Lord, out of His sheer goodness, will not send down fresh rain, then you must give up the garden for lost. It has been like this with me more than once, and I am amazed at it. If all this had not happened to me, I could not believe it. I write this for the comfort of weak souls like myself, that they may never despair or lose their trust in God's greatness. Even if they fall after the Lord has raised them as high as this, they must not faint unless they wish to be utterly lost. For tears gain everything; and one kind of water attracts another.

This has been one of the chief things that has given me courage, even being what I am, to obey my superiors and write this account of my wretched life, also of the favours which the Lord has done me, who have not served Him but sinned against Him. I wish that I were a person of great authority so that my words might be believed: and I implore the Lord God to grant me this grace. Let no one, I repeat, who has started to pray be discouraged and say: 'If I fall back into sin, it will be better for me not to go on practising prayer'. I believe it will be worse for such a person to give up prayer and continue in his evil ways. But, if he persists in prayer, he may be sure that it will bring him to the haven of light.

This was the devil's pretext for making his great assault on me; and I suffered so severely from the thought that it showed a lack of humility to persist in prayer when I was so wicked that, as I have said, for a year and a half I gave up prayer – or for a year at least, I am not very sure about the last six months. This would have meant – and did mean – neither more nor less than plunging into hell, without the need of any devils to drag me there. O my Lord, how very blind I was, and how well the devil achieves his purpose when he begins to meddle like this! The deceiver knows that any soul who resolutely persists in prayer is lost to him, and that, thanks to the goodness of God, every time he brings it down he only helps it to leap up again even higher in His service. This is a matter of some concern to Satan.

O my Jesus, what a sight it is to see a soul that has risen so high and has fallen into sin, raised up again when You stretch out Your hand to it. Then it is conscious of Your manifold greatness and mercy, and of its own wretchedness. Then it truly dissolves, and recognizes Your power. It dares not lift up its eyes; it raises them only to acknowledge its great debt to You. It devoutly prays the Queen of Heaven to intercede with You. It invokes the help of the saints, who also fell after You had called them. Now it considers You too bountiful in Your gifts, because it feels itself unworthy of the ground it treads. It resorts to the Sacraments, and burns with a living faith when it sees what virtues God has implanted in them. It praises You for having left us such medicines and ointments for our wounds as not only heal them on the surface but entirely remove them. It is amazed at this. And who, Lord of my soul, would not be amazed at such great compassion and such high mercy shown to such foul and abominable treason? I cannot think why my heart does not break as I write these lines, for I am wicked.

With these poor tears that I am weeping now, and that are Your gift – water from a most impure well in so far as it is mine – I seem to be paying You for my repeated treacheries in always doing evil, and in labouring to wipe out the graces that You have granted me. Give my tears virtue, O my Lord; purify this muddy water; if only that I may not tempt others to judge me, as I have been tempted myself to judge others. For once I used to ask: 'Why, O Lord, do You pass by some most holy persons who have always served You and have been tried; persons brought up in Religion, who have true feeling and are not like myself, who am only religious in name? I cannot see why You do not grant them the mercies that You grant me.'

But then, O my sole Good, it became clear to me that You are keeping back the reward, to give it to them all at once, and that my weakness has need of it here. They are strong enough to serve You without it, and You treat them as brave souls that are free from self-seeking. Yet You know, O my Lord, that I would often cry out to You, offering excuses for those who spoke ill of me, since they seemed to me to have ample cause. This was when You, of Your goodness, had restrained me from offending You greatly, and when I was abandoning all those practices that I thought could cause You displeasure. It was when I did this, O Lord, that You began to open Your treasures for Your servant. It seemed that all You were waiting for was that I should be willing and prepared to receive them. Accordingly, You began after a short time, not only to give them, but to wish others to know that You were doing so.

When this was known, people began to have a good opinion of one whose wickedness they had never clearly realized, though much of it was evident enough. Then calumny and persecution began at once, and in my opinion with good reason. Therefore I felt no hostility to anyone, but implored You, O Lord, to consider how right they were. They said that I wanted to be a saint, and that I introduced innovations, although in many respects I had not yet managed even to comply fully with my rule. They said that I had not attained the goodness and sanctity of the nuns in my own house; and I do not believe that I ever shall, unless God brings it about of His own goodness. They said that, on the contrary, I was for abolishing what was good, and introducing customs which were not so; or at least that I did my best to introduce them, and had a great deal of ability for evil. So they were innocent in blaming me – and I do not mean only the nuns, but other people as well. They showed me truths about myself, since it was Your will.

Once after undergoing this temptation for some time, I was reciting the Hours and came to the words, 'Righteous art Thou, O Lord, and upright are Thy judgements',[1] and began to think what a great truth this is. For the devil never had the strength to tempt me into doubting

1. Psalm cxix [Vulg. cxviii], 137.

that You have every treasure, or into questioning any article of the Faith. It seemed to me, on the contrary, that the less natural foundation they had, the more firmly I believed them and the more devotion they inspired in me. When I thought of You as all powerful, I accepted all the wondrous works that You have done; and in this respect, as I have said, I had never a doubt. At that moment, as I considered how You could with justice allow so many who, as I have said, are Your most faithful servants to remain without those gifts and mercies that You conferred on me, being such as I am, You answered me, O Lord: 'Do not pry into this, but serve Me'.

These were the first words that I ever heard You say to me, and I was very frightened. But as I shall speak later of this way of hearing, together with other matters, I shall say no more about it here. To do so would be a digression, and I think that I have digressed enough already. I hardly know what I have said, and it could not be otherwise. But you, sir, must bear with these lapses. When I think what God has suffered from me and see my present state, I am not surprised that I lose the thread of what I am saying and have still to say. May it please the Lord that any foolishness I talk may always be of this kind; and may His Majesty never allow me the power to oppose Him in the slightest degree. Rather than that, let Him destroy me just as I am.

His great mercies are abundantly proved by His having forgiven my great ingratitude not once but many times. He forgave St Peter once, but has forgiven me often. The devil had good reason for tempting me; I should never have pretended to be the close friend of One whom I treated so publicly as an enemy. Was ever blindness as great as mine? Where could I expect to find a remedy, O Lord, except in You? What folly to run away from the light, in order to go on stumbling! What proud humility did the devil plant in me, when I gave up my hold on that pillar and staff whose support I needed to save me from making a great fall.

I cross myself as I write. I do not think that I have ever passed through so great a danger as when the devil put these ideas into my head under the false cloak of humility. How could one who was still so wicked be asked, even after receiving such great favours, to approach God in prayer? It was enough, he said, for me to recite the Office like all the other nuns. But even this I did not do properly. Why then did I want to do more? This showed a lack of reverence, indeed a contempt for God's favours.

It was right for me to consider these arguments and accept them, but it was very wrong to translate it into deeds. Blessings on You, O Lord, for coming to my help. For this seems to me, in principle, to be the temptation of Judas, only that the traitor did not dare to tempt me so openly. But he would little by little have prevailed over me as he did over Judas. For the love of God, let all those who practise prayer reflect well on this, and realize that when I gave up prayer my life became much more depraved. Let them consider what a fine remedy and what a pretty humility the devil gave me. I was greatly disturbed. But how could my spirit be calm? Miserable creature that it was, it was going further and further from its true rest. It remembered graces and mercies that it had received, and felt a disgust for the pleasures of this world. I am astonished that I was able to endure this. Only hope enabled me to do so. For I do not think – so far as I remember now, and this must have been twenty-one years ago – that I ever gave up my resolution to resume prayer, but merely postponed my resumption until I should be quite free from sins. How very far astray this hope led me! The devil would have dangled it in front of me till Judgement Day, so that he could then bear me off to hell. But, though I had recourse to prayer and reading, which revealed truths to me and showed me the evil path that I was treading, and though I importuned the Lord with tears, I was too wicked for this to avail me at all. When I abandoned these practices and took to amusing myself, which gave me plenty of opportunities for sin and little help – I will venture to say no help at all except to my ruin – what could I expect but the events that I have described?

I think much credit in God's sight is due to a certain Dominican friar,[1] a man of great learning, for waking me from this slumber. It was he who made me, as I believe I have said, take Communion fortnightly, and devote myself less to evil. I began to come to my senses, though I did not cease to offend the Lord. However as I had not lost the path, I continued on it, though slowly, first falling and then picking myself up again. Still, anyone who does not stop walking onwards arrives in the end, though late. To lose the path seems to me the same thing as giving up of prayer. May God, of His mercy, keep us from this!

It will be evident from this – and note it carefully, for the love of God – that though a soul may come so far as to receive great graces from God in prayer, it must not trust in itself, because it may fall; nor

1. Father Barrón.

must it expose itself to any sort of occasions for sin. This should be well pondered, for it is most important: even though a favour may certainly come from God, the devil can subsequently delude us by using all his ability to make treacherous use of that very favour, against such persons as have not grown strong in the virtues, and are not mortified or detached. Such people have not the strength to confront occasions for sin and other such dangers, however great their desires and resolutions.

This is excellent doctrine, and not my own but taught me by God, and so I should like ignorant people like myself to know it. Even if a soul is in the state I have just described, it must not trust itself so far as to go out to battle, because it will have enough to do to defend itself. What it needs is armour to protect it from the devils; it has not yet strength enough to engage them and trample them underfoot, as those who are in the state that I shall describe next can do.,

This is the deception with which the devil catches his prey. When a soul sees itself so near to God, and perceives the difference between the things of heaven and the things of earth, also what love the Lord is showing it, from this love springs confidence together with the assurance that it cannot lose the fruit it possesses. It seems distinctly to see its reward, and to feel that it cannot possibly leave something that even in this life is so delicious and sweet for anything as mean and impure as worldly pleasure. Because of this confidence the devil robs it of the distrust that it should have of itself. Then the soul, as I have said, runs into danger and, in its ardour, begins to give away its fruit without stint, in the belief that now it has nothing to fear for itself. This rashness does not come from pride, for the soul perfectly well knows that it can do nothing of itself. It comes from an extreme and immoderate trust in God. The soul does not see that it is itself unfledged. It can leave the nest, and God is taking it out, but it is not yet able to fly, for its virtues are still not strong, it has not enough experience to recognize danger, and it does not know what harm self-confidence does it. This is what ruined me.

Now because of this and for other reasons, we have great need of a director and of conversation with spiritual persons. If God raises a soul to this state, I firmly believe that He will never cease to favour it nor let it perish, unless it utterly forsakes Him. But if, as I have said, it has fallen, let it be very careful – let it be very careful, for the love of God – that the devil does not trick it into giving up prayer, as he tricked me by means of that false humility of which I have spoken and would gladly speak again and again. Let it rely on God's goodness, which is greater than all the evil we can do. When we know ourselves and want to return to His friendship, He does not remember our ingratitude, or how we have misused the favours He has granted us. He might well punish us, but in fact our sins only make Him forgive us the more readily, as He would those who have been members of His household and who have eaten, as they say, of His bread.

Let men remember His words and consider what He has done for me, who grew tired of offending before He grew tired of forgiving. He never tires of giving, nor can His mercies ever be exhausted. Let us, then, not grow weary of receiving them. May He be blessed for ever, Amen, and may all things praise Him.

CHAPTER 20

*She treats of the difference between union and rapture, and explains
what a rapture is. She also says something about the good that a soul
derives from being, by the Lord's goodness, brought to it. She
speaks of its effects*

I WISH that I could explain, with God's help, the difference between
union and rapture, or elevation, or flight of the spirit or transport –
for they are all one. I mean that these are all different names for the same
thing, which is also called ecstasy. It is much more beneficial than
union, its results are much greater, and it has very many other effects as
well. Union seems to be the same at the beginning, the middle, and the
end, and is altogether inward. But the ends of rapture are of a much
higher nature, and their effects are both inward and outward. As the
Lord has explained things hitherto, let Him do so now. For if His
Majesty had not shown me ways and means of saying something, I
certainly should never have found any.

Let us now reflect that this last water of which I have spoken is so
abundant that, if the ground did not refuse to receive it, we might suppose the cloud of His great Majesty to be with us here on earth. But
when we are thanking Him for this great blessing, and drawing near to
Him by means of such works as are in our power, the Lord catches up
the soul just as one might say the clouds gather up the mists of the earth,
and carries it right out of itself, just as I have heard it said the clouds or
the sun actually do catch up the mists. Then the cloud rises to heaven,
taking the soul with it, and begins to show it the features of the kingdom
He has prepared for it. I do not know whether this is an accurate comparison, but in point of fact that is how it happens.

In these raptures, the soul no longer seems to animate the body; its
natural heat therefore is felt to diminish and it gradually gets cold,
though with a feeling of very great joy and sweetness. Here there is no
possibility of resisting, as there is in union, in which we are on our own
ground. Against union, resistance is almost always possible though it
costs pain and effort. But rapture is, as a rule, irresistible. Before you
can be warned by a thought or help yourself in any way, it comes as a
quick and violent shock; you see and feel this cloud, or this powerful
eagle rising and bearing you up on its wings.

You realize, I repeat, and indeed see that you are being carried away you know not where. For although this is delightful, the weakness of our nature makes us afraid at first, and we need a much more determined and courageous spirit than for the previous stages of prayer. Come what may, we must risk everything and leave ourselves in God's hands. We have to go willingly wherever we are carried, for in fact, we are being born off whether we like it or not. In this emergency very often I should like to resist, and I exert all my strength to do so, especially at such times as I am in a public place, and very often when I am in private also, because I am afraid of delusions. Sometimes with a great struggle I have been able to do something against it. But it has been like fighting a great giant, and has left me utterly exhausted. At other times resistance has been impossible; my soul has been carried away, and usually my head as well, without my being able to prevent it; and sometimes it has affected my whole body, which has been lifted from the ground.

This has only happened rarely. Once, however, it took place when we were all together in the choir, and I was on my knees, about to take Communion. This distressed me very much, for it seemed a most extraordinary thing and likely to arouse considerable talk. So I ordered the nuns – for it happened after I was made prioress – not to speak of it. On other occasions, when I felt that the Lord was about to enrapture me again, and once in particular during a sermon – it was our patron's feast and some great ladies were present – I lay on the ground and the sisters came to hold me down, but all the same the rapture was observed. Then I earnestly beseeched the Lord to grant me no more favours if they must have outward and visible signs. For worries on this score exhausted me, and whenever He gave me these raptures I was observed. It seems that, of His goodness, He has been pleased to hear me. For I have never had them since, although it is true that this was not long ago.

It seemed to me when I tried to resist that a great force, for which I can find no comparison, was lifting me up from beneath my feet. It came with greater violence than any other spiritual experience, and left me quite shattered. Resistance requires a great struggle, and is of little use in the end when the Lord wills otherwise, for there is no power that can resist His power. At other times He is graciously satisfied with our seeing that He desires to grant us this grace, and that it is not His Majesty that is withholding it. Then, when we resist out of humility, the same effects follow as if we had given a complete assent.

The effects of rapture are great. One is that the mighty power of the Lord is made manifest. We see that against His Majesty's will we can do nothing to control either the soul or the body. We are not the masters; whether we like it or not, we see that there is One mightier than we, that these favours are given by Him, and that, of ourselves we can do absolutely nothing. This imprints a deep humility upon us. I confess that in me it aroused a great fear, at first a very great fear. One sees one's body being lifted from the ground; and though the spirit draws it up after itself, and does so most gently if it does not resist, one does not lose consciousness. At least I myself was sufficiently aware to realize that I was being lifted. The majesty of One who can do this is so manifest that one's hair stands on end, and a great fear comes over one of offending so great a God. But this fear is stifled by very great love, newly enkindled, for One who has, as we see, so great a love for so vile a worm, that He does not seem satisfied with actually raising the soul to Himself, but will have the body also, mortal though it is, and though its clay is befouled by all the sins we have committed.

Rapture leaves behind a certain strange detachment also, the real nature of which I shall never be able to describe. All that I can say is that it is somewhat different from that caused by purely spiritual graces. For although they produce a complete detachment of the spirit from all things, here the Lord seems to wish the body to be detached also. Thus a new estrangement from the world takes place, which makes life much more painful. It also leaves a distress behind, which we cannot bring about ourselves and which we can never remove, once it has come. I should very much like to explain this great distress, but I do not think I shall be able to. Still I will say something about it, if I can.

It must be noted that these events are much more recent than the visions and revelations of which I am now going to write, and which belong to the time when I was practising prayer and the Lord was giving me such great joys and favours. Although I still have these occasionally, this distress that I am going to describe is now a far more frequent and ordinary experience with me. Its intensity varies, but I will speak of it at its most severe. Later I shall describe the great shocks I used to suffer when the Lord chose to throw me into these transports, but they have, in my opinion, no more connexion with this distress of mine than has any completely physical experience with one that is entirely spiritual. I do not think that I am greatly exaggerating. For although the distress caused by these shocks is felt by the soul, it is also felt by the body. Both seem to share in it. It does not cause the extreme abandonment, however, that comes with this purely spiritual distress.

We play no part, as I have said, in bringing a rapture on. Very often there comes an unexpected desire – I do not know what impels it – and with that desire, which permeates the whole soul in a moment, it begins to become so weary that it rises far above itself and above all creation. God then so strips it of everything that, strive though it may, it can find no companion on earth. Nor, indeed does it wish for one; it would rather die in its solitude. It may be spoken to and make every possible effort to reply, but all to no avail. Whatever the spirit may do, it does not escape from its solitude; and although God seems at that moment very far from the soul, He sometimes reveals His grandeur to it in the strangest way imaginable. This way is indescribable; and I do not think that anyone could believe or understand it who has not already experienced it. It is a communication made not to comfort the soul, but to show it the reason why it is weary – which is because it is absent from that Good that contains all good things within itself.

In this communication the desire grows, and so does the extreme loneliness in which the soul finds itself, and with it there comes a distress so subtle and piercing that, placed as it is in this desert, the soul can, I think, say literally with the Royal Prophet: 'I watch, and am as a sparrow alone upon the house top'.[1] It is possible that King David was experiencing this same loneliness when he wrote although, since he was a saint, the Lord may have granted him this experience in a higher measure. This verse comes to my mind at these times in such a way that it seems to be fulfilled in me. It is a comfort to me to know that others have felt these extremes of loneliness, and an even greater comfort that they have been people of such quality. The soul, then, seems to be not in itself but on a house-top or roof, raised above itself and all created things. I think it is far above even its own highest part.

At other times the soul seems to be in a state of destitution, and to be asking itself: 'Where is Thy God?'[2] It must be remembered that I did not know the Spanish meaning of this verse, and that later, when I found out, it used to comfort me to think that the Lord had brought them to my mind without any effort of mine. At other times I used to remember St Paul's saying that he was 'crucified unto the world'.[3] I do

1. Psalm cii, 7. [Vulg. ci. 7]   2. Psalm xlii, 3. [Vulg. xli, 4]
3. Galatians vi, 14.

not mean that this is true of me - I clearly see that it is not. But the soul seems to me to be in this state when no comfort comes to it from heaven and it is not there itself, and when it desires none from the earth and is not there either. Then it is as if crucified between heaven and earth, suffering and receiving no help from either.

The help that comes from heaven is, as I have said, a most wonderful knowledge of God, so far above anything that we can desire that it brings with it greater torment. For the desire then grows so intense that its extreme distress, as I see it, sometimes robs it of all consciousness. But such states last only a short time. One seems to be on the point of death; only the agony carries with it so great a joy that I do not know of any proper comparison. It is a harsh yet sweet martyrdom. If any earthly thing is then offered to the soul, even one that it usually finds most sweet, it will not accept it, but seems to throw it away at once. It clearly realizes that it wants nothing but God, but loves no particular one of His attributes. It wants Him entire, and has no knowledge of what it desires. I say that it has no knowledge because the imagination can picture nothing; and indeed, I think that during much of this time the faculties are in suspense. As joy suspends them in union and rapture, here they are suspended by their distress.

O Jesus! How I wish that someone could really explain this to you, my Father, if only so that you could tell me what it means. For this is the habitual state of my soul, nowadays. Whenever I am not busy with something, it is plunged into these death-like yearnings; and I am afraid when I feel them coming on, because I know that I shall not die. But once I am in them, I long to suffer like this for the rest of my life, although the pain is so extreme as to be nearly unbearable. Sometimes my pulse almost ceases to beat at all, as I have been told by the sisters who sometimes see me in this state, and so understand better now. My bones are all disjointed and my hands are so rigid that sometimes I cannot clasp them together. Even next day I feel a pain in my wrists and over my whole body, as if my bones were still out of joint.

Sometimes I really think that if things continue as they are at present, it must be the Lord's will to end them by putting an end to my life. The pain seems to me enough to cause death; only, I do not deserve it. All my longing at these times is to die. I do not remember purgatory or the great sins that I have committed, for which I deserve hell. I forget everything in my longing to see God; and this abandonment and lone-liness seems better than all the company in the world. If there can be any comfort for one in this condition, it is to talk with some person who has passed through the same torment. Then she finds that, despite her complaints, nobody seems to believe her.

The soul in this state is further tormented because its distress has now so increased that it no longer seeks solitude as it did before, or company, except of those to whom it can complain. It is like a person with a rope round his neck, who is strangling but tries to take breath. The desire for company seems to me the product of our weakness, for our distress puts us in peril of death. This I know for certain since, as I have said, I have several times been in this situation myself during the crises of my severe illnesses, and I think I can say that the peril is as great as any I have known. The desire for the body and soul not to be parted, therefore, is like a voice crying out for help to take breath. By speaking of its pain, and complaining and seeking distractions, the soul is endeavouring to live, though much against the will of the spirit, or of the higher part of the soul, which wishes never to come out of this distress.

I am not sure if I am correct in what I say, or if I am expressing it properly, but to the best of my belief things happen in that way. I ask your Reverence what rest I can have in this life, now that the relief I once had in prayer and solitude, in which the Lord used to comfort me, has turned to an habitual torment. Yet at the same time this pain is so sweet, and the soul is so conscious of its value, that it now desires this suffering more than all the gifts that it used to receive. It believes this to be the safer state, too, because it is the way of the Cross; and, in my opinion, it contains a joy of exceeding worth, because the body has no part in it but agony, whereas the soul, even while suffering, rejoices alone in the bliss and contentment that this suffering brings.

I do not know how this can be, but it is so. This grace comes from the Lord; and I do not think I would exchange this favour which the Lord bestows on me – for it is highly supernatural and comes from His hand and, as I have said, is in no way acquired by me – for any of the favours of which I shall speak later on; I do not say for all of them at once, but for any one of them separately. It must not be forgotten that this state, in which the Lord is keeping me now has come after all the others described in this book; I mean that these transports have succeeded the favours that I received from the Lord and have written of already.

In the beginning I was afraid, as is almost always the case with me when the Lord grants me a new grace, until His Majesty reassures me as I proceed. He told me to have no fear, and to value this favour above all those that He had given me before, for the soul was purified by this pain; it was burnished or refined, like gold in the crucible, the better to take the enamel of His gifts, and the dross was being burnt away here instead of in purgatory. I had perfectly understood that this was a great favour, but I was much more certain of it now; and my confessor tells me that all is well. But though I was afraid because I was so wicked, I could never believe that it was anything bad. On the contrary, the supreme greatness of the blessing frightened me, when I remembered how little I deserved it. Blessed be the Lord who is so good! Amen.

I seem to have wandered from my subject. I began by speaking of raptures, and what I have been describing is something greater than a rapture, and so leaves behind the effects that I have recorded.

Now let us return to raptures, and to their most usual characteristics. Very often they seemed to leave my body as light as if it had lost all its weight, and sometimes so light that I hardly knew whether my feet were touching the ground. But during the rapture itself, the body is very often like a corpse, unable to do anything of itself. It remains all the time in whatever attitude it was in when the rapture came on it; seated, for example, and with the hands open or closed. The subject rarely loses consciousness; I have occasionally lost it entirely, but not very often and only for a short time. Generally the senses are disturbed; and though absolutely powerless to perform any outward action the subject still sees and hears things, though only dimly, as if from far away. I do not say that he can see and hear when the rapture is at its height; and by 'its height' I mean those times when the faculties are lost, because closely united with God. Then, in my opinion, it neither sees nor hears nor feels. But, as I said in describing the previous prayer of union, this complete transformation of the soul in God is of short duration. While it lasts, however, none of the senses perceives or knows what is taking place. We can have no way of understanding this, while we are on earth at least – or rather God cannot wish us to, since we have not the capacity for such understanding. This I have learnt for myself.

You will ask me, Father, how it is that a rapture sometimes lasts for many hours. Very often my experience is as I have described it in relation to the previous stage of prayer, the rapture is discontinuous. And very often the soul is absorbed, or – to put it better – the Lord absorbs it into Himself. But after He has held it for a moment, the will alone remains in union. The two other faculties appear to be always moving, like the pointer on a sundial, which is never at rest, though if the Sun of Righteousness wishes, He can make them stand still.

What I am describing lasts only a moment. But as the surge and impulse of the spirit have been violent, the will remains absorbed, even when the other faculties begin to stir again, and remains mistress over all these workings in the body. For though the two restless faculties try to disturb it, it thinks that the fewer enemies it has the better, and so takes care that they shall not do so. Therefore it suspends them entirely, that being the Lord's wish. The eyes are generally closed, although we may not wish to close them, and if occasionally they remain open, the soul, as I have just said, does not perceive anything or pay attention to what it sees.

A person can do very little in this condition, and so will not be capable of doing much when the faculties come to themselves again. But let him to whom the Lord grants this favour not be discouraged when he finds himself in this state, with his body unable to move for many hours, and with his understanding and memory wandering at times. True, generally they are absorbed in the praise of God, or in an attempt to comprehend or understand what has happened to them. Yet even for this they are not sufficiently awake, but are like people who have slept and dreamed for a long time, and have not yet properly woken up.

I stress this point because I know that there are persons now, even in this place, to whom the Lord is granting these favours; and if their directors have no experience of this – more especially if they have no learning – they may suppose that persons enraptured should be as if dead. It is a shame that such suffering should be caused by confessors who do not understand what I am saying. But, if I have spoken at all to the point, you will understand me, sir, since the Lord has already granted you this experience, though, as this happened only recently, perhaps you have not considered these matters as much as I have. So then, however hard I try, my body has not enough strength to move for quite a long time; the soul has taken it all away. But often a person who was previously very ill, and racked with severe pain, is left healthy at the end and stronger than before. For a very great gift is received in rapture, and the Lord sometimes wishes the body, as I have said, to enjoy it also, because at such times it is obedient to the will of the soul. When one comes to one's senses, it sometimes happens, if the rapture has been deep, that for a day or two, or even three, the faculties are so absorbed or in such a state of stupor that they seem no longer to be themselves.

Now comes the distress of having to return to life. Now the soul has grown wings that can bear it, and has shed its weak feathers. Now the standard is lifted high for Christ, and it really seems as if the captain of the fort is climbing, or being lifted, to the highest tower, there to raise it aloft in God's name. The soul looks down on those below, like one in a safe place who fears no dangers now, but courts them instead, since they seem to give it the certain assurance of victory. This is clearly shown by the soul's contempt, in this state, for the things of this world, which it values at nothing. One who is high up attains many things. The soul has no desire to seek or possess free-will; all it wants is to perform the Lord's will, and it prays Him that it may, giving Him at the same time the keys of its own will. Behold, our gardener has now become the captain of a fortress, and wants nothing but to obey the orders of his Commander. He does not wish to be his own master or anyone else's; he does not want even one pippin from the orchard. If there is any good thing there, may the Lord divide it among others. Henceforth the soul wants nothing of its own, only to do everything for His greater glory, and according to His will.

This is how things actually happen. If the raptures are true raptures, the fruits and advantages mentioned remain with the soul; if they do not, I should very much doubt if they came from God. Indeed I should be afraid that they were frenzies of the kind that St Vincent[1] speaks of. I have myself seen and I know by experience that the soul in rapture is mistress of everything, and gains such freedom in one hour or even less that it cannot recognize itself. It perfectly well sees that this is not its own achievement, and does not know how it has come to possess such a blessing. But it clearly realizes the very great benefit that each of these raptures brings. No one will believe this who has not experienced it; and so people do not believe the poor soul that lately they saw so wicked, when they suddenly see it aspire to such heroic heights. For now it is not content to serve the Lord in small things, but wishes to do so in the greatest way it can. This they consider a temptation and a folly. If they knew that this ambition arises not from the soul but from the Lord, to whom it has surrendered the keys of its will, they would not be so astounded.

It is my belief that a soul which reaches this state neither speaks nor

1. St Vincent Ferrer, *De Vita Spirituali*, xiv.

acts of itself, but that its sovereign Lord takes care of all it has to do. O my God, how right the Psalmist was – and how right we shall all be! – to ask for the wings of a dove.[1] The meaning of that verse is very clear; and it is clear too that he is referring to the flight of the spirit, as it rises above all created things and above itself first of all. But it is a gentle flight, a delightful flight – a flight without noise.

What power the soul has when the Lord raises it to a height from which it looks down on everything and is not enmeshed in it! How ashamed it is of the time when it was so enmeshed! It is indeed amazed at its own blindness, and feels pity for those who are still blind, especially if they are men of prayer to whom God is granting consolations. It longs to cry aloud and call their attention to their delusions; and sometimes it actually does so, only to bring down a storm of persecutions on its head. Particularly if the person in question is a woman, it is accused of lacking humility, and of wishing to teach those from whom it should learn. So they condemn it, and not without reason, for they know nothing of the force that impels it. At times it cannot help itself, or refrain from enlightening those whom it loves and wishes to see freed from the prison of this life. For the state in which it has once been living is neither more nor less than a prison, and this it realizes.

The soul is weary of the time when it was concerned with points of honour, and of the delusion which led it to believe that what the world calls by that name is honour at all. It sees that this is just a great lie, and that we are all taken in by it. It understands that true honour is not illusory but real; that it esteems what has value, and despises what has none. For all transitory things are as nothing or less than nothing, and are displeasing to God. The soul laughs at itself when it thinks of the time when it valued money and desired it; though, for myself, I really do not think that I ever had to confess to being covetous. It was quite bad enough that I should have given any thought to money at all. If the blessing that I now see within me could be bought with money I should set great store by it. But I know that it can only be gained by abandoning everything.

What can be bought with this money that we desire? Can it be anything of value? Anything that is permanent? If not, what do we want it for? All that it provides is a dismal ease which costs us very dear. What it often obtains for us is hell; what it buys is fire everlasting and torment without end. If all would agree to regard it as useless dross, how

1. Psalm lv, 6 [Vulg. liv, 7].

smoothly the world would run and how little bargaining there would be! All men would be friendly, one to another, if the world were to lose interest in honour and money. I really believe that this would be a remedy for everything.

The soul perceives man's blindness to the nature of pleasure, and his failure to realize that even in this life it purchases trials and disquiet. What restlessness! What discontent! What useless labour! Not only is the soul aware of the cobwebs that cover it, but the sunlight is so bright that it sees every little speck of dust besides, even the most minute. However hard it may have laboured to perfect itself, therefore, once the sun really strikes it, it views itself as most unclean. It is like the water in a glass, which seems quite clear when the sun is not shining on it but, if it does, is seen to be full of tiny specks.

This comparison is quite literal. Before the soul attains this rapture, it thinks that it is being careful not to offend God, and does what it can in so far as its strength allows. But once it reaches this stage, the Sun of Justice strikes it and makes it open its eyes. Then it sees so many of these specks that it would like to close them again. For it is not yet so completely the child of that mighty eagle that it can gaze straight into the sun. In the few moments that it can keep its eyes open, it sees that it is quite unclean. Then it remembers the verse that runs: 'Who shall be just in Thy presence?'[1]

When it looks on this divine Sun, it is dazzled by the brightness; when it looks on itself, dust clouds its eyes and the little dove is blind. So it happens very often that the soul is utterly blinded, absorbed, amazed, and dazzled by the wonders that it sees. Thus it acquires true humility that will never allow it to say any good of itself, or to permit others to do so. Not it but the Lord of the garden distributes the garden's fruit; and so none sticks to its hands. All the good that is in it is directed to God; if it says anything about itself, it is for His glory. It knows that it possesses nothing here and that it cannot ignore this knowledge which it has acquired by direct vision, even if it wishes to. Therefore it shuts its eyes to the things of this world, and opens them to take in the truth.

1. Probably a reference to Job xxv, 4.

CHAPTER 21

*She continues and concludes her account of this last stage of prayer,
telling what the soul who has reached it feels when it returns to live in
the world. She describes the light God throws on the world's deceits.
All of this is good doctrine.*

IN conclusion, I will say that in this state the soul does not have to give
its consent. This it has already given. It knows that it has voluntarily
placed itself in His hands, and that it cannot deceive Him, since He
knows everything. Here it is not as it is in the world, which is so full of
deceits and duplicities, that when, judging from outward signs, you
think that you have gained a man's good will, you very quickly realize
that all was a lie. Nobody can live amidst so much scheming, especially
if he has himself some small interest in it all.

A soul is blessed indeed when the Lord brings it to an understanding
of the truth. What a state this would be for kings! They would do better
to strive after this than after great dominions. Then justice would rule
in their kingdoms, and great crimes would be prevented – many in fact
might have been prevented already. In this state no one fears to lose his
life or honour for the love of God. What a grand thing this would be
for one who is more obliged than lesser men to consider the Lord's
honour – for subjects will always follow kings! To advance the Faith
by one step, or to show one ray of light to heretics, I would give up a
thousand kingdoms, and with good reason. For the winning of an everlasting kingdom is gain of another sort; and if the soul but tastes one
drop of the water of that kingdom, all the things of this world appear
loathsome thereafter. What then if the soul should be utterly engulfed
in such water?

O Lord, if You were to make it my vocation to proclaim this aloud,
I should be disbelieved, as are many others who can speak of these
things in other ways, but at least I should satisfy myself. If I could make
a single one of these truths plain to others, I think I should count my life
as nothing. I do not know what I should do afterwards, for I cannot rely
on myself. Yet, although I am what I am, I keep experiencing a violent
desire to tell these truths to my superiors. But since this is all that I can
do, O Lord, I turn to You and pray You to set all things right. You
know very well that, provided I were left in such a state as never to

offend You, I would gladly divest myself of all the favours that You have given me, and transfer them to the kings of this world. For I know that if I did they could not possibly allow the things that they allow to-day; nor could they fail to possess the greatest blessings.

O my God, let kings understand how great their obligations are. You have been pleased to distinguish them on earth in such a way that, as I have heard, signs appear in the heavens when You take one of them from the earth. It stirs my devotion indeed, O my King, to consider that it is Your will to teach them in this way how they must imitate You in their lives, since these signs that appear at their deaths are the same as those that appeared at Yours.

I am being very bold and your Reverence must tear this page out if you think it wrong, but, believe me, I should express this better in the presence of kings, if I might speak to them or if I thought that they would listen to me. For I pray to God most earnestly for them, and wish that I might be of service to them. All this makes one careless of one's life – and I often wish I could lose mine. It would be a very small risk to run for so great a gain, since there is no real living once we see with our own eyes the great illusion in which we walk and the blindness from which we suffer.

When a soul has reached this point, it does not merely desire to serve God; His Majesty also gives it the strength to put its desire into effect. If any way occurs to it in which it thinks it may do God a service, it will perform that service; and all this is nothing because, I repeat, nothing except doing God's pleasure is of any value. The trouble is that no opportunities occur to people as worthless as myself. May it be Your pleasure, O Lord, that the time may come when I shall be able to pay You at least one farthing of the great sum I owe You. Be pleased to ordain that this servant of Yours, O Lord, may serve You in some way. There have been other women who have done heroic deeds for love of You. I myself am only fit to talk, and so You have not been willing, O God, to test me by deeds. All my will to serve You leaks away, and even here I have no freedom, since it is always possible that I may fail altogether.

First strengthen my soul, and prepare it, O Jesus, my supreme Good, and then ordain the means whereby I may do something for You. No one could bear to receive so much and pay nothing in return. Cost what it may, O Lord, I pray You not to let me appear before You so empty-handed, since a man's reward must be proportionate to his works. Here is my life; here is my honour; here is my will; I have given them all to You; I am Yours; do with me what You will. I know very well, my Lord, how little I can do. But now that I have come to You, now that I have climbed that watch-tower from which all truth can be seen, I shall be capable of all things so long as You do not depart from me. But if You depart from me, even for a moment, I shall fall back to where I was; which was in hell.

Oh, how it pains a soul which has been in this state to return to the business of the world, to look at the disorderly farce of this life, to waste time attending to such bodily needs as those of eating and sleeping! Everything wearies it; it cannot run away; it sees itself a prisoner in chains, and it is then that it feels most keenly the captivity in which our bodies hold us, and the wretchedness of this life. It understands why St Paul prayed God to deliver him from it;[1] it joins its cries to his and, as I have said before, begs God to give it freedom. Such is its violence on these occasions that it often seems as if the soul is straining to leave the body and go out in search of freedom, since no one is delivering it. It wanders like one sold into a foreign land, and what most distresses it is that it finds so few to join it in its complaints and prayers, since men as a rule desire to live. Oh, if we were utterly detached, and never based our happiness on the things of this world, then the distress caused by our continually living without God would temper our fear of death with the desire to enjoy life. If a woman like myself to whom the Lord has given this light, but whose charity is so lukewarm and whose works have won her no certainty of true repose, is nevertheless so often sad at finding herself in this exile, I often wonder what the sorrow of the saints must have been. What must St Paul and the Magdalen and others of their kind have suffered when this flaming love of God burst so strong within them? Their lives must have been a continual martyrdom. I think that the only people who give me any comfort, and whose conversation relieves me, are those in whom I find these desires. I mean desires accompanied by works, and stress the works because I am thinking of some who imagine themselves detached, and claim to be. They must be so, of course, since their vocation demands it, and so do the long years that have passed since many of them began to tread the way of perfection. But my soul can distinguish from afar between those who are detached in words, and those who have confirmed these words by deeds. It knows very well how little is achieved by the one sort and

1. Romans vii, 24.

how much by the other; and this is a difference that can be clearly discerned by anyone with experience.

I have described the effects of these raptures that come from the spirit of God. Actually, some of these may be greater and some less; by less I mean that at the beginning, although the effects take place, they are not expressed by deeds, and so their presence is not obvious. Also perfection is a thing of growth; the cobwebs have to be brushed away from the memory, and this requires some time. Meanwhile as love and humility grow in the soul, so these flowers of virtue give off a greater scent for the benefit both of the soul itself and of others. Indeed the Lord can so work on a soul in one of these raptures that there remains little for it to do in order to achieve perfection. Except from experience, no one will ever believe how much the Lord gives to a soul in that moment; no effort of ours, in my opinion, will achieve it. I do not mean to say that, with the Lord's help, persons who over many years work according to the directions given by writers on prayer, and make use of their principles and methods, will not reach perfection and great detachment. But it will cost them great labour, and much more time. In rapture, however, without any effort of ours, the Lord deliberately raises the soul from the earth and gives it dominion over all earthly things, even though there may be no more merits in such a soul than there were in mine – and I cannot speak more strongly than that, for I had hardly any.

The reason why His Majesty does this is that it is His pleasure, and that He wishes to do so. Even if the soul is not prepared, He makes it fit to receive the blessing that He is giving it. Although He certainly never fails to give comfort to such as make proper preparation and strive after detachment, He does not always give it to those who have earned it by cultivating their gardens. Sometimes, as I have said, He chooses to display His greatness on poorer ground, and so thoroughly to prepare it for every blessing that it almost seems as if it would be impossible for the soul to return to its old life of sin against God.

The mind is now so used to dwelling upon real truth, that everything else seems to it childish. It laughs to itself at times when it sees serious men – men of prayer and religion – paying great attention to points of honour, which it long ago trampled underfoot. They say that prudence and the dignity of their calling requires them to behave in this way, in order that they may be able to do greater good. But the soul knows very well that they would achieve far more in one day by putting the love of God above their dignity than in ten years of prudent care for their authority. So this soul continues to lead a troubled life, and always has its crosses, but it is a life of continuous growth. Those with whom it has most to do keep on thinking that it has reached the summit, but soon they see it raised even higher, for God is always granting it new favours. God is the soul of that soul; and as He has it in His keeping, so He gives it light. He seems to be watching over it, always taking care that it shall not offend Him, assisting it and rousing it to serve Him. When my soul reached this state in which God granted it this great mercy, my troubles ceased; His Majesty gave me strength to escape from them. Meeting with occasions for sin, and even the company of those people who had formerly distracted me now did me no more harm than if they had never been. Indeed, what had once harmed me now helped me. Everything was a means of increasing my knowledge of God and my love for Him. Everything made me realize how much I owed Him, and grieve for what I had been.

I perfectly understood that none of this was due to myself, and that I had not won it by my own efforts; the time had been far too short for that. His Majesty, out of His own goodness, had given me the necessary strength. From the time that the Lord began to grant me the favour of these raptures until now, this strength has continued to grow in me, and He, in His kindness, had held me with His hand to prevent my turning back. This being the case, I do not imagine that I am doing anything of myself, but entirely understand that this is the Lord's work. I think, therefore, that any soul to which the Lord is granting these favours and who walks in humility and fear, always realizing that all this is the Lord's own doing and that we play next to no part in it, may mix with any sort of people. However disturbing and vicious its company may be, it will not be affected or moved in any way. On the contrary, as I have said, distractions will be a help and a source from which the soul may derive great profit. It is the strong that are chosen by the Lord to benefit others, even though their strength does not come from themselves, and when the Lord brings a soul to this state, little by little He communicates very great secrets to it.

In ecstasy come true revelations, great favours, and visions, all of which help to humble and strengthen the soul, to make it despise the things of this life and more clearly realize the greatness of the reward that the Lord reserves for those who serve Him. May it please His Majesty that the immense bounty which He has heaped on this miserable sinner may help to strengthen and embolden those who read this, so that they may give up absolutely everything for God's sake. If His Majesty so amply rewards us even in this life that we can clearly see the prize which is gained by those who serve Him, how immense will it be in the life to come?

CHAPTER 22

She shows how safe a path it is for contemplatives not to raise their spirits to lofty things, and how the approach to the most exalted contemplation must be by way of Christ's humanity. She tells of an incident in which she was herself deceived. This is a very profitable chapter.

I WANT to say one thing, if your Reverence will allow me to do so, which is, in my opinion, very important, and will serve as a lesson that may well be necessary. In some books on the subject of prayer, it is said that although the soul cannot reach this state of itself, since the work that the Lord performs in it is entirely supernatural, yet it can help itself by lifting the spirit above all created things and raising it with humility, once it has spent some years in the purgative life and made some progress in the illuminative. I do not quite know what they mean by 'the illuminative', but I understand it to be the life of those who are making progress. They earnestly advise us to put aside all bodily imagination and directly to approach the contemplation of the Divinity, saying that even the thought of Christ's humanity will embarrass those who have arrived at this point, and hinder their attainment of perfect contemplation. They quote Our Lord's words to the Apostles at the coming of the Holy Ghost [1] – I mean after His ascent into heaven. But it seems to me that if they had believed, then, as they did after the coming of the Holy Ghost, that He was both God and man, it would have been no hindrance to them. Moreover, these words were not spoken to the Mother of God, though she loved Him more than all the rest. But these writers think that as this is an entirely spiritual work anything bodily may prevent or impede it, and that contemplatives ought to think of themselves as circumscribed, but of God of being everywhere. Their endeavour must then be to be engulfed in Him. This seems to me right enough for some occasions, but I cannot bear the idea that we should withdraw ourselves completely from Christ, and put His divine body on a level with our miseries and all created things. May His Majesty grant me the ability to explain myself!

I do not oppose this view, for they are spiritual men and learned, and know what they are saying. Besides God leads souls along many roads

1. St John xvi, 7 *et seq.*

and paths, as He has led mine. It is of mine that I wish to speak here –
I will not meddle with the souls of others – and of the danger that I
found myself in through trying to conform with what I read. I can well
believe that those who have reached union and gone no further – I
mean those who have had raptures and visions and other favours that
God grants to the soul – will suppose this view to be the best, as I once
did myself. But if I had adhered to it, I do not think that I should ever
have reached my present state, for I believe it to be mistaken. Of course,
it may be I who am mistaken – but I will describe what happened to me.

As I had no director, I used to read these books, and little by little
came to think I was learning something from them. Later I discovered
that I should have learnt very little from my reading if the Lord had not
shown me the way. For until His Majesty taught me by experience, I
understood nothing and had no idea what I was doing. When I began
to have a little experience of supernatural prayer – I mean of the prayer
of quiet – I tried to banish all bodily things, but I did not dare to lift up
my soul, for I saw that in my state of wickedness this would be presumption. Still, I thought that I was experiencing the presence of God –
as proved to be true – and contrived to remain with Him in a recollected state. If God assists at this prayer, it is very sweet and brings great
joy. So conscious was I of the gain I was deriving from it and of my
pleasure in it, that no one could have made me return to my medita-
tions on the Humanity, which seemed to me to present a positive
hindrance. O Lord of my soul and my Good, Jesus Christ crucified, I
never recall this old belief of mine that it does not give me pain. I think
that it was an act of high treason, though one committed in ignorance.

All through my life I had been deeply devoted to Christ – for this
happened only recently. By 'recently' I mean before the Lord granted
me the favour of raptures and visions. So I did not hold this opinion for
very long, and soon returned to my habit of rejoicing in the Lord.
Especially when I took Communion, I would wish to have His image
and portrait before my eyes, since I could not have it as deeply graven
on my soul as I should have liked. Is it possible, my Lord, that I could
have harboured the thought, even for so much as an hour, that You
could hinder my greatest good? Where did all my blessings come from,
if not from You? I will not think that I was to blame for this, since I was
very sorry for it, and it was certainly the product of ignorance. You
were pleased, therefore, in Your goodness, to remedy matters by giving me someone to cure me of this error, and by afterwards permitting

me to see You often, as I shall tell later on, in order that I might clearly realize how gravely wrong I was and tell many people of my mistake – as I have already done – and also in order that I might put it all down here at this moment.

This, in my opinion, is the reason why many souls who have reached the prayer of union advance no further and fail to achieve very great liberty of the spirit. There are two reasons, I think, on which I can base my opinion. Of course I may be quite wrong, but what I say I have learnt by experience, for my soul was in a very bad way until the Lord gave it light. All its joys came in little sips; and once these were over, it never found any companionship, as it did later, in its trials and temptations. My first reason is that   hatever little humility the soul possesses is so disguised and concealed as not to be observed. Could there be anyone as miserably proud as I was, one who after labouring all his life at every imaginable kind of penance and prayer and after suffering every kind of persecution, would not count himself very rich and amply rewarded if the Lord allowed him to stand at the foot of the Cross with St John? I do not know how anyone could take it into his head not to be content with this, except myself, for the result was that things went wrong with me just when they should have gone right.

There may be times when our temperament or some indisposition finds the Passion too painful a subject to be dwelt on. But what can hinder us from being with Him after His Resurrection, since we have Him so near us in the Sacrament, in which He is already glorified? Here we shall not see Him wearied and broken and pouring with blood, as He lies exhausted by the roadside, persecuted by those to whom He was doing good and not even believed in by the Apostles. Certainly one cannot always bear to think of the great trials He suffered. But here He is free from pain, full of glory, strengthening some and bringing courage to others before He ascends into heaven. In the most holy Sacrament, He is our companion, and it would seem impossible for Him to withdraw from us even for a moment. Was it possible for me, then, O my Lord, to withdraw from You in the hope of serving You better? True, when I offended You I did not know You. But once I did know You, how could I suppose that I should gain more in this way? O, what an evil path I was pursuing, Lord! Indeed, I think that I should have lost the road altogether, if You had not brought me back to it. When I have seen You beside me, my eyes have rested on all blessings at once. No trial has come to me that I cannot suffer gladly when I gaze at You as You stood before Your judges. In the presence of so good a Friend, of a Captain so brave that He Himself stepped out first to suffer, one is capable of bearing anything. He helps us and gives us strength; He never fails and is a true friend.

I clearly see, and have done so ever since, that if we are to please God and He is to grant us great favours, it is His will that this should be through His most sacred Humanity, in whom His Majesty said He is well pleased.[1] I have learnt this indeed by repeated experiences; the Lord has told it me. I have clearly seen that it is by this door we must enter, if we wish His sovereign Majesty to reveal great secrets to us. Therefore, your Reverence, even if you are at the summit of contemplation, you must seek no other way; this one alone is safe. It is through this Lord of ours that all good things come to us. He will show us the way. If we consider His life, that is our best example. What more can we ask than have so good a friend at our side, who will not leave us in trials and tribulations, as worldly friends do? Blessed is he who truly loves Him, and always has Him by his side. Let us consider the glorious St Paul, from whose lips the name of Jesus seems never to have been absent, so firmly did he hold it in his heart. Since realizing this, I have looked carefully into the lives of several saints who were great contemplatives, and they travelled by no other road. St Francis proves this by his stigmata, as does St Antony of Padua with the Infant Jesus. St Bernard too rejoiced in the Humanity, and so did St Catherine of Siena and many others of whom your Reverence will know better than I.

Withdrawal from bodily objects must no doubt be good, since it is recommended by such spiritual persons. But, in my opinion, it is right only when the soul is very far advanced. Until then it must, of course, seek the Creator through His creatures. All this depends on the grace that the Lord gives to each soul: a subject into which I will not enter. But what I should like to make clear is that Christ's Humanity must not be reckoned among these bodily objects. This must be clearly understood, and I wish I knew how to explain it.

When God is pleased to suspend all the faculties, as we have seen He does in the kinds of prayer already described, it is evident that, even against our will, this Presence is taken from us. We accept this at such a time. It is a blessed loss since it enables us to enjoy more than we seem to be losing. For then the soul is wholly occupied in loving One whom

1. Matt. iii, 17.

the understanding has been working hard to know. It is loving what it has not comprehended, and rejoicing in what it could not rejoice in so well if it had not lost itself, in order, as I say, the better to gain itself. But that we should painfully and laboriously accustom ourselves to give up trying with all our strength to keep always before us – and the Lord grant we always may! – this most sacred Humanity; this, I insist, seems to me wrong. It leaves the soul, as they say, in the air; it has no support, I think, however full it may think itself to be of God.

While we live as human beings, it is very important for us to keep Christ's Humanity before us. Here I come to that second hindrance that I mentioned. The first, which I began to explain, is a certain lack of humility, in that the soul desires to rise of itself before the Lord raises it, and is dissatisfied with meditating even on anything so precious, and longs to be Mary before it has laboured with Martha. When the Lord wishes it to be Mary, even on the very first day there is no need for fear, but we must prepare ourselves properly, as I think I have already said. This small grain of insufficient humility may seem to be of little importance, but it does great harm to those who want to advance in contemplation.

To come now to the second point, we are not angels but have bodies, and it is madness for us to want to become angels while we are still on earth, and as much on earth as I was. Generally, our thoughts must have something to support them, though sometimes the soul may go out from itself, and it may often be so full of God that it will need no created thing to bring it to recollection. But this is not very usual. When we are busy, or suffering persecutions or trials, when we cannot get enough quiet, and in times of dryness, Christ is our very good friend. We look at Him as a man, we see Him weak and in trouble, and He is our companion. Once we have got this habit, it is very easy to find Him beside us, though times will come when we can do neither the one nor the other. To this end, it is advisable to do as I have said, and not show ourselves to be trying after spiritual consolations. Come what may, the great thing is to embrace the Cross. The Lord was deprived of all consolation, and forsaken in His trials. Let us not forsake Him; His hand will help us to rise better than our own efforts; and, as I have already said, He will withdraw Himself when He sees that it is good for us and when the Lord wishes to take the soul out of itself.

It greatly pleases God to see a soul humbly take His Son as mediator, and yet love Him so much that even when His Majesty is pleased to raise it, as I have said, to the highest contemplation, it realizes its un-worthiness and says with St Peter: 'Depart from me, for I am a sinful man, O Lord'.[1] This I have proved, for it is in this way that God has led my soul. Others may, as I have said, find another and shorter cut; but what I have learnt is that the entire edifice of prayer must be founded on humility, and that the lower a soul abases itself in prayer, the higher God raises it. I do not remember His ever having granted me the re-markable favours of which I shall speak later except when I have been overwhelmed by the sight of my own wickedness; and His Majesty has even managed to help me towards this self-knowledge by revealing things to me that I could not have suspected myself. It is my opinion that though a soul may seem to be deriving some immediate benefit when it does anything to further itself in this prayer of union, it will in fact very quickly fall again, like a building without foundations. I am afraid too that it will never achieve true poverty of spirit, which lies in not seeking comfort or pleasure in prayer, since it has already given up earthly comforts and pleasures. It must find its consolation in trials, undergone for the sake of Him who lived a life of trials; and these it must endure, remaining calm in times of dryness, though it may grieve at having to suffer them. But they should not cause us the disquietude and distress that are felt by some who, if they are not always working with their intellect and stimulating feelings of devotion, think that all is lost, as if their efforts merited some great blessing. I do not mean that such things should not be sought for, or that we should not be careful how we approach God, but merely, as I have said elsewhere, that we should not worry ourselves to death even if we cannot think a single good thought. We are unprofitable servants. So what do we suppose we can do?

But it is Our Lord's will that we shall know this, and be like the little donkeys that work the water-wheel I have mentioned. Though their eyes are blinkered and they have no idea what they are doing, they water more than the gardener can with all his efforts. Once we have placed ourselves in God's hands, we must walk freely along this road. If His Majesty is pleased to promote us to His household or Privy Council, we must go willingly. But if He tells us to serve Him in minor offices and, as I have said elsewhere, not sit down in the highest room.[2] God is more careful for us than we are for ourselves, and He knows what each of us is good for. What is the use of a man's governing him-

1. Luke v, 8.   2. Luke xiv, 8.

self if he has already given over his entire will to God? This, in my view, is much less permissible here than at the first stage of prayer, and does much more harm; for these blessings are supernatural. If one has a bad voice one cannot make it good, however much one forces oneself to sing; whereas if God is pleased to give one a good voice, one has no need to try it twice. So let us continually pray Him to grant us favours, and resign our spirit while trusting in His greatness. Since the soul is permitted to sit at Christ's feet, let it take care not to stir from there, but stay as it will. Let it imitate the Magdalen and, when it is strong, God will lead it into the desert.

Your Reverence must be satisfied with this explanation until you find someone with more experience than I, who knows these things better. Do not believe people who are beginning to taste of God, but who think they are making more progress and receiving greater consolations by helping themselves. How well God can reveal Himself, when He chooses without these petty efforts of ours! Do what we may, He can transport the spirit like a giant lifting a straw, and all resistance is useless. What a strange kind of belief it is that if God wishes a toad to fly, He will wait for it to do so by its own efforts! I think that our spirits would find it even harder and more painful than that to raise themselves up if God did not do it for them, since they are weighed down with earth and countless encumbrances, and the mere desire to fly is not of uch use to them. For though flying is more natural to them than it is to a toad, they are so sunk in the mire that by their own fault they have lost the ability.

I will conclude then by saying that whenever we think of Christ, we should remember the love with which He has bestowed all these favours on us, and what great love our Lord God has revealed to us also in giving us this pledge of His love for us, for love calls out love. So, although we may be very much at the beginning and very wicked, let us try always to think of this and to arouse love in ourselves. For if once the Lord grants us the favour of imprinting this love on our hearts, everything will be easy for us, and we shall do great things in a very short time and with very little labour. May His Majesty grant us this love, since He knows how much we need it, for the sake of that love which He bore us and for His glorious Son, who revealed it to us at such great cost to Himself. Amen.

I should like to ask your Reverence one question. Why, when the Lord begins to grant a soul such a sublime favour as to raise it to perfect contemplation, does it not, as by rights it should, become perfect immediately? There is certainly no doubt that it should, for anyone who receives such a favour should never again seek earthly consolations. Why is it then that raptures and the soul's growing accustomed to receive favours, appear only to bring results of increasing sublimity – and the more detached it is the greater they are – when the Lord might leave the soul sanctified at the very moment when He comes to it? How is it that this same Lord does not perfect it in the virtues until later, and by the passage of time? I do not know the answer, but should like to do so. I do know, however, that there is a difference between the degree of fortitude that God gives us in the early stages, when a rapture is over in the twinkling of an eye, and is almost imperceptible except through the effects that it leaves behind, and what we receive later on when our raptures are of longer duration. I often think that this must be because the soul does not completely prepare itself at once. The Lord gradually trains it, giving it resolution and manly strength to trample all earthly things underfoot. This He did in the shortest time for the Magdalen, and He has done the same for other persons, according to the measure in which they have allowed Him freedom to act yet cannot bring ourselves to believe that even in this life God will reward us a hundredfold.

I have also been thinking out another comparison. Supposing that the same amount is given to beginners as to those who have progressed further, it is like a meal shared by many people. Those who eat very little are left with a pleasant taste for a short while; those who eat more receive some sustenance; and those who eat much receive life and strength. Moreover, it is possible for the soul to eat of this food of life so often and so plentifully as to consider that no other food nourishes it. It now sees what good this food is doing it, and its palate has become so accustomed to its sweetness that it would rather not live than have to eat anything else, for that would only take away the pleasant taste left by the good food. Again, the conversation of godly people does not bring us as much profit in one day as in many; and if we are long enough in their company, we may so benefit, with God's help, as to become like them. Everything, in fact, depends on His Majesty's pleasure, and on whom He chooses to confer this favour. But it is important that anyone who is beginning to receive it shall make up his mind to detach himself from everything and esteem it as he should.

I think too that His Majesty goes about trying to prove who loves

Him – whether this person or that – revealing Himself to us in such sublime joy in order to rouse our belief, if it is dead, in what He is going to give us. 'Look,' He says, 'this is one drop of an immense sea of blessings.' Indeed He leaves nothing undone for those He loves, and when He sees that they accept His gifts, He gives Himself continuously. He loves all who love Him – and how well they are loved! What a good friend He is! O Lord of my soul, if only one had the words to explain what You give to those who trust in You, and what is lost by those who reach this state yet keep themselves to themselves! It is not Your will, Lord, that they should. For You do more than this when You come to a lodging as mean as mine. May You be blessed for ever and ever!

I beseech your Reverence once more that if you discuss my writings about prayer with spiritual persons, you make sure that they really are spiritual persons. For if they only know one path or have stuck half-way, they will never guess my meaning. There are some whom God leads immediately by a very exalted road, and they think that others can make progress in the same way, by quietening the mind and making no use of bodily aids, but this will make them as dry as sticks. There are others, too, who when they have attained a little quiet, at once think that as they have got this they can get all the rest. But in this way, instead of gaining they will, as I have said, lose. So, experience and discretion are necessary in all things. May the Lord, in His goodness, give them to us.

CHAPTER 23

She returns to the history of her life, and tells how she began to strive
for greater perfection. This is profitable matter for those who have to
direct souls engaged in the practice of prayer, and teaches them how to
deal with beginners. She tells of the profit that she derived
from this knowledge.

I SHALL now return to the point in my life where I broke off. For I have digressed for longer, I think, than I should have done, in order that what is to follow may be more clearly understood. From now onwards this is a new book – I mean another and new life. Up to now the life I described was my own. But the life I have been living since I began to expound these methods of prayer is one which God has been living in me – or so it has seemed to me. For I cannot think it possible that I can have myself escaped in so short a time from such wicked habits and deeds. The Lord be praised who rescued me from myself!

Now when I began to avoid occasions for sin and to devote myself more to prayer, the Lord began to grant me favours, as though He desired to make me willing to receive them. His Majesty began to give me the prayer of quiet very frequently, and often the prayer of union too, which lasted for some time. Since there have been cases lately of women who have been grossly deceived and subjected to great illusions through the machinations of the devil, I was very much afraid.[1] For I felt very great delight and sweetness, which it was often beyond my power to avoid. On the other hand I was conscious of a deep inward assurance that this was of God, especially when I was engaged in prayer, and I found that I was the better for these experiences and had developed greater fortitude. But as soon as I became a little distracted, I would be afraid again, and would wonder whether it was not the devil that was suspending my understanding and making me think this a good thing, in order to deprive me of mental prayer, to stop me from my meditating on the Passion, and to prevent my using my mind. I did not understand things at all, and felt that I was making a loss rather than a gain. But when His Majesty was pleased to give me light, so that I

1. This refers to Magdalena de la Cruz, a nun of Córdoba, who was convicted of wilful deceptions by the Inquisition, and burnt in 1541.

should not offend Him and should recognize the extent of my debt to Him, my fears so increased that they made me search diligently for spiritual persons with whom to talk. I already knew of some, for members of the Company of Jesus had come here [1] and, though I knew none of them, I was greatly attracted to them simply by my knowledge of their way of life and prayer. But I did not consider myself worthy to speak to them, or strong enough to obey them; and this made me even more afraid. To discuss things with them, I being what I was, seemed to me a little too presumptuous.

I spent some time in this state. But after a great inward tussle and more fears, I finally decided to consult a spiritual person and ask him what kind of prayer I was practising, also to make things clear to me if I were going astray. I decided that I must do everything in my power not to offend God, for, as I have said, this lack of fortitude that I found in myself made me extremely fearful. Heaven preserve me, how deluded I was to depart so far from what was good in my anxiety to become good! The devil must attach great importance to this moment when the virtues are beginning to grow, for I could not shake myself free. He knows that a soul's whole relief lies in conversation with the friends of God, and this explains why I could not make up my mind to consult somebody. I put off doing so until I had amended my life first, just as I had done before when I gave up prayer. It may be that I should never have come to a decision, for I was so subjugated by little bad habits, that I could not bring myself to realize that they were bad at all. For this I needed the help of others, and their hands as well to raise me up. Blessed be the Lord, for in the end His was the first hand.

When I found my fear growing so fast because I was making progress in prayer, it seemed to me that there must either be something very good or something extremely bad about it. I was quite certain that my experiences were supernatural, since I was sometimes unable to resist them and could not have them whenever I wanted them. I thought to myself that all I could do was to keep my conscience clear and avoid all occasions for even venial sin. For if the spirit of God was at work, the gain was clear; whereas if it was the devil, so long as I tried to please God and not to offend Him, he could do me little harm and would himself be the loser. Having decided this, I strove for some days to live in this way, begging God all the time to help me. But I saw that my soul had not the strength to achieve such great perfection alone, on account

1. They founded a college at Ávila in 1554.

of certain attachments that I felt for things which, though not bad in themselves, were enough to spoil everything.

I was told of a learned cleric [1] living in the place, whose goodness and holy life the Lord was beginning to make known to the world. Through a pious gentleman [2] who also lived there, I contrived to make his acquaintance. This gentleman is married, but so exemplary and virtuous in his life and so devoted to prayer and charity that his goodness and perfection shine out from everything he does; and with good reason, for he has brought great benefits to many souls. Indeed, he has such talents that, although his married state is a hindrance, he cannot do otherwise than use them. He is a man of great intelligence, and very gentle with everybody, and his conversation is never wearisome, but so sweet and gracious, as well as honest and pious, that it greatly delights anyone who has dealings with him. All that he says is directly for the benefit of those souls with whom he is talking; and he seems to have no other object but to do whatever he can for everyone he meets, and to please everybody.

This diligent and holy man took such pains on my behalf, that I think it was he who began my soul's salvation. His humility towards me is astounding, for he has, I believe, been practising prayer for nearly forty years – it may be two or three years less – and his life seems to be as perfect as his married state permits. His wife is a great servant of God also, and so charitable that he loses nothing on her account; indeed, she was chosen by God to be the wife of one whom He knew would be a very great servant of His. They were connected by marriage with some relatives of mine.

I had much to do also with another great servant of God who was married to a cousin of mine; and thus I contrived that this cleric who, as I have said, was such a servant of God, should come and talk to me. He was a great friend of this gentleman, and I thought of taking him as my confessor and director. When he brought this cleric to me, I was extremely confused at finding myself in the presence of so holy a man. I spoke to him about my soul and my prayers, but he would not take my confession. He said that he was very busy, and indeed he was. He began in fact with the pious determination to treat me as if I were strong – and I should have been, considering the method of prayer that he saw I practised – and to see that I should not offend God in any way.

1. Gaspar Díaz, who was for some time Santa Teresa's confessor.
2. Don Francesco de Salcedo, a family connexion who had studied theology.

But when I saw how resolutely and promptly he attacked those little habits of mine that I have already mentioned, and realized that I had not the courage to adopt a more perfect way of life, I was distressed. Realizing that he was treating me in spiritual matters as if I were capable of immediate perfection, I saw that I should have to be much more circumspect.

In time I recognized that the methods he employed with me would not lead to my improvement, since they were intended for a soul that was more perfect, and I, though advanced in divine favours, was a beginner in the virtues and in mortification. Really, if I had only had him to consult, I do not think that my soul would ever have prospered. For the distress I felt when I saw that I was not doing, and seemed to be incapable of doing, what he told me, was enough to make me lose hope and give up the whole thing. It astounds me sometimes that, though he was a person with a special gift for turning beginners towards God, it was not God's will that he should understand my soul or desire to take charge of it. I see that this was all for my good, so that I should get to know and consult those holy people, the members of the Society of Jesus.

So I made an arrangement with this pious gentleman that he should sometimes come to see me. It showed his great humility that he should have been willing to have dealings with anyone as wicked as I. He began to visit me and to encourage me, and told me not to think I could get rid of all my imperfections in a day. He said that God would do it for me little by little, and that he himself had for many years been troubled by some quite trivial habits which he had not been able to shake off. O humility, what great blessings you bring to those who possess you, and also to those who have to do with them! In order to help me, this saintly man – for I think I may rightly call him so – told me of his own weaknesses, or of what his humility made him think to be such. Considered in relation to his state of life, they were neither faults nor imperfections, though in mine they would have been very great faults indeed. I am not saying this without a purpose. I may seem to be making much of small matters, yet they are most important if a still unfledged soul – as they say – is to begin to progress and to learn to fly, though no one will believe this without the experience. But as I hope in God that your Reverence will benefit many souls, I speak of these matters here. For I owe my whole salvation to the fact that this gentleman knew how to help me. He had the necessary humility and charity to deal with me, and the patience to bear with my only partial amendment. Discreetly and gradually, he showed me ways of overcoming the devil, and I began to be so fond of him that I never felt more composed than on the days when I saw him. These, however, were few. When there was a long interval, I used to become very distressed and to imagine that he was staying away on account of my wickedness.

When he began to realize how great my imperfections were – and they may even have been sins, though after my conversations with him began I considerably improved – and when, in order to obtain light from him, I described to him the favours God was bestowing on me, he warned me that the two things were inconsistent. He said that these favours were for persons very far advanced and greatly mortified, and that he could not help being somewhat disturbed. He thought that an evil spirit might have something to do with it, but could not be sure. He asked me to think carefully over my whole experience of prayer, and to tell him about it. The trouble was that I simply could not describe the nature of my prayer. For not until recently has God granted me the grace of understanding it and describing it.

When he said this to me, frightened as I was already, I was even more greatly distressed and burst into tears, for I truly desired to please God and could not persuade myself that this was the devil's work. But I was afraid that God might be closing my eyes to this on account of my great sins. Looking through some books, to see if I could learn some way of describing my prayer, I found one called *The Ascent of Mount Sion* 1 which touches on the union of the soul with God. Here I read a full description of my own state when, in the midst of this prayer, I could think of nothing at all. I underlined the relevant passage and gave him the book, so that he and that cleric I have mentioned,2 a holy man and a servant of God, might look at it, and tell me what I ought to do. I would give up this method of prayer altogether, if they thought I should, for why should I court these dangers? If after almost twenty years of prayer, I had gained nothing, but had only been deceived by the devil, it would have been better not to pray at all, even though this would have been very hard for me since I already learnt what my soul was like without prayer. Wherever I looked, there were trials all around me. I was like someone who has fallen into a river, and fears that whichever way he swims he will only get into greater danger, yet who is almost drown-

1. By Bernardo de Laredo, translated into English by E. Allison Peers.
2. Master Daza, who was one of the 'five friends'.

ing. This is a very great trial, and I have been through many such, as I shall tell later. For though it seems unimportant, it may possibly be of some use for me to explain how the spirit is to be tried.

This is certainly a great trial to undergo, and requires cautious treatment, especially from those in charge of women. For we are very weak and could come to great harm if we were told outright that the devil was deluding us. These cases should be very carefully considered, and women should be removed from all possible dangers. They should be advised to keep their experiences to themselves, and their advisers should keep them secret too. I speak as one who has suffered grave trials from the indiscretions of certain persons with whom I have discussed my prayers. By making quite honest inquiries, one of another, they have done me great harm. For they have divulged things which should rightly have been kept private, since they are not for everyone; and it has looked as if I were proclaiming them myself. I do not think that the fault was theirs; all this was permitted by the Lord in order that I might suffer. I do not mean that they revealed what I told them in confession. But as they were people whom I had consulted about my fears and whom I had asked for enlightenment, I think they should have kept completely silent. Nevertheless, I never dared hide anything from such persons. I think then that women should be directed with great discretion, and should receive encouragement. Directors must wait for the right moment, and then the Lord will help others as He helped me. Had He not done so, my fears and my timidity would have led me into great harm. Considering the serious heart trouble from which I suffered, I am surprised that I was not gravely upset.

Well, when I had handed him the book, and given him the best account I could of my life and sins – not in confession, since he was a layman, although I fully explained to him how wicked I was – these two servants of God considered with great charity and love what would be best for me. At length I received the reply that I had awaited with such fear. In the intervening days I had begged many people to pray to God for me, and had prayed hard myself. But when this gentleman called it was to inform me with great distress, that as far as they could both see I was being deluded by the devil. What they advised me to do was to discuss matters with a member of the Society of Jesus, who would come if I asked him to do so and told him that I was in trouble. I could then give him a perfectly clear account of my whole life and condition in the form of a general confession; and by virtue of the sacrament of

Confession, God would enlighten him more fully, for the Jesuits were great experts in spiritual matters. They said that I must adhere faithfully to his instructions, for so long as I had no one to direct me, I was in great peril.

This so alarmed and distressed me that I did not know what to do. I could do nothing but weep. But while I was in an oratory, in a state of great affliction, not knowing what might become of me, I read in a book that seemed to have been put into my hands by the Lord Himself St Paul's words: 'But God is faithful, who will not suffer you to be tempted above that ye are able'.[1] This thought, that God would not suffer those who love Him to be deluded by the devil, gave me great comfort. I began to think over my general confession and to write down all that was evil about me and all that was good. Thus I prepared as clear an account of my life as I knew how to, leaving nothing unsaid. When it was done, I remember feeling the very greatest misery and affliction, because I had found so much that was bad to record, and so little that was good. I was also greatly perturbed that my sisters in the house should see me consulting with such saintly people as these Jesuits. For now my wickedness frightened me, and I felt that I should be obliged to abandon it and to give up my amusements, because if I did not do so I should grow worse. So I arranged with the sacristan and the portress that they should say nothing to anyone. But this was of no use, since the person who was at the door when I was sent for talked about it all over the convent. What difficulties and fears the devil puts in the way of those who wish to come to God!

I gave that servant of God [2] – he was a true servant and a very prudent one – a full account of my soul, and he, being conversant with these matters, told me what was wrong and greatly encouraged me. He said that my experiences were quite patently the work of the spirit of God, and that what I needed was to start praying again, because I had not laid a good foundation, nor had I yet begun to understand the nature of mortification. This was true; I do not think I even knew the meaning of the word. He said that I must never on any account abandon prayer; on the contrary I ust work hard at it, since God was granting me such special favours. How did I know, he asked me, that the Lord did not wish to benefit many people and to do much else through me? Here I think he was foretelling the uses that God was afterwards to make of me. He added that I should be greatly to blame if I did not respond to the

1. 1 Corinthians x, 13.   2. Father Juan de Prádanos.

favours that God was showing me. Judging by the way in which his words impressed themselves on me, I concluded that the Holy Ghost was saying all this through him, for the good of my soul.

This made me very much ashamed, and led me along paths that seemed to turn me into a very different woman. What a great thing it is to understand a soul! He told me that I must base my prayer each day on one incident of the Passion, and get all I could out of it. He said that I must think only of Christ's Humanity and, as far as possible, resist recollections and delights. These I must not accept until he should tell me otherwise.

He left me comforted and encouraged; the Lord had helped me, and had helped him also to understand my condition and know how to direct me. I was now determined not to depart from his instructions in any particular, and I have adhered to this determination until this day. Praised be the Lord who has given me the strength to obey my confessors, although imperfectly! They have almost always been members of the blessed Company of Jesus. Although, as I have said, I only obeyed them imperfectly, my soul began to make a notable improvement, as I shall now relate.

CHAPTER 24

She continues the same subject and tells how her soul went on improving, once she had begun to obey; also how little use it was for her to resist God's favours, since His Majesty went on giving them to her in more liberal measure.

THIS confession left my soul so amenable that I thought there could be nothing which I should not be prepared to do. So I began to make many changes in my habits, although my confessor did not press me, and indeed appeared to make very light of the whole matter. I was deeply influenced by his treatment, however, because he led me by way of the love of God, which brought me, not oppression, as it would have done if I had not acted out of love, but freedom; and I remained in this condition for almost two months, doing everything in my power to resist God's gifts and favours. The change in me was visible even superficially, for the Lord was already giving me the courage to suffer things which those who knew me, and even the nuns of my own house, considered and described as extreme. Compared with what I had been doing before, these could rightly be called extreme, but they fell short of what was required of me by my habit and profession.

By resisting God's gifts and favours, I gained one thing: instruction from His Majesty Himself. Previously I had thought that if I wished to receive favours in prayer, I must often remain apart, and so I had scarcely dared to stir. Then I saw how little this had to do with it; for the more I tried to turn my mind to other things, the more the Lord enveloped me in that sweetness and glory, until I felt entirely surrounded by it. I could not flee from it in any direction, and so things went on. All this so concerned me that I was quite distressed. But the Lord was much more concerned on my behalf in those two months; He granted me favours and revealed Himself to me to a far greater degree than He had done before, in order to show me that resistance was no longer within my power. I began to feel a new love for the most sacred Humanity; my prayers began to settle, like a house that now had some foundations; and I began to be more addicted to penances, which I had neglected because of my severe illnesses.

That holy man who heard my confessions told me that there were certain things that could not hurt me, and that perhaps God was giving me my ill-health because I did not perform penances. His Majesty, he suggested, might possibly have decided to inflict some penances on me Himself. He ordered me, therefore, to practise certain mortifications, which I did not find very pleasant. But I performed them all because they seemed to be commanded by the Lord; and I thanked Him for giving them to me in such a way as to make me obey Him. My soul was so sensitive to any tiny offence I might be committing against the Lord that, if I had any superfluous possession, I could not become recollected until I had got rid of it. I prayed frequently that the Lord would take me in His hand and, now that I was on terms with His servants, would not allow me to fall again. For to fall now, I thought, would be a very great failure, since they would lose credit through me.

During this time Father Francis, who was once Duke of Gandia, [1] came here. He had given everything up some years before and entered the Company of Jesus. My confessor and the gentleman I have spoken of arranged for him to visit me, so that I might talk to him and give him an account of my experiences; for they knew that he was very advanced in prayer and that he received great favours and graces from God, as rewards, even in this life, for all that he had given up for Him. When he had heard my story, he told me that my experiences came from the spirit of God and that I should be wrong to struggle any longer against them. Up to now, he said, I had been right in resisting. But henceforth I must always begin my prayer with a meditation on some incident in the Passion; and then if the Lord should transport my spirit I should not struggle against Him, but should allow His Majesty to take it, since the rapture was not of my seeking. He gave me this medicine and advice as one who had made great progress himself; and experience counts for a great deal in such matters. He insisted that it would be a mistake for me to go on resisting. I was greatly comforted by this, and so was that gentleman, who was delighted that Father Francis had found my experiences to be the work of God, and who continued to help and advise me to the best of his ability, which was very great.

At this moment my confessor was moved away from the town; and this very much grieved me, because I thought I was bound to return to my wickedness, and felt it would be impossible to find another like him. My soul was, as it were, in a desert, very disconsolate and fearful, and I did not know what would become of me. But a relation of mine

1. St Francis Borgia, then Commissary of the Society of Jesus in Spain.

arranged for me to go and stay with her, and I immediately managed to obtain another Jesuit confessor. It pleased our Lord that I should strike up a friendship with a widowed lady [1] of good family, who was greatly given to prayer and had much to do with the Fathers. She got me to confess to her confessor and I stayed in her house, which was quite close, for quite a few days. I was delighted by the many conversations I had with the Jesuits, for my soul profited greatly by observing the holiness of their way of life.

This Father [2] began to lead me towards greater perfection. He told me to leave nothing undone that might make me entirely pleasing to God; and he treated me with great skill, though gently at the same time. For my soul was not at all strong, but very sensitive, especially in respect to abandoning certain friendships. Although these were not the cause of any offence against God, they involved a great deal of affection, and I thought that I should be ungrateful if I were to give them up. I asked my confessor why I must behave so ungratefully since I was committing no sin. He told me to put the matter before God for some days, and to recite the hymn *Veni, Creator*, that God might show me the better course. Having spent a great part of one day in prayer, beseeching the Lord to help me content Him in every way, I began the hymn; and as I was reciting it a rapture came on me so suddenly that it almost carried me away; it was so plain that I could make no mistake about it. This was the first time that the Lord had granted me this grace of ecstasy, and I heard these words: 'I want you to converse now not with men but with angels'. This absolutely amazed me, for my soul was greatly moved and these words were spoken to me in the depths of the spirit. They made me afraid therefore, though on the other hand they brought me much comfort, after the fear – which seems to have been caused by the novelty of the experience – had departed.

These words have been fulfilled. For I have never since been able to form a firm friendship, or to take any comfort in, or to feel particular love for, any people except those whom I believe to love God and to be trying to serve Him. This has been something beyond my control; and it has made no difference if the people have been relatives or friends. Unless I know that a person loves God or practises prayer, it is a painful

1. Doña Guiomar de Ulloa, a very close friend of Santa Teresa's, who later helped her to found the Convent of St Joseph.
2. Father Baltasar Álvarez, who was Santa Teresa's confessor from 1559 to 1564.

cross to me to have to do with him. There have been, so far as I can remember, no exceptions to this rule.

Since that day I have had the courage to give up everything for God, who in that moment – for I think it was no more than a moment – was pleased to make His servant another person. So there was no need for my confessor to give me any more commands. When he had found me so firmly attached to these friendships, he had not ventured to tell me definitely to give them up. He had been forced to wait until our Lord did the work, which He did. For myself, I had never thought that I should be able to break with them, since I had already tried, and the attempt had afforded me such distress that I had abandoned it on the grounds that there was really nothing wrong with these attachments. But now the Lord set me free and gave me strength to do the work. So I told my confessor, and gave everything up, as he had commanded me to. It did the people in question a great deal of good to see my determination.

Blessed be God for ever, for giving me in one moment the freedom that I had been unable to attain for myself, despite all my efforts during so many years, in which I had sometimes done such violence to myself as to affect my health. As this was the work of One who is almighty and the true Lord of all, it gave me no pain at all.

CHAPTER 25

She treats of the means and manner whereby these words that God speaks to the soul are perceived without being actually heard, and of some possible deceptions in regard to them. She tells how false locutions are to be distinguished from true. This is a most profitable chapter for any who may have reached this stage of prayer, because the explanation is very clear and contains much teaching.

I T will be as well, I think, to explain the nature of these locutions which God bestows on the soul and to describe the soul's feelings when it receives them, in order that your Reverence may understand them. For since the occasion of which I am speaking, on which the Lord granted me this favour, it has become a common occurrence with me; and it is so to-day, as will be seen in what I have still to say. The words are perfectly formed, but are not heard with the physical ear. Yet they are received much more clearly than if they were so heard; and however hard one resists it is impossible to shut them out. For when, in ordinary life, we do not wish to hear, we can close our ears or attend to something else; and in that way although we may hear we do not understand. But when God speaks to the soul like this, there is no alternative; I have to listen whether I like it or not, and to devote my whole attention to understanding what God wishes me to understand. It makes no difference whether I want to or not. Since He who is all-powerful wishes us to understand, we have to do what He wishes; and here He reveals Himself as our true Lord. This I know from repeated experience, for such was my fear that I put up a resistance for almost two years; and sometimes I still try to resist, though with little success.

I want to describe the delusions that may occur here, though I do not think that anyone with adequate experience will often, if ever, be deceived. But his experience must be adequate. I will explain also how those locutions that come from good spirits differ from those that come from evil ones, and how they may be – as sometimes occurs – caused by the intellect itself, or by the spirit talking to itself. I do not know whether this is possible, but only to-day it has struck me that it is. I have plenty of proof concerning those cases when the locutions are of God. I have been told things two or three years beforehand that have afterwards been fulfilled, and so far none of them has proved untrue.

There are other ways too in which the spirit of God can be plainly detected, as I shall tell later.

I think it possible that a person who has laid some request before God with most loving concern may imagine that he hears a voice telling him whether his prayer will be granted or not. This may well be, though once he has heard some genuine message, he will see clearly what this voice is, for there is a great difference between the two experiences. If his answer has been invented by the understanding, however subtly it may be contrived, he perceives the intellect ordering the words and speaking them. It is just as if a person were composing a speech, or listening to what someone else says; and the understanding will then realize that it is not listening but working, and that the words it is inventing are imprecise and fanciful; they have not the clarity of the real locution. In such cases it is in our power to deflect our attention, just as we can stop speaking and be silent. But in the true locution, this cannot be done. Another sign, which is the surest of all, is that these false locutions leave no results, whereas when the Lord speaks, words lead to deeds; and although the words may be of reproof and not of devotion, they prepare the soul, make it ready, and move it to tenderness. They give it light, and make it quiet and happy. If it has been dry and disordered and restless, the Lord seems to remove its troubles with a wave of His hand; or better still, He seems to explain to it that He is all-powerful and that His words are deeds.

There seems to me to be the same difference as between speaking and listening, neither more nor less. For, as I have said, when I am speaking, my intellect goes on arranging what I am saying; but if I am spoken to, I do no more than effortlessly listen. The false locution is like something that we cannot clearly make out; it is as if we were asleep; but when God speaks, the voice is so clear that not a syllable of what He says is lost. It happens at times that the understanding and the soul are so perturbed and distracted that they could not put together a satisfactory sentence, and yet the soul finds itself addressed in grand speeches that it could not compose for itself even if it were completely recollected; and at the first word, as I have said, it is completely changed. How, since it is in ecstasy and its faculties are suspended, could it possibly understand things that have never come into its mind before? How could they come at a time when the memory is hardly working, and the imagination is more or less stupefied?

It should be noted that if we see visions and hear words like this, it is never, in my opinion, at a time when the soul is in union or during the rapture itself. For then, as I have already explained – I think when speaking of the second water – all the senses are completely lost and, as I believe, there can be no seeing or understanding or hearing at all. The soul is wholly in Another's power, and during this very brief period the Lord does not seem to leave it free for any experience whatever. But when this brief time is over, and the soul is still enraptured, then is the time I am speaking of. The faculties, though not lost, remain in such a state that they can hardly do anything. They are, as it were, absorbed and incapable of composing arguments. But there are so many ways of telling the difference between true and false locutions that, even if we are mistaken once, we shall not be mistaken often.

I mean that if a soul is experienced and on its guard, it will see the difference very clearly; for apart from other points which prove the truth of what I say, the false locutions have no effect and the soul does not accept them, as it has to accept divine locutions even against its will. It does not believe in them, but on the contrary knows that they are the ravings of the mind, and takes no more notice of them than of someone whom it knows to be a lunatic. But to the true locution we listen as to a saintly and learned person of great authority who we know will not lie to us. But even this is a poor comparison, for sometimes these words are of such majesty that, even if we do not know from whom they come, they make us tremble if they are spoken in reproof, and if they are words of love consume us with love. Furthermore, as I have said, they speak of things that were very far from being in our memory, and take the form of such long sentences spoken so quickly that it would have taken us a very long time to make them up ourselves; and if we had done so, I do not think that we could possibly have been unaware that they were of our own composition. So there is no reason why I should dwell any longer on this matter, for I think it would be a marvel if any experienced person were taken in, unless he deliberately wanted to be.

When I have been in doubt I have often disbelieved what was said to me, and wondered if I had been imagining it – I mean after the experience was over, for at the time it was impossible – and then, a long time afterwards, I have found it all fulfilled. For the Lord makes the words stay in the memory so that we cannot forget them, whereas those that originate in our own minds are like a first stirring of thought that passes and is forgotten. A divine locution may, as it were, fade with the passage of time, yet not so completely that one loses the memory of its having been spoken. It is only after a long interval, or if the words relate only to some favour or some instruction, that they can disappear entirely. But words of prophecy, in my opinion, can never be forgotten – at least by me, although I have a poor memory.

I repeat then, that unless a soul is so wicked as wilfully to pretend that it has received this favour – which would be extremely wicked – or to say that it understands something when it does not, I think there is no possibility of its failing to recognize that it has made the words up and is speaking them to itself, assuming, of course, that it has once heard the spirit of God. If it has not, it may continue in its delusion for the whole of its life, and imagine that it is understanding something. But how this can be I do not know. Either a soul wishes to understand or it does not. If it is rejecting what it hears, and is far too frightened to want to hear anything, or has other reasons for preferring to be quiet during its times of prayer and not have these experiences, how can the intellect have the time to make up speeches? For this requires time. But when the locutions are genuine, they instruct us without any cost in time, and make us understand things which it would probably take us a month to put in order for ourselves. What is more, the mind and soul themselves are amazed at some of the things they understand.

This is how things are, and anyone with experience will know that what I have said is literally true. Praise be to God that I have been able to explain it like this. I will conclude by saying that if all locutions came from the intellect, I think we could hear them whenever we liked, and every time we prayed we might think we heard them. But this is not the case with divine locutions. I may listen for many days and, although I want to hear something, cannot do so; while at other times when, as I have said, I do not want to, I am forced to listen. It seems to me that anyone anxious to deceive others by saying that he has heard from God what actually came from himself, might very well claim to have heard it with his physical ears. For I certainly never thought that there was any other way of hearing or understanding, until I had the experience myself; and so, as I have said, it has cost me considerable trials.

Locutions that come from the devil not only lead to no good, but leave bad effects behind them. These I have experienced, though only on two or three occasions, and each time I have had an immediate warning from the Lord that they came from the devil. Not only is the soul left in great dryness, but there is also a certain disquiet, such as I have experienced on many other occasions when the Lord has allowed me to be subjected to great temptations and spiritual trials of various sorts. But although this disquiet torments me very often, as I shall say later, it is not easy to know where it comes from. The soul seems to resist the experience and is upset and afflicted without knowing why, for what is actually said is not evil but good. I think that one spirit must recognize the other.

The pleasures and joys which the devil bestows are, I believe, most various; and with his pleasures he might well deceive anyone who has not experienced, or is not experiencing, pleasures from God. I actually mean pleasures, for they bring a sweet, strong, impressive, delightful, and calm refreshment. Mild bursts of feeling, that come with tears, and other such weak manifestations are good beginnings and show true emotion. But at the first breath of persecution these little flowers wither. I do not call them real devotions, and they are useless as a means of distinguishing between the effects of a good spirit and a bad one. So it is as well for us always to proceed with great caution, for if persons no further advanced in prayer than this experience visions or revelations, they may very easily be deceived. I myself had never known anything of the kind until God gave me, of His goodness alone, the prayer of union, always excepting that first experience of which I have spoken, when many years ago I saw Christ. I wish His Majesty had then been pleased to inform me that this was a true vision, as I have since realized it was. That would have been no small blessing to me. After visions of the other kind, the soul is not left in a calm state, but in a kind of bewilderment and most perturbed.

I am positively certain that the devil will not deceive, nor will God permit him to deceive, a soul that puts no trust whatever in itself, that is fortified in the faith, and that is absolutely certain that it would suffer a thousand deaths for any single article of it. With this love for the faith, which God then infuses into it, comes a living and strong belief. The soul always tries to act in conformity with the Church's teaching, asking advice from this person and that, and acting as one already so deeply grounded in these truths that no imaginable revelation, even if it saw the heavens open, would cause it to swerve an inch from the doctrine of the Church. If it should ever feel its thoughts wavering on this point, or stopping to say, 'If God says this to me, it may well be true, just as what He said to the saints was true', I do not say that it will believe what it is saying, but that the devil will be beginning to tempt it; and this is his first step. To stop and say this is clearly very wrong. But even this first step will not be taken when the soul is strong in this respect, as the Lord makes it in those to whom He grants these gifts. Then it feels able to crush the evil spirits, in defence even of one of the Church's smallest truths.

I mean that if this great strength does not arise in a soul, and if it is not helped by devotions or by visions, it must not consider itself secure. For although it may not feel the harm immediately, it may suffer great harm by slow degrees. For from what I can see and know by experience, the proof that something comes from God lies in its conformity to Holy Scripture. If it diverges in the least from that, I think I should feel incomparably more certain that it came from the devil than I had previously been of its divine origin, great though my belief in this may have been. In such cases there is no need to go in search of signs, or to ask from what spirit it comes. For this is so clear a sign that it comes from the devil that if afterwards the whole world were to assure me that it was of God, I should not believe it. The position is that when it is of the devil, all good things seem to be hidden from the soul and to flee from it; it becomes restless and touchy, and suffers nothing but bad effects. It may seem to have good desires, but they are not strong; and the humility that remains behind is false, excitable, and lacking in tranquillity. I believe that anyone with experience of the good spirit will understand this.

The devil can play plenty of tricks all the same; and so there is nothing more certain than that we must always be fearful and proceed with caution. We must have a learned man as our director, and hide nothing from him; and then no harm can befall us – although plenty has befallen me through the excessive fears of certain persons. This was especially so on one occasion when there was a meeting of a number of people in whom I felt a great and justifiable confidence. I had dealings with only one of them, but he ordered me to speak freely to the rest. Then they had long discussions among themselves about means of helping me, for they were very fond of me and were afraid that I might be deceived. I was much afraid of this myself when I was not at prayer, but when I prayed, God always granted me some favour and I was immediately reassured. I think there were five or six of these people, all great servants of God; and they had all decided, as my confessor told me, that my experiences were of the devil, that I ought not to take such frequent Communions, and that I ought to find distractions so as not to be so much alone. I was very much alarmed, as I have said, and my heart trouble made things so much worse that very often I did not dare to stay alone in a room by day. When I found them all affirming this and myself disbelieving them, I felt a very serious scruple, and believed myself to be lacking in humility. All of them were leading incomparably better lives than I, and were men of learning. How could I do anything else but believe them? I made every possible effort to do so and, thinking how wicked I was, concluded that what they said must be true.

In deep distress, I left the church and went into an oratory. For many days I had not taken Communion and had refrained from seeking solitude, which was my chief comfort. I had no one to discuss matters with, since they were all against me. When I spoke to them about my experiences, I thought they were mocking me, as if it were all my fancy. There were some who said that it was clearly the devil's work. Only my confessor constantly comforted me, although he took their side. This, as I afterwards learnt, was in order to test me. He told me that, even if it was the devil, my prayer could do me no harm so long as I did not offend against God, who would deliver me from him. He said that I must pray to God frequently. My confessor and all his penitents and many more prayed for me, and I myself, as well as many whom I knew to be servants of God, spent the whole of our prayers in begging His Majesty to lead me by some other path. This continued for about two years, during the whole of which time I made this continual petition to the Lord.

When I reflected that what I heard so often might be the devil's words, nothing was of any consolation to me. As I now no longer spent solitary hours in prayer, the Lord would make me recollected during conversation. He said what He pleased, and I could not avoid it; much though it distressed me, I had to listen. Now when I was alone, with no company to give me relaxation, I could neither pray nor read, but was as if stunned by all these trials and by fear that the devil might be deceiving me. I was utterly disquieted and exhausted, and did not know what to do. I have several times – indeed, often – been in this sort of state, but never, I think, in such distress as then. I would remain in this condition for four or five hours on end, and there was no comfort for me, either in heaven or on earth: Our Lord left me to suffer my fear of a thousand dangers. O my Lord, what a true friend You are, and how powerful! You can do everything when You will. and you never cease to will if we love You! Let all things praise You, Lord of the world. O that a voice might go forth over the earth, proclaiming how faithful You are to Your friends! All things fail, but You, Lord of them all, never fail. Small is the suffering that You allow to those who love You. O my Lord, how delicately and gently and sweetly You know how to deal with them! If only we had none of us stopped to love anyone but You! You seem, Lord, to inflict severe tests on those who love You, but only in order that in the worst of their trials they may know the depth of Your love for them.

O my Lord, had I but the understanding and learning, and fresh words as well with which to extol Your works as my soul knows them! Alas, I lack all these, but if You do not abandon me, let all created things persecute me, let the devils torment me, but do not fail me, Lord, for I have experience of the benefits and the deliverance You bring to those who trust in You alone. When I was in this state of great exhaustion – at that time I had not begun to have visions – these words alone were enough to dispel it and to quiet me completely: 'Have no fear, daughter, for it is I, and I will not forsake you. Have no fear.'

In the state I was then in, I think it would have taken many hours to persuade me to be calm, and that one person would not have been enough to do it. But here I was, calmed by just these few words. I received strength and courage, security, tranquillity, and enlightenment, and in one moment found my soul transformed. I think I would have maintained against the whole world that this was God's work. Oh, how good God is! Oh, how good the Lord is and how powerful! He gives not only counsel but relief. His words are deeds. As He strengthens our faith, see how our love grows!

This is certain, and I would often remember how when a storm arose on the sea, the Lord commanded the winds to be still. Then I would say to myself: 'Who is this whom all my faculties thus obey? Who is it that in a moment sheds light amidst such great darkness, who softens a heart that seemed to be of stone and sheds the water of gentle tears where for so long it had seemed to be dry? Who gives these desires? Who gives this courage? What have I been thinking of? What am I afraid of? What is this? I wish to serve this Lord, and have no other aim but to please Him. I seek no contentment, no rest, no other blessing but to do His will.' I seemed to feel so confident of this that I could affirm it.

So, I reflected, if this Lord is powerful, as I see He is and know He is, and if the devils are His slaves – and of this there can be no doubt, since it is an article of faith – what harm can they do me, who am a servant of this Lord and King? Why should not I have the strength to fight against all hell? I took a cross in my hand, and God really seemed to give me courage. In a short time I found myself so transformed that I should not have been afraid to wrestle with devils, for I felt that I could easily defeat a whole host of them with that cross. 'Come on now, all of you,' I cried, 'I am a servant of the Lord, and I should like to see what you can do to me.'

They certainly seemed to be afraid of me, for I became quite calm and had no more fear of them. In fact I lost all my habitual fears for good. For although I have sometimes seen devils, as I shall tell by and by, I have hardly been afraid of them since. In fact, they have seemed to be afraid of me. I have acquired an authority over them, given me by the Lord of all things, and now I take no more notice of them than of flies. They appear to be such cowards, that their strength fails when they see anyone who despises them. They are enemies that are only capable of making an attack on people whom they see giving in to them, or on God's servants whom He allows them to try and torment for those servants' greater good. May it please His Majesty to make us fear Him whom we ought to fear, and to understand that greater harm can come to us from one venial sin than from all hell combined – for that is the truth.

These devils keep us in terror, because we lay ourselves open to being terrorized. We become attached to honours, possessions, and pleasures. Then they join forces with us, since by loving and desiring what we should loathe we have become our own enemies. Then they will do us great harm. We make them fight against us with our own weapons, which we put into their hands instead of using them in our own defence. This is most deplorable. But if we hate everything for God's sake, embrace the Cross and try to serve Him truly, the devil will fly from such realities as from the plague. He is himself a lie and a lover of lies, and will have no dealings with anyone who lives with the truth. When he sees a person's understanding darkened, he deftly helps him to lose his sight altogether. If he sees anyone already blind enough to find comfort in vanities – and in such vanities, for the things of this world are no more than toys – he knows that he is a child, treats him as such, and makes bold to wrestle with him, not once but many times.

Please God I may not be one of these! May His Majesty help me to take as comfort what is true comfort, to take as honour what is true honour, and what is really delightful as delight – and not the other way round. Then I snap my fingers at all the devils; they shall be afraid of me. I do not understand these fears which make us cry: 'The devil! the devil!', when we might be saying, 'God! God!', and making the devil tremble. For we know very well that he cannot stir without the Lord's permission. What are we thinking of? I am sure I am more afraid of these people who are so frightened of the devil than I am of the devil himself. He cannot do me any harm, but they, especially if they are confessors, can be most disturbing. For several years they were such a trial to me that now I am astonished that I was able to bear it. Blessed be the Lord, who so truly helped me!

CHAPTER 26

*She continues with the same subject, relating and describing certain
events which rid her of her fears, and convinced her that the spirit
which spoke to her was a good one*

I LOOK upon the courage which the Lord gave me to fight the devils
as one of the greatest favours that He has bestowed on me. It is very
wrong for a soul to behave like a coward or to fear anything except
offending God, since we have an all-powerful King and a Lord so
mighty that He can do everything and make all men His subjects. There
is, as I have said, nothing to fear so long as we walk truthfully in His
Majesty's presence with a clean conscience. For this reason, as I have
said, I would wish always to be in awe, so as never for a moment to
offend Him who in that same moment might destroy us. If His Majesty
is pleased with us there is not one of our enemies that will not tear his
hair. This can be accepted as true. But what soul is upright enough to
please Him entirely? Here lies the reason for our fear. Certainly my
soul is not. It is most wretched and useless and overflowing with
miseries. But God's ways are not men's ways. He understands our weaknesses; the soul knows by a strong inward surmise whether it truly loves
Him. For the love of those who reach this stage is no longer hidden, as
it was at the beginning, but comes with a great impulse and a longing to
see God, which I have already described and shall describe again. Everything wearies and exhausts such a soul; everything torments it. If its rest
is not in God, and does not come from God, it is mere restlessness, for it
sees that its true rest is far away. Its love is, therefore, something most
evident; as I say, it cannot be hidden.

It happened at times that I was greatly tried and maligned about a
certain matter that I shall describe later, by almost everyone in the town
where I live and by my Order. I was greatly distressed by many things
which arose to disturb me. But the Lord said to me then: 'What are you
afraid of? Do you not know that I am all-powerful? I will fulfil my
promises to you.' And they were fulfilled shortly afterwards. Then I
began to have such strength that I believe I could have undertaken new
enterprises in His service, even if they had cost me more trials and
caused me to suffer afresh. This has happened to me so many times that
I cannot count them. He has often reproached me like this, and He does
so still when I fall into imperfections great enough to destroy a soul. His

words always lead to amendment, for, as I have said, His Majesty gives both counsel and relief. At other times the Lord recalls my past sins to me, especially when he wishes to grant me some special favour; and then I feel as if my soul were really before the Judgement; for the truth is presented to it with such complete insight that it does not know where to hide. Sometimes I am warned of perils to myself and others, and frequently I have been told of things that were to happen three or four years afterwards; all have come true, and it would be possible to detail some of these cases. There are so many signs, in fact, to show that these locutions are of God that I do not think the fact can be doubted.

The safest thing is to follow the course that I do. If I did not, I should have no peace – not that it is right for us women to have peace, since we have no learning. When I do this I cannot come to any harm, but must reap great benefits, as the Lord has often told me. What I am saying is that I reveal my whole soul to a confessor, and describe to him the favours which the Lord grants me. I choose a man of learning and obey him; I confess frequently, and never give it up. I once had a confessor[1] who subjected me to great mortifications, and who would sometimes distress me and greatly try me by disquieting my mind. But I believe it is he who has done me the most good. I was very fond of him, yet I was several times tempted to leave him, for I thought that the distress he caused me disturbed my prayer. But each time I decided to give him up, I at once realized that I must not, and received a divine reproof that upset me more than any action of my confessor. Sometimes questions on the one hand and reproofs on the other utterly exhausted me. But I needed them all, for my will was not bent to obedience. Once the Lord told me that it was no true obedience if I was not determined to suffer, and that I must fix my eyes on His suffering. Then everything would come easy.

A confessor to whom I had gone at the beginning advised me on one occasion, that since my experiences were now proved to be due to a good spirit, I ought to keep silent and say nothing about them to anybody, as it was better not to speak about such things. This did not seem wrong to me, for whenever I spoke of them to this confessor I used to feel most distressed and abashed. In fact it sometimes upset me more to mention these favours, especially if they were considerable ones, than to confess to grave sins – for I expected to be disbelieved and to be made fun of. This grieved me greatly, and to speak of God's marvels now

1. Father Baltasar Álvarez, then a man of only twenty-five.

seemed to me an irreverence. So I preferred to keep quiet. But I came to realize that I had been very badly advised by that confessor, and that when I confessed I must on no account keep anything back. If I told everything, I knew that I should be absolutely safe; if I did not I might sometimes be deceived.

Whenever the Lord told me in prayer to do one thing and my confessor said something else, the Lord would speak again and tell me to obey him. Then His Majesty would change that confessor's mind, so that he would come back and tell me to do the opposite. When a number of books in Spanish were taken away from us, and we were told not to read them,[1] I felt it deeply because some of them gave me recreation and I could not go on reading them, since now I only had them in Latin. Then the Lord said to me: 'Do not be distressed, for I will give you a living book'. I could not understand why this had been said to me, for I had not yet had visions. But a very few days afterwards I understood perfectly. What I saw before me gave me so much to think about and so many subjects for recollection, and the Lord showed me such love and taught me in so many ways, that I have had very little or no need of books since. His Majesty has been a veritable book in which I have read the truth. Blessed be this book, which imprints on our minds in an unforgettable way what we must read and do. Who can see the Lord afflicted, persecuted, and covered with wounds without embracing, loving, and longing for those wounds? Who can see anything of the glory that He gives to those who serve Him, without recognizing that any deeds or sufferings of ours are nothing compared with the expectation of that reward? Who can see the torments of the damned without feeling that all earthly torments are by comparison pure delights, and without realizing how much we owe to the Lord for having so often delivered us from that place?

Since, with God's help, I mean to say more about some of these things later, I shall now continue the account of my life. May the Lord graciously have enabled me to make clear what I have said. I am sure that anyone with experience will understand me and will see that I have succeeded in saying at least something. But I shall not be surprised if the inexperienced think it nonsense. The fact that it is I who am the narrator will be enough to excuse them, and I shall not blame anybody who criticizes me in that way. May the Lord allow me to carry out His will exactly. Amen.

1. By a decree of the Grand Inquisitor, 1559.

CHAPTER 27

*She describes another way in which the Lord teaches the soul and,
without speech, makes His will known to it in a wondrous manner.
She also speaks of a vision and of a great favour, which was not
imaginary, that the Lord granted her. This is a most
noteworthy chapter*

To return to the account of my life, I have already spoken of my
great distress and affliction and of the many people who were
praying that the Lord might lead me by another and surer path since,
as they told me, there was so much doubt about this one. The truth is
that though I was begging God to do this, and was most anxious to feel
some desire for another path, once I saw how much my soul was
benefiting, I could not truly desire it, except occasionally when I was
troubled by what they said to me, and by the fears that they aroused in
me. I kept on praying for it, nevertheless. But I realized that I was entirely changed, and could only put myself into the hands of God, who
knew what was good for me and would perform His will in me in all
respects. I saw that this road led to heaven, and that previously I had
been going to hell. So I could not compel myself to desire a change of
path, or believe that the devil was deceiving me, although I did everything in my power to desire the former and to believe the latter. But it
was completely impossible. I offered up all my actions, if there should
be anything good in them, to this end. I implored the saints to whom I
was devoted to save me from the devil. I made *novenas* [1] and commended myself to St Hilarion and to St Michael the Angel, for whom I
undertook fresh devotions with this in view; and I begged many other
saints that the Lord might show me the truth – I mean to prevail on His
Majesty to do so.

At the end of two years, during the whole of which both other
people and myself had prayed continually that the Lord might either
lead me by another path or reveal the truth – and all the time the locutions which, as I have said, the Lord was giving me were very frequent –
I had the following experience. One day when I was at prayer – it was
the feastday of the glorious St Peter – I saw Christ at my side – or, to
put it better, I was conscious of Him, for I saw nothing with the eyes

1. A special nine days devoted to a particular form of prayer.

187

of the body or the eyes of the soul. He seemed quite close to me, and I saw that it was He. As I thought, He was speaking to me. Being completely ignorant that such visions were possible, I was very much afraid at first, and could do nothing but weep, though as soon as He spoke His first word of assurance to me, I regained my usual calm, and became cheerful and free from fear. All the time Jesus Christ seemed to be at my side, but as this was not an imaginary vision I could not see in what form. But I most clearly felt that He was all the time on my right, and was a witness of everything that I was doing. Each time I became a little recollected, or was not entirely distracted, I could not but be aware that He was beside me.

In great trouble, I went at once to my confessor to tell him about this. He asked me in what form I had seen Him, and I replied that I had not seen Him. He asked me how I knew it was Christ, and I replied that I did not know how, but that I could not help being aware that He was beside me, that I had plainly seen and felt it, and that when I prayed my soul was now much more deeply and continuously recollected. I said that the effects of my prayer were quite different from those I had experienced hitherto, and that this was perfectly evident to me. I had no way of explaining myself except by using comparisons; and no comparison, I think, can help one much to describe this kind of vision, for it is one of the highest possible kinds. This was told me afterwards by a holy man of great spirituality called Friar Peter of Alcántara,[1] whom I shall mention again, and other men of great learning have told me the same thing. It is, of all the kinds of vision, the one with which the devil can least interfere, and so there are no terms in which we unlearned women can describe it; men of learning will explain it better. For if I say that I do not see Him with the eyes of the body or the eyes of the soul, because this is no imaginary vision, how then can I know and affirm that he is beside me with greater certainty than if I saw Him? If one says that one is like a person in the dark who cannot see someone though he is beside him, or that one is like somebody who is blind, it is not right. There is some similarity here, but not much, because a person in the dark can perceive with the other senses, or hear his neighbour speak or move, or can touch him. Here this is not so, nor is there any feeling of darkness. On the contrary, He appears to the soul by a knowledge brighter than the sun. I do not mean that any sun is seen, or any brightness, but there is a light which, though unseen, illumines the

1. The Franciscan saint and reformer.

understanding so that the soul may enjoy this great blessing, which brings very great blessings with it.

It is not like the presence of God, which is often experienced, especially by those who have the prayer of union and the prayer of quiet. It is as if when we are on the point of praying we discover the Person to whom we were going to speak. We seem to know that He is listening by the spiritual effects, by the feelings of great love and faith of which we then become conscious, also by the good resolutions, with their accompaniment of sweetness, that we then make. This great favour comes from God, and anyone who receives it should value it highly, for it is a very high form of prayer. But it is not a vision. God is understood to be present, as I have said, by the effects which He produces on the soul, for that is the way in which His Majesty wishes to make His presence felt. But in a vision the soul distinctly sees that Jesus Christ, the Virgin's son, is present. In the other kind of prayer influences come to it from the Divinity; but in this not only do we receive these but we find that the most holy Humanity has become our companion and is also pleased to grant us favours.

Then my confessor asked me: 'Who said that it was Jesus Christ?' 'He often tells me so Himself,' I answered, 'but before ever He said it, it was impressed on my understanding that it was He, and even before that He used to tell me He was there when I could not see Him.' If someone I had never seen or heard about were to come and speak to me when I was blind or in thick darkness and were to tell me who he was, I should believe him, but I should not be able to affirm that he was that person as positively as if I had seen him. But here one can, for though He is unseen He imprints so clear a knowledge on the soul that there seems to be no possibility of doubt. The Lord is pleased to engrave it so deeply on the understanding that one can no more doubt it than one can doubt the evidence of one's eyes. In fact it is easier to doubt one's eyes. For sometimes we wonder whether we have not imagined something seen, whereas here, though that suspicion may arise momentarily, so great a certainty remains behind that the doubt has no validity.

It is the same with another of God's methods of instructing the soul, that by which He speaks to it without words, as I have already said. He uses so celestial a language that it is difficult to explain it to mortals, however much one may wish to, unless the Lord Himself teaches us how. He introduces into the innermost parts of the soul what He wants it to understand, presenting it not in pictures or in the form of words, but in the manner of this vision that I have described. Consider carefully this way in which God reveals to the soul not only His wishes, but also great truths and mysteries. Often when He explains some vision that He has been pleased to grant me, the instruction comes in this way. This, I think, is the state with which the devil can least interfere, for reasons which I will set out – and if they are not good ones I must be under a delusion.

This kind of vision and language is of so spiritual a nature that I think there is no excitement in the faculties or the senses that could give the devil any advantage. It is only occasionally and fleetingly that these experiences occur. For the rest of the time, I believe, the faculties are not suspended or the senses put to sleep. They remain very active, which is not always the case in contemplation – indeed it is very seldom so. But when they are suspended, we are, I believe, ourselves inactive and accomplish nothing; everything seems to be the work of the Lord. It is as if food has been put in our stomachs without our eating it or knowing how it got there. We know very well that it is there although we do not know what the food is or how it entered. For my soul has seen nothing and felt nothing; it had never been moved to desire this, nor had it come to my knowledge that such an experience was possible.

In the locutions which we dealt with previously, God makes the understanding listen, even against its will, and take in what is said to it. The soul now seems to have other ears to hear with, and He makes it listen, preventing its attention from wandering. It is like someone with good hearing whose friends will not allow him to stop his ears, but talk to him all together and loudly, so that he cannot help attending. He, however, plays a part, since he takes in what they are saying. But here the soul plays none; it is relieved now even of the minor activity of listening, which it performed in the past. It finds everything cooked and eaten for it; it has only to enjoy its nourishment. It is like a man who has had no schooling, and has never even taken the trouble to learn to read, yet who finds himself, without any study, in possession of all living knowledge. He does not know how or whence it came, since he has never done even so much work as would be necessary for learning the alphabet.

This last comparison gives some idea, I think, of this heavenly gift. For the soul suddenly finds itself learned, and such exalted mysteries as that of the Holy Trinity are so plain to it that it would boldly argue against any theologian in defence of these miraculous truths. The soul is so astounded that a single one of these favours is enough to transform it entirely, and to make it love nothing but Him, who, as it sees, without any labour on its part, makes it capable of receiving these great blessings. The secrets which God communicates to it, and the love and friendship with which He treats it are impossible to describe. Some of the favours He bestows on it are so wonderful in themselves that when granted to one who has not deserved them, they may arouse suspicion. No one, indeed, who has not a very lively faith will believe in them. So, unless I am commanded otherwise, I intend to speak only of a few that were granted to me. I will limit myself to a description of certain visions, which may be of some use to others, or may prevent those to whom the Lord gives these experiences from being surprised and thinking them impossible, as I used to. This may explain how and by what path the Lord has led me; which is what I have been commanded to write.

To return to this way of understanding, the Lord, as I see it, wishes the soul to have at any rate some idea of what happens in Heaven. Therefore, just as souls there understand one another without speaking – which I never knew for certain till the Lord of His goodness revealed it to me, unworthy though I am, in a rapture – even so it is on earth. Here too, God and the soul understand one another simply because it is His Majesty's will, and no other means is necessary to express the love that exists between these two friends. If two people, in this life, love one another and are of good intelligence, they seem to understand one another without signs, merely by the exchange of a glance; and this must be the case too in the experience I have been speaking of. For without seeing one another, we look on one another face to face, as two lovers do. It is as the Bridegroom says to the Bride in the *Song of Songs*, I believe; at least I have been told that it is said there.

How wondrous is God's loving kindness, that He permits Himself to be looked at with eyes that have looked on things in as sinful a way as the eyes of my soul! After such a sight, Lord, may they never grow accustomed again to looking on base things, may nothing content them but You! How great is man's ingratitude and to what extremes will it go! I know by experience that what I say is true, and that only the smallest part of what You do for a soul that You lead to such states can be expressed in words. O souls that have begun to pray and that possess true faith, what blessings can you pursue in this life – not to mention those that you may gain in eternity – that are equal to the least of these?

Reflect on this truth: that God gives Himself to those who give up everything for Him. He is no respecter of persons, but loves everyone, with no exceptions, as He was pleased, in His goodness, that I should see. For He revealed it to me in a rapture. Reflect that what I am saying is not a fraction of what could be said. I have only written as much as is needful to explain the kind of vision and favour that God gives to the soul. But I cannot describe what the soul feels when the Lord allows it to understand His secrets and wonders. The joy is so much above all others felt on earth that it gives us a rightful loathing for the pleasures of this life, all of which are but dross; and it is odious to bring them into the comparison, even if we might enjoy them for ever. And what are these joys that the Lord gives us? Only one drop of water from the great, overflowing river that He has prepared for us.

It is shameful, and I certainly feel ashamed. What is more, if it were possible to be ashamed in Heaven I should rightfully be the most ashamed there. Why should we desire all these blessings and delights and eternal glory, all at the cost of our good Jesus? Even if we are not helping Him to carry His Cross with the Cyrenean, shall we not at least weep with the daughters of Jerusalem?[1] Is it by pleasures and pastimes that we shall come to enjoy what He won for us with so much blood? That is impossible. Can we think that by pursuing vain honours, we can recompense Him for the scorn He suffered in order that we might reign for ever? That is not the way. It leads far, far astray, and we shall never get there by it. Proclaim these truths aloud, your Reverence, since God has not made me free to do so. I should like to proclaim them for ever. But God heard me and I understood Him so late, as will be clear from what I have written, that I feel deeply ashamed to speak of it and prefer to keep silence. I will merely dwell on a subject about which I meditate from time to time.

May it please the Lord to bring me to a state in which I can enjoy this blessing. What will be the incidental glory and pleasure of the blessed who already enjoy it when they see that, late though they are, they have left nothing undone that they could possibly do for God, that they have kept nothing back that they might have given Him in any possible way, according to their power and position, and that the more they had the more they have given? How rich will a man find himself who has given up all his riches for Christ! What honour will he receive who for His sake desired no honours, but has been pleased to see himself

1. Luke xxiii, 26, 28.

humbled! How wise will he be who was glad to be considered mad, since He who was wisdom itself was called so! How few of these are living to-day – because of our sins! Alas, there seem to be no more of those whom people once accounted mad, when they saw them performing heroic deeds, like true lovers of Christ! O world, world, how much of your reputation is due to those few who really know you!

We think that God is best pleased if we acquire a reputation for wisdom and discretion, and that may be so. It depends what we mean by discretion. We at once conclude that we are failing to set an example if each one of us does not exercise great dignity and authority in our calling. We think it very odd and disconcerting to the weak, if a friar, a cleric, or a nun wears old patched clothes, or even if they are often recollected and given to prayer. Such is the state of the world to-day, and so forgotten are the perfections and the mighty raptures of the saints of old, that I do not think things could be made any worse if those in religion were to put into practice what they say about despising the things of this world. For the Lord turns any such scandals to great advantage. If some were scandalized indeed, others would be struck with remorse; and we should at least have some illustration of what Christ and His Apostles suffered, of which we have more need to-day than ever.

What a grand illustration God has just taken from us in the shape of the blessed friar, Peter of Alcántara. The world is not yet fit to bear such perfection. They say that people's health is poorer nowadays, and that times are not what they were. But this holy person was a man of our day, and yet he had as robust a spirit as those of the olden times, and so he trampled on the world. Now although everyone does not go about barefoot or perform such severe penances as he did, there are many ways, as I have said elsewhere, of treading the world underfoot, and the Lord teaches them to those in whom He sees courage. And what great courage His Majesty gave to this holy man, that he could perform, as is common knowledge, such severe penances for forty-six years. I should like to say something about this, for I know that it is all true.

He spoke of it to me, and to another person from whom he concealed very little. In me he confided out of love, for the Lord was pleased that he should feel love for me, and should stand up for me, and encourage me at a time when I was in great need. This I have spoken of and shall speak of again. He said, I think, that for forty years he had never slept more than an hour and a half between nightfall and morning, and that at the beginning the hardest part of his penance had been the conquering of sleep. For this reason he always remained standing or on his knees. Such sleep as he had, he took sitting down, with his head propped against a piece of wood, which he had fixed to the wall. He could not lie down to sleep even if he wished to, for his cell, as is well known, was only four and a half feet long. During all those years, however hot the sun or heavy the rain, he never wore his hood or anything on his feet. He was always clothed in a sackcloth habit with nothing between it and his skin; and this he wore as tight as he could bear it, with a cloak of the same material over it. He told me that in the bitterest cold he would take off his cloak and leave the door and window of his cell open, so as to gain some physical relief afterwards from the increased warmth, when he put it on again and closed the door. He usually ate only once in three days, and he wondered why this surprised me. He said that it was perfectly possible once one got used to it, and a companion of his told me that sometimes he would go eight days without food. This must have been when he was at prayer, for he used to have great raptures and transports of love for God, of which I was once a witness.

His poverty was extreme, and so, even in his youth, was his mortification. He told me that he had lived for three years in a house of his Order, and had not known a single friar except by his voice. For he never raised his eyes, and so when he had to go to any part of the house, he could only do so by following the other friars; it was the same thing out of doors. For many years he had never looked at a woman. He told me that it was all one to him whether he looked at things or not; but he was very old when I came to know him, and so extremely thin that he looked like nothing more than a knotted root. With all his holiness, he was very courteous, though he used very few words except when answering questions. Then he was a delight, for he had a very lively intelligence. There are many other things about him that I should like to say, but I am afraid that your Reverence will ask me what this has to do with me – I have been afraid of that even as I have been writing. So I will stop here, adding only that he died as he had lived, preaching and admonishing his friars. As he saw that his end was approaching, he recited the psalm, *I was glad when they said unto me.*[1] Then he fell on his knees and died.

It has been the Lord's pleasure that I should have more to do with

1. Psalm cxxii [Vulg. cxxi].

him since his death than in his life, and that he should advise me on many subjects. I have often seen him in the greatest glory. The first time he appeared to me, he spoke of the blessedness of his penance, which had won him so great a prize, and of many other things as well. A year before his death he appeared to me, when I was on a journey. I knew that he was soon to die and told him so, though we were many miles apart. As he drew his last breath, he appeared to me again and said that he was going to rest. I did not believe in this experience, but related it to a number of people, and a week later came the news that he was dead – or, to put it better, had entered into eternal life.

See then how his life of hardships has ended in great glory. I think that he is a much greater comfort to me now than when he was here. The Lord once told me that no petition made in his name would fail to be heard. I have had many things granted that I have asked him to ask of the Lord. Blessed be He for ever! Amen.

But what a lot I have been saying in order to incite your Reverence to despise the things of this life, as though you did not already know all this, and were not determined to abandon everything in order to put your resolutions into effect. I see so much perdition in the world that even if my writing has no other effect than to weary this hand that wields the pen, it brings me some comfort. For all that I say is in criticism of myself. May the Lord pardon me for any offence to Him in this matter, and may your Reverence forgive me too, for wearying you to no purpose. I seem to be exacting a penance from you for the sins I have myself committed.

CHAPTER 28

She tells of the great favours that the Lord bestowed on her, and of His first appearance to her. She defines an imaginary vision, and speaks of the great effects and signs produced by one that is from God. This is a most profitable and noteworthy chapter

To return to our subject, I spent some few days with that vision continually before me, and it did me so much good that I never emerged from the state of prayer, and contrived to act in such a way as not to displease Him whose presence as a witness had been so clear to me. Although I was occasionally frightened by the quantity of advice that was offered to me, my fears were short-lived, for the Lord reassured me. One day when I was at prayer, He was pleased to show me His hands only; their beauty was beyond description. This put me in great fear, as does every new experience at the beginning, whatever supernatural favour the Lord may be granting me. A few days later I saw that divine face also, which seems to leave me completely entranced. I could not understand why the Lord was revealing Himself to me gradually like this, since He was afterwards to grant me the favour of seeing Him whole. But finally I realized that His Majesty was pandering to the weakness of my nature. May He be blessed for ever. So base and vile a creature as I would not have been able to bear all this glory at once and, knowing this, in His compassion, He gradually prepared me.

Your Reverence may imagine that it would have required no great effort to behold those hands and that beautiful face. But such is the beauty of glorified bodies, and such the supernatural glory which surrounds them, that it throws all who gaze upon them into confusion. I was so awe-struck, indeed, as to be completely upset and bewildered. Soon afterwards, however, I felt quite certain and secure; the effects quickly dispelled all my fears.

Once when I was at Mass on St Paul's Day, there stood before me the most sacred Humanity, in all the beauty and majesty of His resurrection body, as it appears in paintings. Of this I gave your Reverence a particular description at the time, at your very urgent request. The writing of it very greatly distressed me, for one can say nothing without doing great violence to oneself. But I wrote the best description that I could, and so there is no reason to repeat it here. I will only remark that if there were nothing else in Heaven to delight the eye but the great beauty of glorified bodies, that alone would be a very great bliss, particularly if it were the Humanity of our Lord Jesus Christ. For if His Majesty reveals Himself on earth to the degree that our wretched state can bear, what will it be like when that blessing is enjoyed in its entirety? Although this vision was imaginary, I never saw it or any other with the eyes of the body, but only with the eyes of the soul.

Those who know better than I say that my previous vision was more perfect than this one, while this in its turn is much nearer to perfection than those that are seen with the eyes of the body. The latter, they say, is the lowest kind, and the one most open to delusions from the devil. I was not aware of this at that time, but as this favour was being granted to me, wished that I could have seen it with my physical eyes, so that my confessor should not tell me that I was imagining it. The moment the vision had passed, at the very instant of its fading, I was myself struck by the thought that these things were all imaginary. It worried me that I had spoken of them to my confessor, and I wondered if I had been deceiving him. Here was more distress. So I went to him, and talked to him about it. He asked me whether I had described the vision as it had appeared to me or if I had meant to deceive him. I replied that I had told him the truth, for I did not think I had been lying. I certainly had not meant to, for I would not have told an untruth for anything in the world. He knew that very well, and so he succeeded in calming me. But it worried me so much to have to go to him over these matters that I do not know how the devil could have put it into my head that I was making them up to drive me into tormenting myself. But the Lord made such haste to bestow this favour on me and to make the reality of it plain to me, that I very soon lost my suspicion that it was all just fancy. Since then I have seen very clearly how silly I was. For if I were to spend many years imagining how I could invent anything so beautiful, I could not do it. I should not know how to begin. For in its whiteness and radiance alone it exceeds anything that we can imagine.

It is not a dazzling radiance but a soft whiteness and infused radiance, which causes the eyes great delight and never tires them; nor are they tired by the brilliance which confronts them as they look on this divine beauty. The brightness and light that appear before the gaze are so different from those of earth that the sun's rays seem quite dim by comparison, and afterwards we never feel like opening our eyes again. It is as if we were to look at a very clear stream running over a crystal bed, in which the sun was reflected, and then to turn to a very muddy brook, with an earthy bottom, running beneath a clouded sky. Not that the sun or anything like sunlight enters into the vision; on the contrary, its light seems the natural light, and the light of this world appears artificial. It is a light that never yields to darkness and, being always light, can never be clouded. It is of such a kind, indeed, that no one, however great his intellect, could imagine its nature in the whole course of his life; and God brings it before us so swiftly that even if we needed to open our eyes in order to see it, we should not have the time. But it does not matter whether they are open or closed; if the Lord wishes us to see it, we shall do so even against our will. No distraction or effort is strong enough to resist it; no diligence or care of our own can attain it. This I have learned from thorough experience, as I shall relate.

Now I should like to say something about the Lord's way of revealing Himself in these visions. I do not mean that I shall describe how it is that He is able to introduce this very strong light into the inner senses, or to present this picture so vividly to the mind that it really seems to be there. That is a matter for the learned: the Lord has not wished to show me how it happens. I am so ignorant and have such a poor understanding that although many attempts have been made to explain it to me, I have never managed to comprehend the way of it. Your Reverence may suppose that I have a lively intelligence, but I certainly have not; I have discovered again and again that I never grasp anything unless it is fed to me, spoonful by spoonful, as they say. Sometimes my confessor would be astounded by my ignorance, and he was never able to explain to me, nor did he even try, how God did this, or how it was possible that He could. Indeed, I have never asked such a question, although, as I have said already, for many years I have been consulting men of sound learning. If there were a question of sin or no sin, I would ask; but, for the rest, all I needed was to realize that God did everything. This made me see that I had nothing to be afraid of, but much to praise Him for. I am merely stimulated to devotion by such difficulties, and the greater they are the greater my devotion becomes.

I will describe, therefore, what my experience has shown me. Your Reverence will explain better than I can the way in which the Lord works; you will make clear all that is obscure and beyond my powers of exposition. At times it certainly seemed to me as if I were looking at a painting, but on many other occasions it appeared to be no painting but Christ Himself, such was the clarity with which He was pleased to appear to me. Yet there were times when the vision was so indistinct that I did think it was a painting, though it bore no resemblance even to the most perfect of earthly pictures, and I have seen some good ones. No, it would be absurd to speak of any resemblance; the vision was no more like a painting than a portrait is like a living man. However well a portrait is painted, it can never look completely natural, for it is plainly a dead thing. But let us pass this over, apposite and truthful though the observation is.

I have not been trying to institute comparisons, for they are never completely accurate; this is the actual truth. Here there is the difference between something living and something painted, neither more nor less. If what I see is an image, it is a living image, no dead man but the living Christ, and He reveals Himself as God and man, not as He was in the tomb, but as He was when He left it, after rising from the dead. Sometimes He comes with such majesty that no one can doubt it is the Lord Himself; this is especially so after Communion, since then we know that He is there, for the Faith says so. Then he shows Himself so much the Lord of that inn, the soul, that it seems to dissolve completely and to be consumed in Christ. O my Jesus, if only one could describe the Majesty with which You reveal Yourself! How utterly You are lord of all the world and the heavens, and of a thousand other worlds; and of countless more worlds and heavens that You have created! And from the majesty with which You appear the soul realizes that it is nothing to You to be lord of all this.

Here it is made plain how small is all the power of hell, compared with Yours, and how he who pleases You can trample all hell beneath his feet. By this we see how right the devils were to tremble when You descended into limbo, and how right they would have been to long for a thousand hells yet lower into which to flee from such a majesty. I see that You are pleased to reveal to the soul the greatness and power of Your most sacred Humanity, united with the Divinity. Here is a clear picture of what the Day of Judgement will be, when we shall see this King in His Majesty, and witness the sternness with which He will treat the wicked. Here is true humility, which allows the soul to see its wretchedness, of which it cannot be ignorant. Here is shame and genuine repentance for sins, for although the soul sees God to be revealing His love, it does not know where to hide and so is utterly confounded. I mean that when the Lord is pleased to reveal so much of His greatness and majesty to it, the vision has such great strength that I think it would be impossible to bear it, unless the Lord were pleased to help the soul in a most supernatural way. He keeps it in a rapture or ecstasy, during the enjoyment of which the sight of that Divine Presence is lost. Though it is true that this vision is afterwards forgotten, that majesty and beauty remain so deeply imprinted on the soul that they are unforgettable except when the Lord is pleased for the soul to suffer such a great dryness and loneliness as I shall later describe; then it seems to forget even God. At all other times, the soul is itself no longer; it is always intoxicated.

This, in my opinion, marks the beginning of a new and living love for God of very high order. For although the earlier vision which, as I have said, reveals God without any image, is higher, yet if the memory is to last, in spite of our weakness, and if the thoughts are to be usefully occupied, it is a great thing that the Divine Presence should be presented to, and should remain in, the imagination. These two kinds of vision almost always occur simultaneously. When they come in this second way, it is in order that the eyes of the soul may see the excellence, the beauty and the glory of the most sacred Humanity; and when they come in the other way, which I described first, we are shown how He is God, that He is powerful, and that He can do all things, command all things, rule all things, and fill all things with His love.

This vision is to be most highly prized and, in my opinion, it brings no dangers, for one can tell by its effects that the devil has no power here. Three or four times, I believe, he has attempted to make a false likeness of the Lord and to present Him to me in this way. He can manage the fleshly form but he cannot imitate the glory that is in this vision when it is from God. He makes these attempts in order to invalidate the true visions that the soul has seen; but the soul resists spontaneously, and becomes troubled, nauseated, and restless. It loses that devotion and joy that it had before, and is unable to pray. This happened to me, as I have said, three or four times, at the beginning. It is something so very different from a true vision that I think even a soul who has only experienced the prayer of quiet will recognize it by its effects, which I described when speaking of locutions. It is very easy to detect and, unless the soul wishes to be deceived, I do not think that the devil will deceive it, so long as it proceeds humbly and in simplicity.

Anyone who has had a true vision from God will detect a false one almost immediately. The devil may begin with consolations and favours, but the soul will push them aside. I think too that the devil's consolations must differ from God's, and will show no trace of pure and holy love. In fact the devil very quickly shows his hand. So, in my opinion, he can do no harm to a soul that has experience.

It is the most impossible of all impossibilities that this can be the work of the imagination. There is no way in which it could be so; the sheer beauty and whiteness of one of His hands is altogether beyond the imagination. We could not, in any case, instantaneously see things of which we have no recollection and that we have never even thought of; things that we could not invent with the imagination, even if we had plenty of time, because, as I have already said, they are far above our earthly understanding. Whether we could in any way be responsible for such a vision will clearly emerge from what I shall say next. If it proceeded from our own mind, not only would it not have the great effects that it has, but it would have none at all. One would be in the position of a man who wants to go to sleep, but is still awake because sleep has not come to him. He may need it, his brain may be tired, and he may long for it. He may settle down to doze and do all that he can to go off to sleep; and sometimes he seems to be succeeding. But if it is not real sleep, it will not restore him or refresh his brain; it will merely exhaust it. The case will be somewhat the same here; instead of being restored and fortified, the soul will become wearier; it will become exhausted and nauseated. But it is impossible to exaggerate the riches that accompany a true vision; it brings health and comfort even to the body.

I advanced this argument, amongst others, when they told me – as they often did – that my visions were of the devil and were all imaginary. I drew such comparisons as I could find and as the Lord showed me. But none of these were of much use, because there were some very holy persons in the place, compared with whom I was a lost soul; and as the Lord was not leading them by this way, they were afraid and thought that what I saw was the result of my sins. Word of it was passed from one to another, so that they all came to know, though I had spoken of it only to my confessor, and to certain others at his request.

I once said to some of these people whom I used to consult: 'If you were to tell me that someone I knew well and to whom I had just been talking is not really himself, and that I was imagining things and you knew what the truth really was, I would believe your statement rather than my own eyes. But if this person had left me some jewels as a pledge of his great love, and if I were still holding them, and if I had possessed no jewels before and now found myself rich where I had been poor, I could not possibly believe that this was a delusion, even if I wanted to.' I said too that I could show them these jewels, for everyone who knew me saw clearly that my soul had changed, and my confessor himself testified to the fact, since it was now very different in every respect, and this was no fancy but something that everyone could most distinctly see. Hitherto, I concluded, I had been extremely wicked; I could not believe, therefore, that if the devil were doing this in order to deceive me and drag me down to hell, he would adopt means so contrary to his purpose as to take away my vices and give me virtues and strength instead. For I clearly saw that these visions had made me a different person.

My confessor who, as I have said, was a very holy father of the Company of Jesus answered them – as I learnt – to the same effect. He was a very discreet man of great humility, and this deep humility of his brought great trials upon me; for he was a man of much prayer and learning, but he did not trust himself, since the Lord was not leading him along this path. He suffered all sorts of severe trials too, on my account. I knew that he was frequently warned to be on his guard against me, and not to let the devil deceive him into believing anything that I said; they quoted instances of others who had been deluded. All this worried me. I was afraid that I should have no one left to confess to, and that they would all avoid me. I could do nothing but weep.

Providentially, he was willing to go on hearing my confessions. So great a servant of God was he that he would have exposed himself to any danger for His sake. He told me therefore that so long as I did not offend God or disobey his injunctions, I need have no fear that he would desert me. He always encouraged me and quieted me. He commanded me also never to conceal anything from him, and in this I obeyed him. He said that if I obeyed him, even the devil himself, if it was the devil, could do me no harm, and that the Lord would turn to good effect any evil that he was trying to work on my soul. That confessor did his utmost to bring my soul to perfection. As I was so much afraid, I obeyed him in every respect, though imperfectly. In the three years and more that he was confessing me, he endured a great deal on account of these trials of mine. For all through the great persecutions that I suffered, and on the numerous occasions when the Lord permitted me to be harshly judged – often undeservedly – they referred everything to him, and he was blamed on my account, though he was utterly blameless.

If he had not been a man of such sanctity, and if the Lord had not given him courage, he could not possibly have borne all this. For he had to answer people who did not believe him and thought I was going to perdition. At the same time he had to calm me, and dispel the terrors that beset me – though sometimes he intensified them. He had also to reassure me, for after each vision that involved a new experience, God allowed me to remain in great fear. All this came from my having been, and my still being, such a great sinner. He comforted me with great compassion, and if he had trusted in himself, my suffering would have been less. For God showed him the truth of it all, and the Sacrament itself gave him light, as I believe.

Those of God's servants who were not convinced had many conversations with me, and I talked carelessly about certain matters, which they took in the wrong sense. I was very much attached to one of them, who was a most holy man to whom my soul was deeply in debt. It greatly distressed me to see that he misunderstood me, since he so greatly desired that I should make progress and that the Lord should enlighten me. Well, as I was saying, I spoke without reflection and, as it seemed to them, with a lack of humility. Finding this one fault in me – and they must have found many more – they condemned me out of hand. They would ask me some questions, which I would answer plainly and without consideration. They then imagined that I was trying to instruct them and thought myself wise. All this went to my confessor, for they certainly desired my good, and then he would scold me.

This continued for some time, and I was afflicted in many ways. But thanks to the favours which the Lord granted me, I endured it all. I am relating all this in order to show what a great trial it is to have as a confessor someone without experience of this spiritual road. If the Lord had not shown me such favour, I do not know what would have become of me. I had enough troubles to drive me out of my mind, and sometimes I found myself in such straits that I could do nothing except lift up my eyes to the Lord. For though these good people's opposition to a weak and wicked woman like myself – and I was fearful into the bargain – may seem nothing when described in this way, it was one of the greatest trials that I have endured in my whole life – and I have met with some severe ones. May the Lord grant that I did His Majesty some service here. For I am quite sure that those who condemned me and argued against me were serving Him and that it was all for my very great good.

CHAPTER 29

*She continues, and describes some great favours which the Lord
showed her, relating also what the Lord said to her, to reassure her
and enable her to answer those who argued against her*

I HAVE wandered far from my subject. I was trying to explain the
reasons why this kind of vision cannot be the work of the imagination. For, how could we picture Christ's Humanity merely through
having dwelt on it, or compose His great beauty out of our own heads?
If such a conception were to be anything like the original, it would take
quite a long time to build up. One can indeed construct such a picture
from the imagination, and can spend quite a while regarding it, and
reflecting on the form and brightness of it. One can gradually perfect
this picture and commit it to the memory. What is there to prevent this,
since it is the work of the intelligence? But when it comes to the visions
I am speaking of, there is no way of building them up. We have to look
at them when the Lord is pleased to show them to us – to look as He
wishes and at what He wishes. We can neither add nor subtract anything, nor can we obtain a vision by any actions of our own. We cannot
look at it when we like or refrain from looking at it; if we try to look at
any particular feature of it, we immediately lose Christ.

For two and a half years, God granted me this favour at frequent
intervals. But more than three years ago He took it from me, in this
form of a continual experience, and gave me something of a higher
kind, of which I shall perhaps speak later. During all that time, though I
saw that He was speaking to me, though I gazed on His very great
beauty, and felt the sweetness with which those words of His, which
were sometimes stern, issued from His fair and divine mouth, and
though, at the same time, I greatly longed to see the colour of His eyes,
or His stature, so as to be able to describe them later, I was never worthy
enough to see them, nor was it any good my trying to do so. On the
contrary, these efforts lost me the vision altogether. Though I sometimes see Him looking at me with compassion, His gaze is so powerful
that my soul cannot endure it. It is caught in so sublime a rapture that it
loses this lovely vision in order to increase its enjoyment of the whole.
So here there is no question of willingness or unwillingness. It is clear

that all the Lord wants of us is humility and shame, and that we shall accept what is given us, with praise for the Giver.

This is true of all visions without exception. There is nothing that we can do about them; no effort of ours makes us see more or less, or calls up or dispels a vision. The Lord desires us to see very clearly that this work is not ours but His Majesty's. We are the less able, therefore, to take pride in it; on the contrary it makes us humble and afraid, when we see that just as the Lord takes away our power of seeing what we will, so He can also remove these favours and His grace, with the result that we are utterly lost. Let us always walk in fear therefore, so long as we are living in this exile.

Almost always Our Lord appeared to me as He rose from the dead, and it was the same when I saw Him in the Host. Only occasionally, to hearten me if I was in tribulation, He would show me His wounds, and then He would appear sometimes on the Cross and sometimes as He was in the Garden. Sometimes too, but rarely, I saw Him wearing the crown of thorns, and sometimes carrying His Cross as well, because of my deeds, let me say, and those of others. But always His body was glorified. Many were the reproaches and trials that I suffered when I spoke of this, and many were my fears and persecutions. They felt so certain of my being possessed by a devil that some of them wanted to exorcize me. This did not worry me much, but I was distressed when I found my confessors unwilling to hear my confession, or when I heard that people were talking to them about me. Nevertheless, I could not be sorry that I had seen these celestial visions. I would not have exchanged a single one of them for all the blessings and delights in the world. I always regarded them as a grand mercy from the Lord, and I think they were a very great treasure. Often the Lord Himself would reassure me, and I found my love for Him growing exceedingly. I would go and complain to Him about all my trials, and I always emerged from prayer comforted and with new strength. But I did not dare to contradict my critics, for I saw that this made things worse, since they attributed my arguments to lack of humility. I discussed things with my confessor, however, and he never failed to give me great comfort if he saw that I was worried.

When the visions became more frequent, one of those who had helped me before, and who had taken my confession sometimes when the minister could not, began to say that clearly I was being deceived by the devil. He ordered me, since I had no power of resistance, always to make the sign of the Cross when I had a vision, and to snap my fingers at it, in the firm conviction that this was the devil's work. Then it would not come again. He told me to have no fear, for God would protect me and take the vision away. This command greatly distressed me, for I could not think that the vision came from anything but God. It was a terrible thing for me to do; and, as I have said, I could not possibly wish my vision to be taken from me. However, in the end I obeyed him. I prayed God frequently to free me from deception; indeed, I did so continually, with many tears, and I also invoked St Peter and St Paul. For the Lord had told me, when He first appeared to me on their festival, that they would preserve me from being deceived. I used often to see them very clearly, on my left, and that was no imaginary vision. These glorious saints were my very true lords.

The duty of snapping my fingers when I had this vision of the Lord deeply distressed me. For when I saw Him before me, I would willingly have been hacked to death rather than believe that this was of the devil. It was a heavy kind of penance for me, and so that I need not be so continually crossing myself, I used to go about with a crucifix in my hand. I carried it almost continually, but I did not snap my fingers very often, because that hurt me too much. It reminded me of the insults He had suffered from the Jews, and I begged Him to pardon me, since I was only acting out of obedience to one who was in His place, and not to blame me, seeing that he was one of the ministers whom He had Himself placed in His Church. He told me not to worry, since I was quite right to obey, and that He would Himself show them the truth. When they forbade me to pray, He seemed to me to be angry. He told me to say to them that this was tyranny. He showed me ways of making sure that these visions were not of the devil, and I will give some of them later.

Once when I was holding the cross of a rosary in my hand, He took it from me into His own; and when He returned it to me, it consisted of four large stones much more precious than diamonds – incomparably so for it is, of course, impossible to make comparisons between things seen supernaturally and the precious stones of this world; diamonds seem imperfect counterfeits beside the precious stones of a vision. On these were exquisitely incised the five wounds of Christ. He told me that henceforth this cross would appear so to me always, and so it has. I have never been able to see the wood of which it was made but only these stones. However, they have been seen by no one but myself. Once they started telling me to test my visions and resist them, these favours became much more frequent. In my efforts to divert my attention, I never ceased praying, and I seemed to be in a state of prayer even when asleep. For now my love was growing, and I would complain to the Lord, saying that I could not bear it. But desire and strive though I might to cease thinking of Him, it was beyond my power; I was as obedient as possible in every way, but I could do little or nothing about it. The Lord never released me from my obedience. But though He told me to do as I was told, He reassured me in another way by telling me how to answer my critics; and this He still does. The arguments He gave me were so strong that I felt perfectly secure.

Shortly afterwards, His Majesty began, as He had promised, to make it even plainer that it was He. There grew so great a love of God within me that I did not know who had planted it there. It was entirely supernatural; I had made no efforts to obtain it. I found myself dying of the desire to see God, and I knew no way of seeking that other life except through death. This love came to me in mighty impulses which, although less unbearable and less valuable than those that I have described before, robbed me of all power of action. Nothing gave me satisfaction, and I could not contain myself; I really felt as if my soul were being torn from me. O supreme cunning of the Lord, with what delicate skill did You work on Your miserable slave! You hid Yourself from me, and out of Your love You afflicted me with so delectable a death that my soul desired it never to cease.

No one who has not experienced these mighty impulses can possibly understand that this is no emotional unrest, nor one of those fits of uncontrollable devotion that frequently occur and seem to overwhelm the spirit. These are very low forms of prayer. Indeed, such quickenings should be checked by a gentle endeavour to become recollected, and to calm the soul. Such prayer is like the violent sobbing of children. They seem to be going to choke, but their rush of emotion is immediately checked if they are given something to drink. In the same way here, reason must step in and take command, for this may merely be a display of temperament. With reflection there comes a fear that there is some imperfection here, which may be largely physical. So the child must be quieted with a loving caress, which will draw out its love in a gentle way and not, as they say, bludgeon it. This love must flow into interior reflection, not boil over like a cooking-pot that has been put on too fierce a fire, and so spills its contents. The source of the fire must be controlled. An endeavour must be made to quench its flames with gentle tears, and not with that painful weeping that springs from the feelings I have described, and does so much damage. I used at first to shed tears of this kind which left my mind so confused and my spirit so weary that I was not fit to resume my prayers for a day or more. Great discretion is needed at first, therefore, so that everything may go on smoothly, and so that spiritual transformations may take place within. All exterior demonstrations should be carefully prevented.

The true impulses are very different. We do not pile the wood beneath the fire ourselves; it is rather as if it were already burning and we were suddenly thrown in to be consumed. The soul makes no effort to feel the pain caused it by the Lord's presence, but is pierced to the depths of its entrails, or sometimes to the heart, by an arrow, so that it does not know what is wrong or what it desires. It knows quite well that it desires God. and that the arrow seems to have been tipped with some poison which makes it so hate itself out of love of the Lord that it is willing to give up its life for Him. It is impossible to describe or explain the way in which God wounds the soul, or the very great pain He inflicts on it, so that it hardly knows what it is doing. But this is so sweet a pain that no delight in the whole world can be more pleasing. The soul, as I have said, would be glad always to be dying of this ill.

This combination of joy and sorrow so bewildered me that I could not understand how such a thing could be. O what it is to see a soul wounded! I mean one that sufficiently understands its condition as to be able to call itself wounded, and for so excellent a cause. It clearly sees that this love has come to it through no action of its own, but that out of the very great love that the Lord has for it a spark seems suddenly to have fallen on it and set it all on fire. O how often, when I am in this state, do I remember that verse of David, *As the heart panteth after the water brooks*,[1] which I seem to see literally fulfilled in myself.

When these impulses are not very strong, things appear to calm down a little, or at least the soul seeks some respite, for it does not know what to do. It performs certain penances, but hardly feels them; even if it draws blood it is no more conscious of pain than if the body were dead. It seeks ways and means to express some of its feelings for the love of God, but its initial pain is so great that I know of no physical torture that could drown it. Such medicines can bring no relief; they are on too low a level for so high a disease. But there is some alleviation and a little

1. Psalm xlii [Vulg. xli].

of the pain passes if the soul prays God to give it some remedy for its suffering, though it can see no way except death by which it can expect to enjoy its blessing complete. But there are other times when the impulses are so strong that it can do absolutely nothing. The entire body contracts; neither foot nor arm can be moved. If one is standing at the time, one falls into a sitting position as though transported, and cannot even take a breath. One only utters a few slight moans, not aloud, for that is impossible, but inwardly, out of pain.

Our Lord was pleased that I should sometimes see a vision of this kind. Beside me, on the left hand, appeared an angel in bodily form, such as I am not in the habit of seeing except very rarely. Though I often have visions of angels, I do not see them. They come to me only after the manner of the first type of vision that I described. But it was our Lord's will that I should see this angel in the following way. He was not tall but short, and very beautiful; and his face was so aflame that he appeared to be one of the highest rank of angels, who seem to be all on fire. They must be of the kind called cherubim, but they do not tell me their names. I know very well that there is a great difference between some angels and others, and between these and others still, but I could not possibly explain it. In his hands I saw a great golden spear, and at the iron tip there appeared to be a point of fire. This he plunged into my heart several times so that it penetrated to my entrails. When he pulled it out, I felt that he took them with it, and left me utterly consumed by the great love of God. The pain was so severe that it made me utter several moans. The sweetness caused by this intense pain is so extreme that one cannot possibly wish it to cease, nor is one's soul then content with anything but God. This is not a physical, but a spiritual pain, though the body has some share in it – even a considerable share. So gentle is this wooing which takes place between God and the soul that if anyone thinks I am lying, I pray God, in His goodness, to grant him some experience of it.

Throughout the days that this lasted I went about in a kind of stupor. I had no wish to look or to speak, only to embrace my pain, which was a greater bliss than all created things could give me. On several occasions when I was in this state the Lord was pleased that I should experience raptures so deep that I could not resist them even though I was not alone. Greatly to my distress, therefore, my raptures began to be talked about. Since I have had them, I have ceased to feel this pain so much, though I still feel the pain that I spoke of in a previous chapter – I do not remember which.[1] The latter is very different in many respects, and much more valuable. But when this pain of which I am now speaking begins, the Lord seems to transport the soul and throw it into an ecstasy. So there is no opportunity for it to feel its pain or suffering, for the enjoyment comes immediately. May He be blessed for ever, who has granted so many favours to one who has so ill repaid these great benefits.

1. Chapter 20.

CHAPTER 30

She returns to the story of her life, and tells how the Lord greatly relieved her trials by bringing her a visit from that holy man, Friar Peter of Alcántara of the Order of the glorious St Francis. She speaks of the great temptations and inner trials which she sometimes suffered

Now when I saw that I could do little or nothing to hold off these very great impulses, I began to be afraid of them, because I could not understand how pleasure and pain could exist together. I already knew that physical pain and spiritual pleasure were compatible, but to experience such extreme spiritual pain and such very great joy together bewildered me. I still did not give up my efforts to resist, but I could do so little that sometimes I became quite exhausted. I would take up the cross for protection, and try to defend myself against Him who with it has been the protector of us all. I saw that no one understood me. But though I was perfectly aware of this myself, I did not dare to tell anyone except my confessor, for this would have amounted to an admission that I was lacking in humility.

The Lord was pleased to relieve me of a great part of my trials, and for a while of them all, by bringing to this place the blessed friar Peter of Alcántara, whom I mentioned earlier, when I said something about his penances; among other things, I have been assured that for twenty years he continuously wore a shirt of iron-plates. He is the author of some little books on prayer, written in Spanish, which are in very great use to-day; as he was a man with great experience of prayer, these are very useful to those who practise it. In addition to the penances of which I have already said something, he kept the original rule of the blessed St Francis in all its rigour.

That widow of whom I have spoken,[1] who was my friend and a true servant of God, learned that the great man was here. Having witnessed my afflictions, in which she was of the greatest comfort to me, she was aware of my plight. Moreover she had such great faith that when everyone else said that my experiences emanated from the devil, she could not help believing them to be the work of God's holy spirit. Not only was she an intelligent and extremely perceptive woman, but she was herself receiving great favours from the Lord in prayer. His Majesty

1. Doña Guiomar de Ulloa.

was pleased to enlighten her, therefore, where learned men remained in the dark. My confessors gave me leave to seek relief by discussing certain things with her, since for many reasons she was a most suitable person. Sometimes she had a share in the favours which the Lord was granting me, and received advice most profitable to her soul. Well, when she heard that this holy man was here, she did not tell me but obtained my Provincial's permission for me to stay with her for a week in order that I should have a better opportunity of consulting him. So during this first visit of his I held several conversations with him, both at her house and in various churches, and later I had a great deal to do with him on many occasions. I gave him a brief account of my life and way of prayer, which was as clear as I could make it. For I have always held to the practice of speaking with the utmost truth and clarity to those whom I consult about my soul. I would always try to reveal its very first impulses to them and over any suspicious or doubtful matters I would take sides against myself and state the adverse case. So I laid my soul bare to him without equivocation or concealment.

Almost from the beginning, I saw that he understood me from experience, and that was all I needed. For I could not understand myself then as I do now, or speak accurately of my state; though, since then, God has allowed me both to understand and to describe the favours which His Majesty sends me. But at that time I needed someone who had gone through it all himself, for no one else could both understand me and explain to me the nature of my experiences. He gave me the greatest enlightenment, particularly in regard to the visions. Except for those that were imaginary, I had been quite unable to understand what they meant. Indeed I did not see how I could ever make anything of visions seen with the eyes of the soul. For, as I have said, I had thought that only those visible with the physical eye are of any consequence, and of this kind I had none.

This holy man enlightened me about the whole matter, explained everything to me, and told me not to worry but to praise God and be quite certain that this was the work of the Spirit. Nothing could be truer, he said, with the exception of the Faith, and nothing more certain or dependable. He took great joy in me, and was most kindly and helpful. He has taken a great interest in me ever since, and has told me about his own affairs and purposes. When he saw in me desires that he had himself already carried into effect – for the Lord had bestowed them on me in great strength – and when He saw too that I had plenty of courage, he enjoyed discussing things with me. Indeed for anyone whom the Lord has brought to this state, there is no pleasure or comfort equal to that of meeting someone whom he believes the Lord to have brought along the first stages of the same path. At the time, I do not think I had gone any further than that, and God grant that I may still be as far forward now.

He felt great compassion for me, and told me that what I had suffered – that is the opposition of good people – was one of the greatest trials in the world, but that I had still plenty awaiting me. I should, therefore, he said, be in continual need of someone who understood me, but there was no such person in the town. He promised, however, to speak to my confessor, and to that married gentleman whom I have mentioned, who was one of those that caused me the greatest pain. For because he had a great affection for me, he attacked me most strongly; since he was a holy and God-fearing soul, and had so recently seen how wicked I was, he could not persuade himself to feel any confidence in me. That holy man fulfilled his promise and spoke to them both, arguing with them and giving them reasons why they should feel reassured and stop worrying me. My confessor scarcely needed this advice; but my noble friend was not entirely convinced. Still what he heard was enough to make him frighten me rather less than he had been doing.

Friar Peter and I agreed that in future I should write and tell him all that happened to me, and that we should frequently commend one another to God. For he was so humble as to attach some value to the prayers of this miserable creature; which made me very much ashamed. He left me greatly comforted and most joyful, telling me to continue my prayers with confidence and to have no doubt that my experiences came from God. If I had any doubts I was to report them, for my greater security, to my confessor, and then I should feel quite safe. I was unable to feel this complete confidence, however, since the Lord was leading me along the road of fear, and so when I was told that the devil was deceiving me I believed it. Still none of my advisers could really inspire me with such fear or confidence as to make me believe in him rather than in the feelings planted by God in my own soul. So, although Friar Peter comforted and calmed me, I did not put sufficient trust in him to be absolutely fearless, especially when the Lord forsook me in the spiritual trials that I shall now describe. But on the whole, as I have said, I was greatly comforted, and I could not give thanks enough to God and my glorious father St Joseph, who seemed to have brought

Friar Peter to the town. For he was Commissary General of the Custody[1] of St Joseph, to whom, as to Our Lady, I used often to commend myself. I sometimes had to endure – and still have to, though to a lesser degree – the greatest spiritual trials, accompanied by bodily pains and tortures so severe that I could scarcely control myself. At other times I suffered from even graver physical ailments, though if I was free from spiritual distress, I bore them with great joy. But when both kinds of pain came on me together, it was a great trial and reduced me to sore straits. I forgot all the favours that the Lord had bestowed on me; all that was left me was a memory, as of something in a dream, and this greatly distressed me. For at such times the understanding becomes dull, and so I was bothered by a thousand doubts and suspicions. I wondered whether I had not misunderstood everything, and whether it was not all my fancy. I felt that it was bad enough for me to be deluded myself without my also deluding those good men. I thought of myself as so wicked that all the evils and heresies which had arisen must be due to my sins.

This was a false humility, invented by the devil in order to disquiet me and to see if he could drive my soul to despair. By now I have had so much experience of the devil's work that he knows I can recognize him and so torments me less in these ways than he used to. His part in an experience can be detected by the restlessness and discomfort with which it begins, by the turmoil that he creates in the soul so long as it lasts, also by the darkness and affliction into which he plunges it, and by its subsequent dryness and indisposition for prayer or anything else that is good. He seems to stifle the soul and constrict the body, making them both useless. In true humility, on the other hand, although the soul knows its wretchedness, and although we are distressed to see what we are, and although we think of our wickedness as extremely grave – as grave as I have described it and as deeply felt – there is no attendant turmoil or spiritual unrest. True humility does not bring darkness or aridity, but on the contrary gives the soul peace, sweetness, and light. It distresses us, but on the other hand we are comforted to see what a great favour the Lord is doing us by sending us this distress and how well the soul is occupied. It is grieved at having offended God, but it is encouraged by His mercy. It is sufficiently enlightened to feel shame, and praises His Majesty for having borne with it so long. But in this other humility which is the work of the devil, there is not enough light

1. A small group of religious houses.

for any good work; God seems always to be wielding fire and sword. The soul dwells upon His justice, but although it believes in His mercy – for the devil is not strong enough to destroy its faith – it is in such a way as to bring no consolation. Indeed when, under these circumstances, my soul considers God's mercy, this only increases my torments, for I feel myself under an even greater obligation than before.

This is one of the most painful, subtle, and deceptive inventions of the devil that I have ever detected; and I should like to warn your Reverence of it, so that if he tempts you in this way, you may have some light and recognize his hand, supposing that he leaves you the understanding to do so. Do not imagine that this will depend upon your knowledge and learning, for although I am quite destitute of both, once I have escaped from his hands, I clearly see that the thing is all folly. Then I realize that the Lord is pleased to give him leave and permission to tempt us, as He allowed him to tempt Job. But, being so wicked, I am, mercifully, not subjected to the rigours of Job.

I was tempted in this way, once, as I remember, on the day before the vigil of Corpus Christi, a festival that I observe with devotion, though not with as much as I should. My trials lasted, that time, only until the feast itself, but on other occasions they have continued for a week, a fortnight, or for as much as three weeks, possibly for even longer. They used to come especially in Holy Week, when I derived particular comfort from prayer. What happens on such occasions is that the devil suddenly seizes upon my thoughts, sometimes on such trivial pretexts that at any other time they would be laughable. He turns the brain upside down and does what he likes with it, and the soul is so fettered that it is no longer its own mistress. It can think of nothing but the nonsense that he suggests to it, things of no importance which neither captivate it nor leave it free, but enslave it in so far as they stupefy it and break its self-control. Sometimes it is as if the devils were playing ball with the soul, and it were incapable of escaping from their power. Its sufferings on these occasions are indescribable. It goes about in search of relief, but God will allow it to find none. There remains still its reasoning-power, which is derived from its free-will, but it cannot make deliberate use of that. I mean that its eyes seem, in a sense, to be blindfolded. It is like someone who has gone very often along the same road and, although the night is dark, knows from past experience where he is likely to stumble. He has seen it all by day, and so is on his guard against this danger. Thus in its avoidance of offences against God, the soul seems to proceed merely by habit. But we are leaving out of account the fact that the Lord is protecting it; which is what really matters.

At such times faith, like all the other virtues, is benumbed and asleep. It is not lost, however, for the soul firmly believes in the Church's teaching. But though it can testify with its lips, it seems in other respects to be oppressed and numbed; it feels as if it knows God only as something heard of from afar off. Its love is so lukewarm that if it hears Him spoken of it listens, knowing that He is who He is because the Church says so; but it has no memory of what it has itself experienced. To go and pray, or to be alone, merely adds to its anguish, for the inward torments that it feels are unbearable, and it does not know their source. I have thought that this is something like hell; and indeed it is so, as the Lord informed me in a vision. The soul burns inwardly, without knowing who has kindled the fire, or whence it comes, or how to escape it, or with what to put it out. When it tries to find a remedy by reading, it seems unable to read a word. Once I happened to pick up the life of a saint in an endeavour to become absorbed and to find some comfort in his sufferings. But I read four or five lines as many times and, though they were in Spanish, understood less of them at the end than at the beginning. So I gave it up. This has happened to me on many occasions, but I remember this one in particular.

To converse with anyone is worse. The devil puts me into such a bad temper that they all think I am longing to eat them up. I cannot help this, and I feel I am doing something if I keep myself under control, or rather that the Lord is doing something when His hand prevents a person in this condition from saying or doing things which will harm his neighbours or offend God. It is certainly useless to go to one's confessor at such times. I can describe the results of that from my own frequent experiences. Saintly though those clerics were whom I was consulting at the time – and whom I still do consult – they would speak to me so sharply and give me such a scolding that they were themselves astonished when I repeated their words to them afterwards. Still they said that they had not been able to do otherwise. Though they had made up their minds beforehand not to use such language to me, and though they were sorry afterwards and even had scruples on account of the physical and spiritual trials that I was undergoing, and though they had made up their minds to console me with words of compassion, they had been quite powerless to do so.

The language they used was not wrong – I mean offensive to God –

but it was the strongest permissible in a confessor. Their intention must have been to mortify me, but though at other times I welcomed mortification and was ready to suffer it, it was pure torture to me then. I used to feel too that I was deceiving them; and would go and warn them most earnestly to be on their guard against me since I might be misleading them. I was well aware that I should not be doing so deliberately, and would not tell them lies, but I was afraid of everything. One of them, realizing the nature of my trials, told me on one occasion not to worry, since even if I wanted to deceive him, he had enough sense not to let himself be misled. This gave me a great deal of comfort.

Sometimes – almost habitually indeed, or at least very frequently – I found relief after taking Communion. There were times when the moment I even approached the Sacrament I felt so much better in body and soul that I was astonished. It was as if all the darkness in my soul had suddenly been dispersed, and the sun had come out; I recognized the stupidities in which I had been living. At other times, a single word from the Lord – if He merely said to me 'Be not troubled, have no fear', as on the occasion that I have described – cured me entirely, or a vision left me as if there had never been anything wrong. I rejoiced in God and complained to Him for allowing me to suffer such tortures. But I was amply rewarded for them, since almost always his mercies descended on me in great abundance afterwards. My soul seemed to emerge from the crucible like gold, with a new purity and brightness that enabled me to see the Lord within it. So, though these trials may seem unbearable, they eventually become light, and the soul desires to suffer them all again, if it can serve the Lord better by doing so. Indeed however many trials and persecutions we undergo, they all contribute to our greater gain, so long as we bear them without offending the Lord, but rejoice that we are suffering for His sake. I do not bear them, however, as they should be borne, but most imperfectly.

On other occasions these temptations came to me – as they still do – in another way. I seem then to have become incapable of thinking a single good thought, or of desiring to put one into practice. My body and soul seem to be completely useless and a burden to me. However I do not have these other temptations and discomforts at the same time, only a feeling of dissatisfaction – I do not know with what – so that my soul takes pleasure in nothing. I used to try outward good works, and half force myself to perform them in order to remain occupied, but I knew very well how little a soul can do when grace is lacking. This caused me no great distress, however, because the realization of my own baseness afforded me some satisfaction. At other times I find myself unable to formulate a single clear or stable thought about God or anything good. I cannot pray even when I am alone. Yet all the same I feel that I know Him.

It is my intellect and my imagination, I think, that are harming me here. My will, I believe, is good, and well-disposed to all that is good. But this intellect of mine is so wild that it seems like a raving lunatic. Nobody can hold it down, and I have not sufficient control over it myself to keep it quiet for a single moment. Sometimes I laugh at myself, and am aware of my wretched state. Then I observe my intellect, and let it alone, to see what it will do; and, miraculously – glory be to God! – it never turns to things that are really wrong, only to indifferent matters, and casts around here, there, and everywhere, for something to think about. I then become more conscious of the very great favour that God bestows on me when he binds this madman in the chains of perfect contemplation. I wonder what would happen if those who think me good were to see me in this distracted state. I am deeply grieved when I find my soul in such bad company. I long to see it free, and so I say to the Lord: 'O God, when shall I finally see my whole soul united in Your praise, and all my faculties enjoying You? Do not allow my soul to be scattered any longer, with each fragment seeming to go its own way.' I have often had this experience, but sometimes I realize that my poor physical health has a great deal to do with it. I often think of the harm done to us by original sin, for it is the cause of our inability to enjoy all benefits at once. My own sins must be to blame also, however, since if I had not committed so many I should have been more perfect in goodness.

I suffered from another great trial as well. I used to think that I understood all the books dealing with prayer that I read, and that I had no further need of them now that the Lord had bestowed the gift of prayer upon me. So I gave up reading them, and read only the lives of the saints. For when I find myself so very inferior to them in my service to God, these books seem to help and encourage me. Then it struck me that it showed a great lack of humility to suppose that I had attained the gift of prayer; and as I could not persuade myself that I had not done so, I was greatly distressed until some learned men, also the blessed friar Peter of Alcántara, told me not to trouble myself. I perfectly realize that even though, in granting me these favours, His Majesty treats me as He does many really good people, I have not yet begun to serve Him. I see that I am nothing but imperfect except in desires and love, though in these, as I am well aware, the Lord has granted me some favours, in order that I may be of some service to Him. I really believe that I love Him, but my deeds, and the many imperfections I find in myself, make me sad.

At other times my soul suffers from what I should call attacks of foolishness, and I seem to be doing neither good nor evil, but to be going with the crowd, as they say. I experience neither torment nor bliss. I do not care if I live or die, suffer pleasure or pain; I do not seem to feel anything. The soul seems to me like a little ass that feeds and keeps alive on the food that is given to it, but eats it without reflection. In this state the soul must be feeding on some of God's great favours, seeing that it does not mind living this miserable life, but does so with equanimity. It does not notice any motions or effects that might show it its condition.

This seems to me now like sailing before a very gentle breeze, when one makes great headway without knowing how. For in the other states the effects are so great that the soul is almost immediately conscious of its betterment, because desires spring up straight away, and the soul is never completely satisfied. This is the result of those violent impulses that I have already spoken of, and that arise in those to whom God grants them. I am reminded of little springs that I have seen flowing, and ceaselessly heaving up the sand all around them. The illustration is telling, and this is a fair comparison to apply to souls who reach this stage. Love goes on bubbling up in them and thinking of the things it will do; it cannot contain itself any more than the spring-water can remain in the ground from which it spouts up. As a general rule, it is the same with the soul, which has such love that it can neither rest nor contain itself; it has soaked the earth all around it and wishes others to drink of its love because there is more than enough for itself, and to join it in praising God. Oh, how often do I remember the living water of which God spoke to the woman of Samaria. I so dearly love that Gospel and have loved it ever since I was quite a child – though, of course, without understanding it then as well as I do now – and I have frequently prayed God to give me that water. I had a picture of the Lord coming to the well, which hung where I often saw it and was inscribed, *Sir, give me this water*.[1]

1. John iv, 15.

This love is also like a great fire, which has always to be fed so that it shall not go out. The souls I am describing are in this situation; whatever it may cost them, they must bring wood to keep that fire alive.

For myself, I am the sort of person who would be glad if she had even straw to throw on it; it is often – indeed very often – like that with me. Sometimes I am laughing, sometimes I am in deep distress. An inner impulse urges me to serve God in some way, but I am not good for anything but decorating images with branches and flowers, or for sweeping and tidying an oratory, or for doing other things so trifling that they make me ashamed. If I performed some penance it was so insignificant that I knew it to be quite worthless unless the Lord would take the will for the deed. Therefore I scoffed at myself. For it is no small trial for those to whom God, in His goodness, abundantly grants this fire of His love, if they have not the physical strength to do anything for Him. This is a very great grief. When a soul lacks the strength to throw a little wood on that fire and is mortally afraid that it may go out, I think it is itself consumed and turns to ash, or melts into tears and burns away; and sweet though this may be, it is a severe torment.

Let the soul praise the Lord exceedingly when it has progressed to this point and when He has granted it the physical strength to perform penances, or given it learning and talents, and freedom to preach, hear confession and lead souls to Him. But it neither knows nor understands the blessing it possesses if it has not learnt by experience what it is to be able to do nothing in the Lord's service, whilst always receiving a great deal from Him. May He be blessed for all things, and may the angels glorify Him! Amen.

I do not know whether I am doing right to enter into such trivial details. As your Reverence has sent me another message, commanding me not to mind writing at some length and to omit nothing, I shall continue to describe clearly and truly all that I remember. But I cannot help leaving a great deal out, for if I did not I should have to spend much more time on my writing and, as I have said, I have so little; and perhaps, after all, nothing would be gained by it.

CHAPTER 31

*She speaks of certain outward temptations and appearances of the
devil, and of the torments which she suffered from him, and also offers
some excellent counsel to persons travelling the way of perfection*

Now that I have recorded some temptations and secret, inner disturbances aroused in me by the devil, I will describe certain
others which he inflicted on me almost in public, and in which it was
impossible not to recognize his agency.

Once when I was in an oratory he appeared on my left hand, in a
hideous form. I particularly noticed his mouth, because he spoke to me,
and it was terrifying. A great flame seemed to issue from his body,
which was intensely bright and cast no shadow. He said to me in a
dreadful voice that I had indeed escaped from his clutches, but that he
would capture me still. I was greatly frightened and made shift to cross
myself, whereupon he disappeared, but immediately came back again.
This happened twice and I did not know what to do. There was some
holy water near by, some drops of which I threw in his direction, and
he did not return again. On another occasion I was tormented for five
hours with such terrible pains and such inward and outward disquiet
that I do not believe I could have stood it any longer. The sisters who
were with me were terrified, and had no more idea what to do for me
than I had of how to help myself.

It is my custom when pains and bodily sufferings are most unbearable
to make the best act of inner resignation that I can, begging the Lord,
if it be His pleasure, to grant me patience – and so long as I have that I
can continue in this state until the end of the world. So this time, when I
found my suffering so cruel I helped myself to bear it by resorting to
these acts and resolutions. The Lord plainly wished me to understand
that this was the devil's work; for I saw close beside me a most hideous
little Negro gnashing his teeth, as if in despair at losing what he had
tried to win. When I saw him, I burst out laughing, and had no fear.
But there were some sisters there who were helpless, and did not know
how to relieve my pain. For he made me thresh about with my body,
head, and arms, and I was powerless to prevent him. But worst of all
was my inner disquiet, from which I could get no relief in any way. I

dared not ask for holy water for fear of alarming my companions and of their realizing what the trouble was.

I have learnt from the experience of several occasions that there is nothing the devils fly from more promptly, never to return, than from holy water. They fly from the Cross also, but return again. So there must be a great virtue in holy water. For my part I feel a special and most notable solace in my soul when I take it up. In fact I am generally conscious of a refreshing power in it which I could not describe; it is like an inner delight that comforts my whole soul. This is not fancy, or something that I have experienced once only; it has happened again and again, and I have observed it with great care. It is as if one were very hot and very thirsty, and were suddenly to drink from a jug of cold water; one's whole being seems to feel refreshed. I often reflect on the great importance of everything ordained by the Church, and it delights me greatly to see that her words are so mighty as to impart their power to this water and make it so very different from water that has not been blessed.

Then as my pains did not stop, I said: 'If you wouldn't laugh at me, I should ask for some holy water.' So they brought me some, and sprinkled it over me, but it did no good. Then I threw some in the direction of the little Negro, and in a second he had gone. All my pain disappeared as if someone had snatched it away, except that I was left as weary as if I had received a severe beating. It was of great service to me to learn that – with the Lord's permission – the devil can do so much harm to a body and soul, even though they do not belong to him. What will he do to them, then, I thought, when they are truly in his possession! This gave me a new desire to deliver myself from such dangerous company.

The same thing happened to me on another occasion not long ago, although it did not last so long and I was alone. I asked for some holy water and the sisters who came in after he had gone – there were two of them, most dependable women who would on no account tell a lie – smelt a very unpleasant smell, like that of brimstone. I did not smell it myself, but it lasted long enough for them to notice it. On another occasion when I was in choir, I felt a great impulse of recollection, and went out so that the sisters should not notice anything. But all who were near me heard sounds where I was, like the noise of great blows, and I myself heard talking, as if something were being discussed, but I did not know what was said. For I was so deep in prayer that I took nothing in, nor was I at all afraid. Almost always this happened at times when the Lord so favoured me as to permit some soul to make progress through my agency. What I am now going to describe is something that actually happened to me. There are many witnesses to it, in particular my present confessor, who saw an account of it in a letter. I did not tell him who had written the letter, but he knew quite well who it was.

A person came to me who had been living for two and a half years in mortal sin of the most abominable kind I have ever heard of; and all that time he never confessed it or ceased from it, yet went on saying Mass. He confessed other sins, but would say to himself of this one: 'How can I confess to anything so foul?' He had a strong desire to be rid of it, but could not bring himself to do so I felt great pity for him, and was deeply grieved to see God offended in this way. I promised him to pray earnestly for his amendment and to request others who were better than I to do the same. I wrote also to a certain person, who – as that priest said – would be able to distribute the letters. So it came about that he made his confession at the first opportunity. For, on account of the many very holy persons to whom I had spoken of him and who had prayed for him, the Lord God was pleased to bestow His mercy on his soul; and I, wretched creature though I am, had taken all possible pains to the same end. He wrote to me that he had so far recovered that days passed without his falling into this sin, but that he was so tormented by the temptation that, to judge by his sufferings, he seemed to be in hell. He asked me to commend him to God. I spoke of him again to my sisters, whose prayers must have caused God to grant me this favour, and they took his plight greatly to heart. Nobody had any idea of his identity. I implored His Majesty to moderate his tortures and temptations, and to let these same devils torment me instead, so long as this did not cause me to sin against Him. Thus it was that I suffered a month of great torments; and it was during that time that the two incidents I have described took place.

The Lord was pleased to deliver him from the devils – as I was informed in a letter – for I had written to tell him what was happening to me during that month. His soul gained strength, and he remained quite free from his sin, for which he could not give enough thanks to Our Lord and to me – as if I had done anything for him, unless he had been helped by the belief that God was granting me favours. He said that when he found himself hard pressed, he read my letters and the tempta-

tion left him; and that he was greatly astonished to hear of my sufferings, also at the manner of his own deliverance. I was astonished too,
but I would have suffered as much for many years more to see that one
soul delivered. May Our Lord be praised for all things. The prayers of
those who serve Him, as I believe the sisters of this house do, can
achieve great things. But the devils must have visited their special
anger on me because all this happened through my agency, and the
Lord permitted them to do so on account of my sins. One night, during
this time, I thought that the devils were suffocating me, and when the
sisters sprinkled a great deal of holy water, I saw a huge crowd of them
running away as if they were going to cast themselves over a precipice.
These accursed creatures have tormented me so often, and I am so little
afraid of them now that I see they cannot stir without Our Lord's permission, that I should weary your Reverence, and myself too, if I were
to write any more about them.

May what I have said help the true servant of God to despise those
bogeys that the devils set up to frighten us. Let him realize that every
time we ignore them they lose some of their power, and the soul gains
greater control. We always derive some benefit from these experiences,
but of this I will not write for fear of being too long. I will only describe
something that happened to me one All Souls' night. I was in an oratory
and, after saying one nocturn, was repeating some very devotional
prayers which come after it and are to be found in our breviary, when
the devil actually alighted on my book to prevent me finishing my
reading. When I crossed myself he went away. But when I began
again he returned. I believe that he did this three times, and I could not
go on until I had sprinkled some holy water. At that moment I saw
several souls coming out of purgatory; their time must have been
almost up, and I thought perhaps the devil was trying to prevent their
deliverance. I have seldom seen him in bodily form, but often in the
sort of vision that I have described when, although he took no form, I
have clearly known that he was there.

I also want to record another incident which greatly frightened me.
One Trinity Sunday, I was in the choir of a certain convent and saw,
while in a rapture, a great battle between angels and devils. I could not
understand the meaning of this vision, but before a fortnight had gone
by I realized that it referred to a dispute between some sisters who
practised prayer and many more who did not, which was doing the
house great harm. The dispute lasted a long time and caused great

disturbance. On another occasion, I saw a huge crowd of devils around me, but I seemed to be completely enveloped in a great light, which prevented their coming near me. I realized that God was guarding me so that they should not approach me and make me sin against Him. From what I had observed about myself on other occasions I knew that this was a true vision. The fact is that I am now aware of how little their power is unless I am fighting against God, and so I am scarcely afraid of them any more. For their strength is nothing if they do not see souls surrendering to them like cowards; only then do they show their power. Sometimes, during these temptations that I have described, I would feel that all my weaknesses and vanities of past times were re-awakening within me; and then I had to commend myself to God indeed. Until my confessor set my mind at rest, I was tortured by the idea that since these ideas arose in my mind I must be wholly possessed by the devil. For it seemed to me that no one who had received such favours from the Lord ought to have even the first impulse towards a wicked thought. At other times I was greatly distressed – as I still am – by finding myself much respected, especially by people of importance, and by hearing myself well spoken of. I have suffered a great deal from this, and I still do. Then I turn to the life of Christ or to those of the saints, and realize that my life is the reverse of theirs, for they met with nothing but contempt and insults. This makes me go forward in fear, like one who does not dare to lift her head, for I do not want to appear to be doing what I am not.

When I am undergoing persecutions, although my body is hurt and I am afflicted in other ways, my soul is completely mistress of itself. I cannot understand how this can be, but that is how it is. The soul seems at such times to be in its own kingdom and to have everything beneath its feet. I had this experience several times and it lasted for quite a few days; it seemed to be a kind of virtue and humility, but now I clearly see that it was a temptation. A Dominican father, a man of great learning, showed me this plainly. When I thought that these favours which the Lord grants me might become public knowledge, my sufferings were so intense as greatly to disturb my soul. They reached such a pitch indeed that at the mere idea of it, I decided that I would rather be buried alive than have these things known. So when these spells of deep recollection or rapture came on me, and I could not resist them even in public, I was so ashamed afterwards that I was unwilling to appear where anyone would see me.

Once when I was extremely worried about this, the Lord asked me what I was afraid of, for only one of two things could happen: either they would speak ill of me or praise Him. By this He meant that those who believed it was His work would praise Him, and those who did not would condemn me, though I should be guiltless. Consequently I should be the gainer in either case, and need not worry. This greatly calmed me, and I am comforted when I think of it. The temptation reached such a pitch that I wanted to leave the place and to take my dowry to another convent, much more strictly enclosed than the one I was in. I had heard this place very well spoken of. It belonged to my own Order and was a long way away. But the distance would have been a great consolation to me, for then I should have been in a place where no one knew me. But my confessor refused to let me go.

These fears deprived me of much freedom of spirit; but later I came to realize that all this disturbance of mind was no true humility. The Lord taught me one truth: if I resolutely and positively believed that anything good in me was not mine at all but came from God, then, just as I was not troubled when I heard other persons praised, but rather delighted and consoled to see that God was revealing Himself through them, so I should not be troubled if He showed His works in me.

I fell into another excess as well, which was to beseech God, and to make it my special prayer, that when a person thought there was any good in me, His Majesty should reveal my sins to him, so that he might see how utterly undeserving I was of these favours. This is always a great desire of mine. My confessor told me that I should not do this, but I have continued the practice almost to this day. Whenever I have noticed anyone thinking very well of me, I have managed, in any roundabout way that I could, to make him aware of my sins. This has seemed to bring me some relief. My sins have made me very scrupulous in the matter.

This practice did not spring from humility, I think, but was very often the result of a temptation. I seemed to be deceiving everybody, though really, when they believed that there was some good in me, they were deceiving themselves, I had no desire to deceive them and never attempted to do so; yet for some reason the Lord permitted these misjudgements. I never discussed anything even with my confessors unless I thought it was necessary; it would have caused me great scruples to do so. I realize now that all these little fears and distresses and semblances of humility were just imperfections, due to my lack of mortification. For a soul resigned into God's hands does not care whether it is well or ill spoken of, so long as it has right understanding. Of course when the Lord is pleased to grant it the favour of understanding, it must clearly realize that it has nothing of its own. Let it trust the Giver, and it will learn why He reveals His gifts; and let it prepare itself for persecution, for it is certain that at times like the present it will come to anyone, when the Lord is pleased to make it known that He is granting him such favours as these. Then a thousand eyes are fixed on such a soul, whereas a thousand souls of a different stamp are observed by none.

In truth there is no small reason here for fear, and I was certainly right to be afraid. But I was being cowardly, not humble. For a soul that God permits to walk thus in the eyes of the world, may well prepare itself to be martyred by the world, since if it will not die to the world of its own free will, the world itself will kill it. Indeed there is nothing in the world that seems good to me, except its refusal to tolerate faults in good people, and its way of perfecting them by speaking ill of them. I declare that one needs more courage to follow the way of perfection if one is not perfect than for suddenly becoming a martyr. Perfection cannot be attained quickly except by one to whom the Lord is pleased to grant this favour as a particular privilege. But when the world sees anyone starting on that road, it expects him to be perfect all at once and can detect a fault in him from a mile away. Yet in him this fault may be a virtue, while his critic, in whom it is a vice, judges others by himself. They will not let this person eat or sleep or, as they say, so much as draw breath; the more highly they think of him, the more they forget that he is still in the body. For however perfect his soul may be, he is still living on earth, and however resolutely he tramples it beneath his feet he is still subject to its miseries. That is why I say that he needs great courage, for his poor soul has as yet hardly begun to walk, and they expect him to be as strong on trying occasions as they read that the saints were after they had been confirmed in grace. All this gives us cause to praise the Lord, and also for great sorrow of heart, since very many souls turn back because, poor things, they do not know how to help themselves. I believe that my soul would have done the same, had not the Lord Himself, in His compassion, done everything for me. Until He had done everything out of His own goodness, all that I did myself, as your Reverence will see, was just to fall and rise again.

I wish that I knew how to express this, because I believe that many souls are deluded at this point by trying to fly before God has given them wings. I think that I have used this comparison before, but it applies here. I will use it again, therefore, for I see some souls very much distressed by this delusion. They begin with strong desires and fervour, determined to advance in virtue, and some of them give up all outward things for God. Then they see, in others more advanced than themselves, notable accessions of virtue, given them by the Lord, for we cannot acquire them ourselves. They find in all the books written on prayer and contemplation, accounts of what we should do in order to rise to that exalted state; and as they cannot immediately accomplish all this, they lose heart. I am speaking of such things as not caring if people speak ill of us, but being more pleased than if they speak well of us; not valuing our own reputation; cultivating a detachment from our relatives, and not desiring their company but, on the other hand, finding it wearisome unless they are given to prayer, and many other things of this kind. These are gifts that must, I think, be bestowed on us by God. For they seem to me to be supernatural blessings that go counter to our natural inclinations. Let these beginners not grow weary but trust in the Lord that, if they pray and do what they can for themselves, His Majesty will make them in very deed what at present they are only in their desires. It is most necessary for our weak nature that we should have great confidence and not be faint-hearted or doubt that if we do our utmost we shall come off victorious.

As I have much experience of these matters, I will give your Reverence a little advice. Do not think – although it may seem so – that anyone has acquired a virtue unless he has tested it with its corresponding vice. We must always be distrustful of ourselves and never grow careless so long as we live. For much that is worldly will stick to us unless, as I say, God gives us the grace fully to understand the nature of everything; and in this life there is nothing which is not attended by plenty of dangers. I believed some years ago, not merely that I was not attached to my relatives, but that they wearied me; and that was certainly true, for I could not bear their conversation. Then an affair of some importance had to be settled, and I had to stay with one of my sisters[1] of whom I had once been very fond. Although she is a better woman than I, I could not get along with her in conversation. For since our conditions are different, she being a married woman, we could not always talk of the things that I should have liked. So I remained alone as much as I

1. Her younger sister Juana, who was married to a difficult and poor man

could. But I found that I was much more affected when she was distressed than when my neighbours were, and that I was quite concerned about her. In the end I realized that I was not as free as I had thought, and that I really had to avoid occasions for sin, in order that this virtue which the Lord had implanted in me might go on growing; and, with His favour, I have endeavoured to do so ever since.

When the Lord begins to implant a virtue in us we must attach a high value to it, and on no account run the danger of losing it. This applies to the matter of our reputation and to many other things. For your Reverence may be quite sure that not all of us who think we are entirely detached really are, and it is necessary never to be careless on this point. If anyone who wants to make progress detects in himself any regard for his reputation, believe me, he should cast this attachment behind him, for it is a chain that no file can sever; only God can destroy it with the aid of prayer and much effort on our part. To my mind, it will impede him on his journey, and I am astounded at the harm it does. I see some persons who are holy in their deeds and perform such wonders that everyone is astonished. God bless me then! Why are souls like that still on earth? Why are they not at the summit of perfection? What is wrong? What can be holding back men who are doing so much for God? Oh, just a little care for the reputation! And the worst of it is that they do not wish to know that they have it, the reason sometimes being that the devil makes them think their punctiliousness is necessary.

Let such persons believe me, let them for God's sake believe this insignificant ant, who speaks because it is the Lord's will that she shall do so. If they do not brush away that caterpillar, it may not damage the whole tree. Some virtues will remain, of course, but they will all be worm-eaten. The tree will not be beautiful; it will not thrive, nor will it let its neighbours thrive, because its fruits of good example are neither sound nor likely to keep. I will repeat once more that however small our concern for reputation, its results will be as bad as when we strike a wrong note or fail to keep time when playing the organ. The whole passage becomes discordant. This concern is a thing most harmful to the soul whenever it occurs, but on this road of perfection it is a pestilence.

We are trying to obtain union with God. We want to follow the words of Christ, who was loaded with reproaches and falsely accused. Can we care then about keeping our own reputation and credit intact?

The two aims are irreconcilable, since they are not on the same road. When we do violence to ourselves, and try in various ways to give up our rights, then the Lord comes to the soul. Some will say: 'I have nothing to give up. I never get opportunities for denying myself'. But if anyone is really determined, I do not think the Lord will let him lose this blessing. His Majesty will arrange so many ways in which he may gain virtue that he will soon have more than he wants. All hands to the task! Set to work, I mean, on some matters of little or no consequence, as I used to do when I began. Try at least to deal with a few of them. These are the straws, as I have said, and I throw them on the fire. That is all I am good for. But the Lord accepts them all. May He be blessed for ever.

One of my faults was this: that I had a very imperfect knowledge of my breviary and of my duties in the choir and in general, simply because I was careless and absorbed in vanities. I saw other novices who could have taught me these things, but I never asked them any questions for fear that they should realize how little I knew. But good example soon prevails; at least it generally does so. Once God had opened my eyes a little, I would ask the girls' opinions, even when I knew a thing, but was in a slight doubt about it; and this did no harm to my reputation or to my credit with them. In fact, I think the Lord has been pleased to improve my memory from that time. I was bad at singing, and was greatly put out if I had not previously studied the part that was assigned to me, not because of my shortcomings in the Lord's eyes, which would have been a virtue, but because of the many who heard me. Merely on account of my reputation, I became so perturbed that I sang worse than I need have done. Later, when I did not know my part very well, I made a point of saying that it was new to me. At first I very much disliked making this admission, but after a time I came to enjoy doing so, and when I began not to mind whether people knew of my ignorance or not, then I sang much better. So this miserable regard for my honour made me unable to perform what I really regarded as an honour, for everyone interprets the word in his own way.

By such nothings as these – and really they are nothing, and I too am certainly nothing, to be hurt by such things – one's efforts begin to improve. Such trivial actions, when performed for God, are of importance in His Majesty's eyes and help Him to greater things. So it was with me in the matter of humility. When I saw that all the nuns were making progress except myself – I was always good for nothing – I would collect their mantles as they left the choir. I felt that in this way I was serving the angels, who had been praising God there. This I did until – I do not know how – they came to hear of it, which made me somewhat ashamed, because I was not yet virtuous enough to be willing that they should know of such a thing. But my shame did not spring from humility, only from the fear that they might laugh at me over a matter so trifling.

O Lord, how ashamed I am to think of all my wickedness, and to number all these little grains of sand which I still did not lift from the river-bed in Your service, but left all embedded in my innumerable meannesses! The water of Your grace was not yet flowing beneath all this sand, to raise it up. O my Creator, if only, among all this wickedness, I had something worth recounting, something to set beside the great favours that I have received from You. But thus it is, my Lord, and I do not know how my heart can bear it, or how anyone who reads this can fail to abhor me when he sees how ill I have repaid Your very great favours, and that I am not ashamed to count any services that I have rendered You as my own. I am ashamed, my Lord, but lack of anything else to enumerate in my favour compels me to speak of these lowly beginnings, if only in order to inspire hope in those who have begun better. For since the Lord seems to have taken notice of my small efforts, He will take still more notice of theirs. May it please His Majesty to give me grace, so that I may not always remain a beginner. Amen.

CHAPTER 32

She tells how it pleased God to carry her in the spirit to a place in hell that she had deserved for her sins. She describes a tithe of what was shown her there and begins to tell of the ways and means by which the convent of St Joseph was founded on its present site

SOME long time after the Lord had bestowed on me many of the favours that I have described, together with others that were very great, one day when I was at prayer, I found myself, without knowing how, plunged, as I thought, into hell. I understood that the Lord wished me to see the place that the devils had ready for me there, and that I had earned by my sins. All this happened in the briefest second; but even if I should live for many years, I do not think I could possibly forget it. The entrance seemed to me like a very long, narrow passage, or a very low, dark, and constricted furnace. The ground appeared to be covered with a filthy wet mud, which smelt abominably and contained many wicked reptiles. At the end was a cavity scooped out of the wall, like a cupboard, and I found myself closely confined in it. But the sight of all this was pleasant compared with my feelings. There is no exaggeration in what I am saying.

I do not think that my feelings could possibly be exaggerated, nor would anyone understand them. I felt a fire inside my soul, the nature of which is beyond my powers of description, and my physical tortures were intolerable. I have endured the severest bodily pains in the course of my life, the worst, so the doctors say, that it is possible to suffer and live, among them the contraction of my nerves during my paralysis, and many other agonies of various kinds, including some, as I have said, caused by the devil. But none of them was in any way comparable to the pains I felt at that time, especially when I realized that they would be endless and unceasing. But even this was nothing to my agony of soul, an oppression, a suffocation, and an affliction so agonizing, and accompanied by such a hopeless and distressing misery that no words I could find would adequately describe it. To say that it was as if my soul were being continuously torn from my body is as nothing. The fact is that I can find no means of describing that inward fire and that despair which is greater than the severest torments or pains. I could not see my torturer, but I seemed to feel myself being burnt and dismembered; and, I repeat, that interior fire and despair were the very worst of all.

In that pestilential spot, deprived of all hope of comfort, it was impossible for me to sit or lie down; there was no room to do so. I had been put in what seemed a hole in the wall, and the very walls, which are hideous to behold, pressed in on me and completely stifled me. There is no light there, only the deepest darkness. Yet, although there was no light, it was possible to see everything that brings pain to the sight; I do not know how this can be. It was not the Lord's will that I should at that time see more of hell itself; since then I have seen another vision of frightful things that are the punishment for certain vices. But although these seemed to me a much more dreadful sight, yet they alarmed me less, for then I felt no physical pain. In the first vision, however, it was the Lord's will that I really should feel these torments and afflictions of spirit, just as if my body were actually suffering them. I do not know how it was, but I quite clearly realized that this was a great favour, and that the Lord wished me to see with my very eyes the place from which His mercy had delivered me. It is nothing to read an account of it, or to think, as I sometimes have – though rarely, for my soul has made little progress by the way of fear – of the various kinds of torment, of how devils tear the flesh with pincers, and of other forms of torture that I have read about. None of these pains is in any way comparable to this, which is a wholly different matter. In fact, they are like a picture set up against the reality, and burning on earth is a trifle compared with this fire.

I was terrified, and though this happened six years ago, I am still terrified as I write; even as I sit here my natural heat seems to be drained away by fear. I can think of no time of trial or torture when everything that we can suffer on earth has not seemed to me trifling in comparison with this. In fact, as I see it, on most occasions, we complain without reason. I repeat that this vision was one of the greatest mercies that the Lord has bestowed on me. It has benefited me very much, both by freeing me from fear of the tribulations and oppositions of this life, and by giving me the strength, whilst bearing them, to give thanks to the Lord, who, as I now believe, has delivered me from these continuous and terrible torments.

Since that time, I repeat, everything has seemed endurable to me in comparison with a single moment of the suffering that I had to bear then. It shocks me to think that after having so often read books which tell something of the pains of hell, I was neither afraid of them, nor realized what they are. What could I have been thinking of? How could I possibly have taken pleasure in things that were driving me directly to that awful place? O God, may You be blessed for ever, for now I see that You loved me far more than I love myself. How often, Lord, did you deliver me from that dread prison, only for me to shut myself in again, in defiance of Your will!

It was this vision that filled me with the very deep distress which I feel on account of the great number of souls who bring damnation on themselves – of the Lutherans in particular, since they were members of the Church by baptism. It has also given me a fervent desire to help other souls. Indeed I believe that if I could free a single one from these dreadful tortures, I would most willingly suffer many deaths. For if we see someone on earth whom we especially love suffering great trials or pains, our very nature seems to awaken our compassion, and the more dire his sufferings the greater our distress. Who, then, could bear to see a soul endlessly tormented in this most terrible trial of all? No heart could possibly endure it without the most hideous affliction. For if earthly tortures, which we know to have their limits and to end with death, move us to such compassion, I do not know how we can look calmly on those others that are endless, and see the devil carrying off as many souls as he does every day.

This vision also makes me wish that in so important a matter we should not be content to do anything less than the best that is in our power. Let us neglect nothing, and may the Lord be pleased to grant us His grace to this end. Despite my very great wickedness, I recall that I took some pains to serve God, and refrained from doing certain things that I see tolerated in the world to-day as matters of no account; that I endured serious illnesses, and bore them with a great patience that was bestowed on me by the Lord; that I was not given to grumbling or slandering people, and that I was, as I think, incapable of wishing anyone ill; that I was not covetous and do not remember ever having felt so much envy as grievously to offend the Lord; that I kept myself free from many other faults, and that, vile creature though I was, I lived in the most constant fear of God. Yet look at the place where the devils had lodged me! It is true, I think, that my sins had merited even worse punishment. Nevertheless, I repeat, the torture was terrible. It is a dangerous thing indeed for a soul to follow its own pleasure, or to be calm and complacent when at every step it is falling into mortal sin.

For the love of God, let us avoid occasions for sin, and the Lord will help us all as He helped me. May it please His Majesty not to let me out of His hand, for fear that I may fall again, now that I have seen the place to which that would bring me. May the Lord not let me fall, for His Majesty's sake. Amen.

After I had seen this vision, and other great and secret things which the Lord, of His kindness, was pleased to show me, concerning the bliss that awaits the good and the pains in store for the wicked, I longed to find some ways and means of doing penance for all my evil deeds, and of becoming in some degree worthy of winning this great blessing. I wanted to avoid human company, and finally to withdraw completely from the world. My spirit was restless, yet not with a disturbing but a pleasant disquiet; I knew quite well that it was of God, and that His Majesty had given my soul this ardour so that I might digest other and stronger meat than I was then eating.

I tried to think what I could do for God, and decided that the first thing was to follow the call to a religious life that the Lord had given me, by keeping my Rule with every possible perfection. Although in the house where I was there were many servants of God and He was well served there, yet, because it was very poor, we nuns often left it for other places where we could live decently and keep our vows. Moreover the Rule was not observed there in its original strictness but, as throughout the Order, in the relaxed form permitted by the Bull of Mitigation. There were other drawbacks too, among them what seemed to me the excessive comfort that we enjoyed, for the house was a large and pleasant one. Now this habit of going on visits, though I was one who frequently indulged in it, was a serious inconvenience to me, because many people whom my superiors could not refuse liked to have me with them, and when I was invited they ordered me to go. Things reached such a pitch, indeed, that I was able to be in the convent very little; the devil must have had a hand in these frequent departures of mine, though at the same time I would always pass on to some of the nuns what I learnt from the people I met, and this was of great benefit to them.

One day, in conversation with myself and one or two other nuns, a certain person[1] asked whether we were prepared to follow the practice of the Barefoot Orders, for it would be quite possible to found a convent of Discalced nuns. I had desired something of the sort myself, and

1. María de Ocampo, the daughter of Santa Teresa's cousin.

so I discussed the idea with a companion who was of the same mind, that widowed lady whom I have already mentioned. She began to think out ways of finding the necessary revenue. But, as I can see now, this would not have got us very far. For my part, however, I was very happy in the house where I was. The place was pleasing to me, and so was my cell, which suited me excellently; and this held me back. Nevertheless we agreed to commend the matter most fervently to God.

One day, after Communion, the Lord earnestly commanded me to pursue this aim with all my strength. He made me great promises; that the house would not fail to be established, that great service would be done Him there, that its name should be St Joseph's; that he would watch over us at one of its doors and Our Lady at the other; that Christ would be with us; that the convent would be a star, and that it would shed the most brilliant light. He said also that although the Rules of the religious orders were mitigated, I must not think that He was poorly served by them. For what would become of the world, if it were not for the religious? He told me to convey His orders to my confessor,[1] with the request that he should not oppose them or in any way hinder my carrying them out.

This vision had a very great effect on me. For these words spoken to me by the Lord were of such a kind as to leave me in no doubt that they were from Him. They distressed me very deeply, because they gave me a partial glimpse of the great anxieties and labours that the task entailed for me. Besides, I was very happy in that house and, although I had discussed the project before, it had never been with any great measure of resolution, or with any certainty that it would be carried out. I now felt that a burden was being laid upon me and, when I saw that, a very disturbing time began for me; I did not know what to do. However, the Lord spoke to me on this subject again and again, and put so many reasons and arguments before me, as to convince me that they were valid and that this was His will. So I dared not do otherwise than speak to my confessor and give him a written account of all that had taken place.

He did not venture definitely to tell me to abandon the project, though he saw that, humanly speaking, there was no way of carrying it out, since my companion who was to undertake it all had very small resources – indeed almost none. He told me to discuss the matter with my director, and to do as he advised me. I did not discuss these visions

1. Father Baltasar Alvarez.

of mine with my director, but the lady who wanted to found the convent had a talk with him, and the Provincial, who is a friend of the religious Orders, took the idea very well. He offered her all necessary support, and told her that he would give the house his sanction. They discussed what income it would require, and for many reasons we decided that it must never contain more than thirteen nuns. Before we began these discussions, we had written to the blessed friar Peter of Alcántara, and told him all that was happening. He advised us to stick to our plans, and gave us his opinion on the whole subject.

Hardly had news of this begun to spread around the place than there fell upon us a persecution so severe that it would not be possible to describe it in a few words. They talked, they laughed at us, and they declared that the idea was absurd. Of me they said that I was in the right place where I was, and they subjected my companion to such a persecution that it quite wore her out. I did not know what to do, for they seemed to me partly right. In this state of exhaustion, I turned to God, and His Majesty began to comfort and encourage me. I could now see, He said, what sufferings those saints who had founded religious orders had gone through, and indeed they had had to endure much more than I could imagine, but we must not let that trouble us. He told me certain things to say to my companion, and to my very great astonishment we at once felt comforted by what had happened, and courageous enough to stand up to everybody. And so we did, for there was hardly anyone among the prayerful, or indeed in the whole place, who was not against us, and did not consider our project absolutely absurd.

There was so much chatter and fuss in my own convent that the Provincial thought it would be difficult to oppose everybody, and so changed his mind. He now withdrew his backing, saying that the income was not assured, that in any case it would be insufficient, and that the plan was meeting with heavy opposition. In all this he seemed to be right. So he put the matter aside and refused to sanction it. We appeared to have taken the first blows and were much distressed, myself in particular at finding the Provincial against me, for his previous approval had justified me in everyone's eyes. My companion was refused absolution if she did not abandon the idea; it was incumbent on her, she was told, to remove the scandal. She went to talk things over with a very learned man who was a great servant of God and of the Order of St Dominic,[1] and told him the whole story. She did this even

1. Brother Pedro Ibáñez.

before the Provincial withdrew his support, for we had no one in the whole place to whom we could look for an opinion; and for that reason people said that the whole idea was our own fancy. The lady gave that holy man an account of everything. She told him how much revenue she derived from her estate, and she very much hoped that he would help us since he was at that time the most learned man in the town, and there were few more learned in his whole Order. I myself told him all that we were proposing to do, and some of our reasons; I did not mention any of my revelations to him, but merely set out the natural reasons that prompted me, for I did not want him to base his opinion on any grounds but these. He said that we must allow him a week before he replied, and asked if we would definitely follow his judgement. I said that we would. But although I said so, and I think that we should have done so, I never for a moment wavered in my confidence that the convent would be founded. My companion had even more faith, and would never have given up the project for anything that might have been said to her.

For my part, although, as I have said, the abandonment of the project seemed to me impossible, I merely believed the revelation to be true in the sense that it was not contrary to what is written in the Holy Scriptures, or to the laws of the Church, which we are obliged to keep. Although I believed that my revelation was really from God, if that learned man had told us that we could not act upon it without offending Him, and that it would be a violation of conscience, I think I should have given the plan up on the spot and sought for some other way. But the Lord showed me no other way. Later, that servant of God told me that at first he had definitely decided that he must urge us to give the project up, because he had become aware of the popular outcry and because the idea seemed as foolish to him as to everyone else. He said that a certain gentleman, having learnt that we had gone to him for advice, had sent him a warning to be careful what he did, and not to help us; but that when he had begun to consider the terms of his answer, to think the matter over and to reflect on the intentions that prompted us, on our way of setting to work and on our concern for our Order, he had decided that we should be rendering God a great service and that the scheme must not be abandoned. His answer was therefore, that we should hasten to carry it out, and he suggested ways and means by which this could be done. He said that, though our resources were small, we must to some extent put our trust in God. He told us to send anyone who opposed us further to him for an answer, and he always helped us in this way, as I shall show by and by.

We were greatly comforted by this, and by the fact that several saintly persons who had hitherto been against us now became reconciled, some of them even helping us. Among these was that pious gentleman of whom I have already written. He now believed that the project, being wholly founded upon prayer – as indeed it was – would be a means of great perfection. Whilst still believing that the foundation would be difficult or even impracticable, he renounced his former view and agreed that the idea might be from God. Here Our Lord Himself must have inspired him, as He inspired that learned cleric and servant of God, to whom, as I have said, I had spoken in the first place, who is an example to the whole town, and whom God keeps there for the help and profit of many souls.[1] He also came forward to help me in this affair. While things were in this state, aided by the continual help of many people's prayers, we practically completed the purchase of a house. It was a small one, but this did not trouble me in the least, for the Lord had told me to start in the best way I could and in due course I should see what His Majesty would do. And how well I have seen it! So, though I knew that our income would be small, I believed that the Lord would manage things in other ways and would give us help.

1. Master Gaspar Daza.

CHAPTER 33

*She continues her account of the foundation of the glorious St Joseph's,
telling how she was commanded to let it drop, how for a time she gave
it up, and how she suffered various trials in the course of which she was
comforted by the Lord*

IT was when the business had reached this stage and was so near to
completion that the deeds were to be signed next day, that the
Father Provincial changed his mind. From what came out later, I
believe that his change of attitude was divinely ordained. For while so
many prayers were being offered up for us, the Lord was perfecting
His work and arranging for its accomplishment in another way. As the
Provincial now refused to sanction the foundation, my confessor at
once told me to let it drop, though the Lord knows what great labours
and afflictions it had cost me to bring it so far. Once it was discontinued
and abandoned, people were even more certain that it had all been an
absurd feminine whimsy, and gossip at my expense increased, even
though up to that time I had been acting on my Provincial's orders.

I was very unpopular throughout the convent for wanting to found
a more strictly enclosed house. The nuns said that this was an insult to
them; that I could serve God just as well where I was, since there were
others there better than myself; that I had no love for my own house,
and that I should have been better employed raising money for it than
for founding another. Some said that I ought to be put in the prison-
cell; but others, though only a few, came out on my side. I saw quite
well that in many respects my opponents were right, and sometimes
I could make allowances for them. But as I could not tell them my
principal argument – that I had been obeying the Lord's commands – I
did not know what to do and was therefore silent. At other times, by
God's great mercy, none of this worried me, and I renounced the project as easily and as contentedly as if it had cost me nothing. This nobody
could believe, not even those given to prayer with whom I talked; they
supposed that I must be very much distressed and ashamed, and even
my own confessor could not really believe that I was not. It seemed to
me that I had done everything in my power to fulfil the Lord's commands, and that I had now no further obligation. So I remained in my
house, where I was quite content and happy, though at the same time I

was never able to give up the conviction that the task would be fulfilled. How, when, and by what means this would be I could not say, but of its eventual accomplishment I was certain.

What greatly distressed me was that my confessor wrote to me on one occasion as if I had been acting against his instructions. It must have been the Lord's will that I should not be exempted from trials arising from the source which would cost me the greatest pain. Among this multitude of persecutions, I had expected that my confessor would console me. But in his letter he said that, as I ought to have realized by now, the whole matter was just a dream. He advised me henceforth to lead a better life, and not to attempt anything more of the kind or even to talk about it, since I now saw what a scandal I had raised. He said some other things too, all of them most painful. This distressed me more than everything else put together, for I wondered whether I had been guilty of leading others into sin, whether these visions were illusory, whether all my prayer had been a deception, and whether I was not utterly lost and deceived. These thoughts so weighed on me that I became quite upset and was plunged into the deepest affliction. But the Lord, who never failed me in any of these trials that I have enumerated, often consoled and strengthened me in ways that I need not describe here. He told me at that time not to be troubled, for I had done God great service and had by no means offended Him in this matter. He also told me to obey my confessor's instructions and to keep quiet for the present, until the time came for the project to be resumed. He left me so consoled and happy that all the persecution I was suffering seemed nothing at all.

The Lord now showed me what a mighty blessing it is to suffer trials and persecutions for Him. I saw such a growth of love for God in my soul, and other graces as well, that I was quite astonished and could not cease to desire even more trials. However, other people thought that I was deeply ashamed; and I should have been if the Lord had not come to my aid in my extremity and granted me these great mercies. Now came the beginning of those stronger impulses of the love of God, of which I have spoken, and of deeper raptures. But I kept silent on the subject, and said nothing to anyone about what I had gained. That saintly Dominican never ceased to share my conviction that the foundation would be made, and as I would not take any further part in the matter, in order not to disobey my confessor, he got in touch with my woman friend. Together they sent an outline of the scheme to Rome.

Now the devil began to spread the news from one person to another, that I had received some revelation about this matter, and people came to me in great alarm, saying that these were difficult times, that some charge might be raised against me, and that I might have to appear before the Inquisitors. But this merely amused me and made me laugh. I never had any fear on that score. I knew quite well that in the matter of faith no one would ever find me failing to observe even the smallest ceremony of the Church, and that for the Church or for any truth in Holy Scripture, I would sacrifice my life a thousand times. So I told them not to be afraid, for my soul would be in a very poor state if there were anything in it that made me fear the Inquisitors. I said that if I thought there were I would go to them myself; furthermore that if any charge were raised against me, the Lord would deliver me and I should be very much the gainer. I discussed all this with the Dominican father who, as I said, was a very learned man, and whose opinions on any subject I could thoroughly trust. I gave him as clear an account as I could of my visions, of my way of prayer, and of the great favours that the Lord was granting me, and I begged him to consider the matter carefully and to tell me if there was anything in them contrary to Holy Scripture, also to give me his general opinion on the whole subject. He greatly reassured me, and I think this conversation was of some benefit to him too. For good man though he then was, from that time onwards he became much more devout in his prayers. He later retired to a friary of his Order, where solitude is much more possible, in order to apply himself more effectually to them; and there he stayed for more than two years. He was so capable, however, that he was needed elsewhere, and was, therefore, compelled under obedience to leave the place, to his great regret.

I was very sorry, in a way, when he left the town, because I had great need of him also. But I did nothing to hinder him, for I realized that this was to his advantage. When I was feeling most grieved by his departure, the Lord told me to take comfort and be grieved no more, for he was under good guidance. His soul benefited so much from his absence, and his spiritual growth was so great, that on his return he told me he would not have missed his stay in that friary for anything in the world. I was able to agree with him. Whereas previously he had reassured and comforted me only through his learning, now he did so also by the ample experience that his spirit had gained of supernatural things. God brought him back at just the right moment, for His Majesty saw that his help would be needed in the foundation of this convent, which His Majesty wished to take place.

For five or six months I kept quiet, making no move towards it and not even speaking about it, and the Lord did not give me a single command. I could not guess the reason for this, but was unable to rid myself of the belief that the foundation would eventually take place. At the end of that time, the then Rector of the Society of Jesus having left, His Majesty replaced him by a very spiritual man of great courage, understanding, and learning,[1] just at the moment when I was in the greatest need. For the priest who was hearing my confessions was subject to a superior, and in the Company they attach great importance to the practice of never taking the slightest action except in conformity with the will of their superiors. So although he thoroughly understood my soul and desired its progress, over certain matters he could not be definite, for very good reasons. My spirit, which was now experiencing very powerful impulses, was greatly troubled by this sort of constraint, but all the same I did not disobey his orders.

One day, when I was in great distress because I thought my confessor did not believe me, the Lord told me not to worry, for my distress would soon be over. I was very glad, since I thought He meant I was to die soon, and the mere thought of this delighted me. Later I realized that He was referring to the coming of the new Rector. For he put no restrictions at all on the priest who confessed me, and so I never suffered from that distress again. On the contrary, he told that minister to comfort me, since there was no cause for fear, and not to lead me by so narrow a road, but to let the spirit of the Lord work in me, for it sometimes seemed as if these great impulses of the spirit were preventing my soul from taking breath.

I went to see this Rector, and my confessor told me to talk to him with all freedom and frankness. I used very much to dislike speaking about these things, and yet when I entered the confessional I felt something in my spirit that I never remember having felt before or since in the presence of anyone else. I cannot possibly describe its nature, or compare it with anything at all. It was a spiritual joy; my soul recognized that here was a soul which would understand and be in harmony with mine, although, as I say, I do not know how this was. If I had ever spoken to him, or had heard great things of him, it would not have been surprising that I felt happy and certain of his understanding

1. Father Gaspar de Salazar.

me. But he had never spoken one word to me, nor I one word to him, nor was he a person of whom I had ever heard before. I discovered later that my spirit had not been wrong, for my conversations with him have been a great benefit to me and to my soul. He is very skilful with persons whom the Lord seems to have brought to an advanced state; he makes them run instead of walking a step at a time. His method is to bring them to complete detachment and to mortification, and the Lord has given him a very great aptitude for this.

When I began to have conversations with him, I immediately recognized what type of director he was, and saw that he had a pure and holy soul, endowed with a special gift from the Lord for the discernment of spirits. This gave me great comfort. Soon after I came under his direction, the Lord began to impress on me again that I must return to the project of the convent, and explain all my reasons and intentions to my confessor, and to the Rector as well, so that they should not stand in my way. Some of the things I said frightened them, but the Rector never doubted that I was prompted by the spirit of God, for he had considered the probable results of such a foundation with very great care. In short, after hearing my many arguments, they dared not risk standing in my way.

My confessor now gave me leave to resume the project with all my might, and I clearly saw what a task I was taking on, for I was quite alone and could do very little. We agreed that things should be done with the utmost secrecy, and so I arranged that a sister of mine,[2] who lived outside the town, should buy the necessary house and furnish it as if it were for herself, with purchase money that the Lord had provided in various ways. It would be a long story to tell how He looked after us. I made a great point of doing nothing to violate my obedience. But I knew that if I spoke of the project to my superiors all would be lost, as it had been on the last occasion; and this time things might be even worse. Getting the money, finding a house, arranging for its purchase and furnishing it was a very trying process, a part of which I had to carry through alone, although my friend did what she could. But she could not do much, hardly more indeed than lend her name to the transaction and give it her approval. All the more difficult work was mine, and I had so many things to do that I wonder now how I could possibly have managed them all. There were times when I exclaimed

2. Doña Juana, the married sister to whom the Saint had found herself to be so attached.

in distress: 'O Lord, why did you command me to do things that seem impossible? If only I were free, woman though I am. . . ! But being tied in so many ways, without money or the means of getting it, either for the Brief or for anything else, what, O Lord, can I do?'

Once when I was in a difficulty and could not think what to do or how to pay certain workmen, St Joseph, my true lord and father, appeared to me, and told me to proceed with my arrangements, for the money would not be lacking. So I went on, without a farthing, and the Lord did provide it in ways that astonished all who heard of them. I thought the house very small, so small indeed that it did not seem possible to turn it into a convent. I wanted to buy another, but had not the means. So there was no way of buying it, and I did not know what to do. There was a little house close to ours, however, also very small, which would have made a chapel. But one day, after I had taken Communion, the Lord said to me, 'I have told you already to move in as best you can', and then added, as a sort of exclamation, 'O the greed of humankind, to imagine that there will not be enough room for you! How often did I sleep in the open air, having nowhere else to lay My head!' I was amazed, and saw that He was right. So I went to survey the little house and found that it would just do for a convent, though a very small one. I did no more about adding to the property, but arranged to have the little house equipped so that we could live in it. It was very rough and ready, and no more was done to it than was necessary to make it healthy to live in. This is always the proper way of doing things.

On St Clare's day, as I was going to Communion, that saint appeared to me in great beauty and told me to take courage. She promised that she would help me if I went forward with what I had begun. I conceived a great devotion for her, and she has truly kept her word. For a convent of her Order, which is close to ours, is at present helping to maintain us. What is more, she has gradually brought this plan of mine to such perfection that the same Rule of poverty which obtains in her house is also observed in ours, and we live on alms. It was essential to get the Holy Father's approval for our existing without any revenue, and the procuring of that cost me no small labour. But the Lord is doing even greater things for us, and it may be at the request of this blessed saint that He is doing them. Without any demand on our part, His Majesty is providing most amply for our needs. May He be blessed for it all. Amen.

At about this same time, on the festival of Our Lady's Assumption, I was in the convent-church of the Order of the glorious St Dominic, thinking of the many sins that I had confessed there in time past, and of other incidents in my wicked life, when I was seized with a rapture so strong that it almost completely took me out of myself. I sat down, and I remember now that I could neither see the Elevation nor hear the Mass; and afterwards I was left with a scruple about this. While in this state I seemed to see myself clothed in a robe of great whiteness and clarity, and at first I could not tell who was putting it on me. But afterwards I saw Our Lady on my right and my father St Joseph on my left, and that it was they who were clothing me. I was given to understand that I was now cleansed of my sins. When I was clothed, and was experiencing the greatest joy and bliss, Our Lady seemed suddenly to seize me by the hands. She told me that I was giving her great pleasure by serving the glorious St Joseph, and promised me that my plans for the convent would be fulfilled. She said that the Lord and they would be greatly served there, and that I need not fear any failure of the project at any time, even though the obedience demanded of us might not be to my liking. She said that they would watch over us and that her Son had already promised to be with us; and that as a sign that this would be so she would give me a jewel. Then she seemed to hang round my neck a very beautiful gold collar, from which hung a cross of great value. The gold and stones were so different from those of this world that there is no comparing them; their beauty is quite unlike anything we can imagine here. Nor can the imagination rise to any understanding of the nature of the robe, or to any conception of its whiteness. Such was the vision that the Lord was pleased to send me that by comparison everything here on earth seems, as you might say, like a smudge of soot.

The beauty that I saw in Our Lady was wonderful, though I could make out no particular detail, only the general shape of her face and the whiteness and amazing splendour of her robes, which was not dazzling but quite soft. I did not see the glorious St Joseph so clearly, although I plainly saw that he was there, as in those visions which I have described already, in which nothing is actually seen. Our Lady looked to me almost like a child. When they had stayed with me for a little while, bringing me the greatest joy and bliss – more I believe than I had ever known before, and I wished it would last for ever – I seemed to see them ascend into the sky with a great multitude of angels. I was left in great solitude, but so comforted and uplifted and recollected in prayer, and so softened that I could not stir or speak for some time, and was quite beside myself. I was left with a passionate longing to be consumed by the love of God, and with other feelings of this sort. All this took place in such a way that I could never doubt, however hard I tried, that this vision was of God. It left me greatly comforted and very peaceful.

The point of what the Queen of the Angels said in regard to our obedience is this. It was a grief to me not to make over the convent to our Order, but the Lord had told me that it would be unwise to do so. He gave me reasons why it would be quite impracticable, but told me to refer to Rome by a certain procedure which He also explained. He promised that in this way I should find security, and so I did. I followed the Lord's instructions – and we should never have concluded our negotiations if I had not – and things turned out very well. In the light of subsequent events, it has proved most convenient that we should be under the Bishop's obedience. But I did not realize this at the time, nor did I know who that prelate would turn out to be.[1] But, as the Lord would have it, he proved a good man, and helpful to this house, as was necessary, in view of all the opposition that it has encountered, as I shall recount later, and in order to bring it to its present state. Blessed be He who has brought all this about. Amen.

1. Don Alvaro de Mendoza.

CHAPTER 34

*She tells how at this time she had to leave the town. She gives the
reasons and tells of her superior's command that she should go and
comfort a very great lady who was in serious distress. She begins
to describe what happened to her there, and to tell how the Lord, in
His mercy, made her the instrument whereby His Majesty roused a
very important person to serve him in earnest, also to say how she
afterwards found help and protection from Him. This is a very
noteworthy chapter*

DESPITE all the care I took to keep people from knowing what I
was doing, the work could not proceed in such secrecy that a
few did not hear of it; and of these some believed in it, and some did not.
I was in great fear that someone would tell the Provincial about it when
he came, and that he might then order me to give the project up; which
would have been the end of everything. But the Lord provided against
this danger in the following way. In a large city, more than sixty miles
away, lived a great lady[1] who was in a state of deep distress because of
the death of her husband. She was in such a desperate condition, indeed,
that fears were entertained for her life. Now she had heard of this miserable sinner. The Lord had ordained that a favourable report of me
should reach her ears, for certain good purposes of His own which were
to result from it. This lady was a most important person, and was on
good terms with the Provincial.[2] Moreover she knew that the nuns of
our house were allowed to go on visits. So the Lord inspired her with a
great desire to see me. She thought that through me she might find that
comfort which she could not discover in herself, and she tried in every
way she knew to get me to visit her. Finally she sent to the Provincial,
who was at a very distant place, and he despatched a message to me that
I must go to her at once, under obedience and with a single companion.
I received this message on Christmas night.

It disturbed me a little and grieved me a great deal to learn that she
wanted me to come to her because she thought there was some good
in me. Knowing myself to be so wicked, I could not bear this. I commended myself earnestly to God, and all through Matins, or for a great

1. Doña Luisa de la Cerda, sister of the Duke of Medinaceli. She was then
living in Toledo.
2. Father Pedro Domenech.

part of it, I was in a profound rapture. The Lord told me that I must certainly go, and must listen to no opinions, for few would give me anything but rash advice; that the visit might bring trials, but would be of great service to God and that, so far as the convent was concerned, it would be to the advantage of the project for me to be absent until the Brief arrived, since the devil was preparing a great plot for the moment of the Provincial's coming. He told me to fear nothing, for He would help me in this. I was greatly encouraged and comforted, and when I spoke to the Rector he told me that I must certainly go. But others said that I should not be able to stand the journey, that it was a plot of the devil to bring some evil on me there, and that I ought to remonstrate with the Provincial.

I obeyed the Rector and, because of what I had learnt in prayer, went without fear, though I was considerably abashed when I thought of their reasons for summoning me, and of how seriously they were deceived. I implored the Lord, therefore, with renewed earnestness, never to abandon me, and was greatly comforted by the fact that the Company of Jesus had a house in the city to which I was going, since I felt that I should be fairly safe if I remained under their direction as I was here.

The Lord was pleased that this lady should be so greatly comforted that she at once began to show a noticeable improvement, and every day her calmness increased. This was a most remarkable thing, because, as I have said, her grief had reduced her to a very sad state. Her improvement must have been the Lord's answer to the many prayers for the success of my enterprise which were being offered up by various pious persons of my acquaintance. She had a profound fear of God, and so Christian a spirit that her goodness must have made up for what was deficient in me. What is more, she conceived a great affection for me, as I did for her when I saw how good she was. But almost everything there was a cross to me; the comfort of the house was a real torture, and the great fuss that was made of me filled me with fear. My soul had such misgivings that I dared not be careless; nor was the Lord careless of me. While I was there, He did me great favours; and these left me so free and enabled me so to despise everything I saw – and the more I saw, the more I despised it – that I never treated those ladies, whom it would have been a great honour to serve, otherwise than with the freedom of an equal. I derived great profit from this, and told that lady so. I saw that, being a woman, she was as subject to passions and weaknesses as myself, and learnt how little importance should be attached to rank.

For the higher a lady's station, the greater are her anxieties and trials, and the more careful she must be to behave according to her position, which hardly allows her even to live. She cannot observe the proper time and order of meals, for everything has to conform with her position rather than with her constitution, and what she eats is more often governed by her rank than by her appetite.

So it was that I came to hate the very thought of being a great lady. God deliver me from this wicked, artificial life – though, despite the fact that she was one of the greatest in the land, I do not believe that there were many humbler or simpler women than she. I was sorry for her, and I still am when I think how often she has to go against her own inclinations, in order to live up to her position. Then again, though she had good servants, one can put very little trust in them. One must not confide in one more than in another, for the favourite is always disliked by the rest. This is slavery, and it is one of the world's greatest lies to call such people masters, when, as I see it, they are slaves in a thousand ways. It was the Lord's pleasure that, during the time I was in that house, its inhabitants should render His Majesty better service. I was not free from difficulties all the same, or from the envy of certain persons who resented my lady's great love for me. They probably felt that I was working for some interest of my own, and the Lord must have permitted their jealousies and other such matters as a trial for me, so that I should not be sucked under by the comforts that I was enjoying there. But He was pleased to extricate me from all this, to my soul's great profit.

While I was there, a very important person happened to arrive, a cleric[1] with whom I had been in touch on various occasions over many years; and whilst I was at Mass in a convent of his Order, which was near my lady's house, I was struck with the desire to know the state of his soul, since I wished him to be a great servant of God. So I got up, meaning to go and talk to him. But as I was then recollected in prayer this seemed to me a waste of time. What business was it of mine, I thought, and sat down again. I think that this happened to me three times, but in the end my good angel prevailed over my evil one, and I went to ask for him. He came to speak to me in one of the confessionals. I began to question him about his life, and he also questioned me about mine, for we had not seen one another for many years. I started to tell him that mine had been a life of great spiritual trials. He pressed me

1. Probably Father García de Toledo.

quite hard to tell him what these trials were. I said that they were not suitable for discussion, and that it was my duty not to say anything about them. He replied that as the Dominican father of whom I have spoken knew of them, and they were great friends, he could easily learn about them from him, and so I need not mind speaking.

The truth is that he could not help pressing me any more than I, I think, could help speaking to him. For despite all the grief and shame that I used to feel when I discussed these things with him and with the Rector whom I have mentioned, this time I was not at all distressed, but greatly comforted. I told him everything under the seal of confession. I had always considered him a man of great intelligence but now he seemed to me more clear-sighted than ever. I considered the magnitude of his gifts and talents, and thought how much good he could do with them if he were to give himself wholly to God. I have had this feeling for many years now. I can never meet anyone whom I like very much without immediately wishing to see him wholly given to God, and sometimes these yearnings of mine are so strong that I cannot resist them. Although I want everyone to serve Him, my desire in regard to those I like is particularly strong, and so I importune the Lord frequently on their behalf. This was the case with respect to the cleric I am speaking of.

He asked me to commend him heartily to God – and he had no need to ask me, for I was in a state in which I could not do otherwise – and so I went to my usual place of solitary prayer and, being extremely recollected, began to speak to the Lord in that foolish way that I often do, without knowing what I am saying. For it is love that speaks, and my soul is so transported that I take no account of the distance between it and God. The love that it knows His Majesty to have for it makes it forget itself. It seems to be in Him, and united to Him without division, and so it talks nonsense. I prayed to him with copious tears that this cleric's soul might become truly devoted to His service. For good though I thought him, I was not satisfied and wanted him to be better; and when I had finished I remember saying 'You must not refuse me this favour, Lord. Think what a good man he is for us to have as a friend.'

O how great is God's goodness and kindness, that He does not judge by the words, but by the will and desires with which they are said! How could He bear a person like me to speak to His Majesty so boldly! May He be blessed for ever and ever.

That night, I remember, I was greatly troubled during my hours of prayer by the thought that I was perhaps no longer His friend. I could not be sure whether I was in grace or not – not that I wanted to know. What I wanted was to die, in order to quit a life in which I was not sure whether I was alive or dead. For I could suffer no worse death than to think that I might have offended God, and this painful suspicion oppressed me. But afterwards I felt happy again and, dissolving in tears, begged Him not to let such a thing be. I soon learnt that I had reason to be comforted and to believe that I was in grace, since my love for God was so strong, and since His Majesty was compassionately granting me these favours, which induced feelings in my soul such as He would never give to one who was in mortal sin. I became confident therefore that the Lord would do for this person what I prayed Him to, and He told me to say certain things to him. This greatly embarrassed me, for I did not know how to say them and, as I have said, I always dislike taking messages to third persons, especially when I am not sure how they will be received, or whether the recipient may not laugh at me. I became very distressed, but in the end decided that I must speak to him without fail. I believe that I promised God to do so, but I felt so abashed that I wrote the message down and gave it to him.

Its effect upon him clearly showed that it came from God. He made a firm resolution to give himself to prayer, though he did not carry it out immediately. As the Lord wanted him for Himself, He used me as an instrument for conveying certain truths to him which, though I did not know it, so exactly applied to his case that he was astonished. The Lord must have disposed him to believe that they came from His Majesty; and for my part, miserable creature though I am, I continued to beseech Him to bring that cleric completely over, and to make him hate the pleasures and activities of this life. And so He did – praise be to God for ever! – to such a degree that each time I speak with him I am quite astounded. If I had not seen it for myself, I should have doubted whether God could possibly have granted him such an increase of favour in so short a time, filling him so full of Himself that he seems to be quite dead to the things of the earth. May His Majesty hold him in His hand, for if he progresses at this rate – which I trust in the Lord he may, for he has a very deep self-knowledge – he will be one of God's most distinguished servants, and a great benefactor to many souls. For he has speedily gained a great deal of experience of spiritual things, these being gifts that God bestows when and how He will irrespective either of time or of service. I do not mean that time and service are unimportant, but very often the Lord will grant one person more contemplation in a single year than He will give to another in twenty. His Majesty knows the reasons why. It is wrong for us to suppose that we shall come to understand, merely through the passage of the years, things that cannot possibly be attained without experience. But many, as I have said, make the mistake of supposing that they can come to understand spirituality without themselves being spiritual. I do not mean that a man who is not spiritual but has learning may not direct someone on the spiritual path. But when dealing with inward or outward conduct, his direction must always be a matter of the intellect, and his criterion the path of nature, while as over supernatural matters he must always refer to the Holy Scriptures. For the rest, he must not worry himself to death, or think that he understands what he does not, or quell spirits which are being guided by another Master greater than he, and so are not left without authority.

He must not be astonished at this, or think such things impossible – to the Lord all things are possible – but try to strengthen his faith and humble himself, because the Lord is perhaps giving to some little old woman a deeper knowledge of this science than to himself, learned man though he is. If he possesses this humility, he will be of greater use both to other souls and to himself, than by trying to be a contemplative if he is not one. Therefore I say once more that unless he has experience, or a very great humility, which will make him realize that he does not understand and that a thing is no less possible for that, he will gain little, and the people he deals with will gain even less. But if he is humble, he need not fear that the Lord will allow him or them to fall into error.

Now this Father of whom I am speaking, who has received a large measure of humility from the Lord, has succeeded in finding out through study all that can be discovered about these things in that way. For he is a good scholar, and when he does not know a thing by experience he refers to others who do; and as the Lord helps him also by giving him great faith, he has been of considerable assistance both to himself and to other souls, my own among them. His Majesty had to call to Himself some of my directors.[1] But, knowing of the trials which I had to undergo, He seems to have provided others to take their places; and they have helped me through numerous trials, doing me at the same

1. St Peter of Alcántara and Brother Ibáñez, who died in 1565.

time a great deal of good. The Lord has almost completely transformed this cleric, to such an extent that he can hardly recognize himself, as they say. He had poor health before, but now the Lord has given him the physical strength to do penances, and the courage to undertake good works. He has done other things for him as well. He seems, indeed, to have received a very special vocation from the Lord. May He be blessed for ever.

All these benefits have come to him, I believe, from the favours that the Lord has granted him in prayer, for there is no doubt about them. Already he has been pleased to test him in a number of situations, from all of which he has emerged as one who already knows what true merit is to be won by suffering persecutions. I hope that the Lord, in His greatness, will cause great good to come through him to members of his Order, and to his Order itself. All this is beginning to spread abroad. I have seen great visions, and the Lord has told me some most wonderful things about him, about that Rector of the Company of Jesus, of whom I have spoken, and about two other friars, of the Order of St Dominic;[1] especially about one to whom the Lord has taught, for his profit, certain things that He had previously taught me. But from this Father[2] I have learnt many things too.

One of these things I will mention here. Once when I was with him in the parlour, my soul and spirit became aware of such a mighty love burning in him that I became almost rapt away, as I thought of the greatness of God, who had raised a soul to this state in so short a time. I was greatly abashed to see him listening with such humility to certain things that I was telling him about prayer, for it was not very humble in me to talk like this to such a person. But because of the great desire I felt to make progress, the Lord must have borne with me. It helped me so much to be with him that there seemed to kindle in my soul a new fire of longing to serve the Lord afresh. O my Jesus, how much can a soul do when ablaze with Your love! What a high value we ought to set on it, and how we ought to pray the Lord to leave it with us for this life! Anyone who has this love should follow after such souls if he can.

It is a great thing for one who is sick to find another afflicted with the same malady. It is a great comfort to discover that one is not alone; and two people can help one another greatly both to suffer and to acquire merit. They form an excellent support to one another in their deter-

1. Pedro Ibáñez (soon to die) and Domingo Báñez.
2. Father García de Toledo.

mination to risk a thousand lives for God, and they long for opportunities of sacrificing themselves.

They are like soldiers who want wars in order to win booty and become rich; they know that they can never be rich without fighting. Trials are their profession. What a grand thing it is, when the Lord lets us see it, to know how much we gain through suffering for Him! But we cannot understand this properly till we have given everything up. If a man clings to a single thing, it is a sign that he values it; and if he values it, he will certainly be sorry to give it up; and in that case all is imperfection and loss. Then there is truth in the saying that he who pursues something that is lost is himself lost. What greater perdition, what greater blindness, what greater misfortune can there be than to set a high value on something that is nothing?

To return then to what I was saying. I was highly delighted when I looked on that soul, and I think the Lord wanted me to have a clear view of the treasures He had laid up in it. When I was aware of the favour that He had done me in making me the instrument of this, I realized how little I had deserved it. But I valued the favours which the Lord had bestowed on him even more highly than before, and felt as deeply indebted for them as if they had been given to me. I gave great praise to the Lord when I saw that His Majesty was fulfilling my desires and had heard my prayer that he should rouse persons like this. Then my soul could no longer contain so much joy; it went out of itself, and lost itself for its own greater gain. Its meditation was broken; when I heard that divine language in which the Holy Spirit seemed to be speaking, I fell into a deep rapture, which lasted for a short time only but caused me almost to lose my senses. I saw Christ in all His majesty and glory, and He showed His great delight in all that was taking place. He told me of it too, and wished me clearly to realize that He was always present at such conversations and was greatly pleased when people found their delight in talking of Him.

Another time, when I was far away from this place, I saw him being carried up to the angels in great glory. From this vision I understood that his soul was making great progress; and so it was. For a cruel slander against his honour had been spread by someone to whom he had done a great service, and whose reputation and soul he had saved. He had endured this accusation most cheerfully, and had done other things most serviceable to God, undergoing other persecutions as well. I do not think it right to say anything more about this just now, but your Reverence knows about it all and, if you think fit, it can all be set down later for the glory of the Lord. All the prophecies which I have mentioned concerning this house, and all those concerning it and other matters of which I shall speak later, have been fulfilled, some of them three years after Our Lord revealed them to me, and others after shorter or longer intervals. I always told them to my confessor and to my friend the widow, with whom I was allowed to discuss them, as I have said. She repeated them, as I have learnt, to other persons, who will know that I am not lying. May God never permit me to speak anything but the whole truth on any subject, especially on one as serious as this.

Once when I was very grieved at the sudden death of one of my brothers-in-law,[1] who had omitted to make a final confession, I was told that my sister would die in the same way, and that I must go to her and make her prepare for death. I told my confessor about this, but he would not let me go. Then I was told the same thing several times more and, when I informed him of this, he gave me permission, since no harm could come of it. She lived in a village, and I went there without saying why, but enlightened her as much as I could on all matters. I got her to make very frequent confessions, and always to think of her soul's profit. She was a very good woman, and did what I said. Some four or five years after she had begun this practice, and had come to keep a strict watch on her conscience, she died with nobody near her and no opportunity of making a confession. It was a good thing that, following her new custom, she had made a confession only a week before; it made me very happy to know that when I heard of her death.

She was only a short time in purgatory. I do not think that it can have been as much as a week later that the Lord appeared to me, just as I had finished taking Communion, and was pleased to let me see her as He raised her to glory. During all those years, between His first speaking to me and my sister's death, neither my companion nor I forgot this prophecy; and when she died, my companion[2] came to me, astonished at the way in which it had been fulfilled. God be praised for ever, who takes such care of souls that they may not be lost!

1. Don Martín de Guzmán y Barrientos, husband of the saint's half-sister María.
2. Dona Guiomar de Ulloa.

CHAPTER 35

She continues the story of the foundation of this house of our glorious father, St Joseph, and of the way in which the Lord ordained that holy poverty should be observed there. She gives her reasons for leaving the lady with whom she was living, and describes several other things that happened to her

WHILE I was with this lady of whom I have spoken, and with whom I stayed for more than six months, the Lord ordained that a blessed woman of our Order,[1] who lived more than two hundred miles away, should hear of me and, happening to travel in that direction, turn some miles out of her way to have a talk with me. The Lord had moved her, in the same month and year as He had moved me, to found another convent of this Order; and when He gave her this desire she had sold all that she had and walked barefoot to Rome to get a patent. She is a woman much given to penance and prayer, to whom the Lord has granted many favours.

Our Lady had appeared to her and commanded her to perform this task, and she had done so much more than I in the service of the Lord that I was ashamed to come into her presence. She showed me the patents that she had brought from Rome, and in the fortnight that we were together we laid our plans for the foundation of these convents. Before I spoke to her, I had never known that before our Rule had been relaxed it had required us to have no possessions. So far it had never occurred to me to found a convent without revenue, my idea being that we ought to have no anxieties about our bare necessities. I had not thought of all the anxieties that arise from the possession of property. This blessed woman was unable to read, yet she knew very well by the Lord's instruction, things that I was ignorant of, although I had read through the Constitutions very often. When she told me this, I thought it quite right. But I was afraid that no one would agree with me, that everyone would call this foolishness, and that I should be told not to do a thing which would cause suffering to others. If I had been the only person involved, nothing on earth would have held me back. On the contrary, it would have been a real joy to me to think that I was follow-

1. Sister María de Jesús, who founded the convent of Discalced Carmelites at Alcalá de Henares.

ing the advice of Christ, Our Lord, for His Majesty had already given me great desires for poverty. For myself I had never doubted that poverty was best, and for days I had been wishing that it were possible for one in my position to go about begging alms for the love of God, and to have no house or other possessions. But I was afraid that if the Lord had not given the same desires to the other sisters they would live in a state of discontent, also that our poverty might be the cause of distractions. I had seen some poor convents which were not places of great recollection, and it had seemed to me that their distracted state arose from their poverty, rather than their poverty from their distracted state. Distraction does not make for riches, nor does God ever fail those who serve Him. In fact my faith was weak, which was not the case with that other servant of God.

I took the opinions of a great many people, but found almost none who agreed with me; certainly not my confessor or the other learned men whom I consulted. They advanced so many arguments against me that I did not know what to do. But now that I knew poverty to be in the Rule, and that it was the most perfect way, I could not persuade myself to accept a revenue. Sometimes, indeed, they convinced me, but when I returned to prayer and saw Christ so poor and naked on His Cross, I could not bear to be rich, and begged Him with tears so to dispose things that I should be as poor as He.

I found the possession of a revenue to be attended by so many inconveniences, and to be the cause of so much disquiet, and even distraction, that I could not stop disputing with the scholars. I sent my arguments in writing to that Dominican friar[1] who was helping us, and he answered me with two sheets of refutation and theology, in which he told me that he had considered the matter carefully and urged me against it. I replied that I had no wish to resort to theology and could feel no gratitude for his learning in this matter if it meant that I was not to follow my vocation, or fulfil the vow of poverty that I had made, or observe Christ's precepts with due perfection. If I found anyone to help me, I was delighted. The lady with whom I was staying was of great assistance to me here. Some people began by telling me that they approved of my plan, but afterwards, when they looked into it further, they found so many drawbacks that they strongly urged me once more to give it up. I told them that, in view of the speed with which they changed their opinions, I preferred to stick to mine.

1. Brother Ibáñez.

It was at this time that, through my entreaties – for my hostess had never seen him – the blessed friar Peter of Alcántara came, at the Lord's pleasure, to visit her house. As a great lover of poverty who had practised it for very many years, he knew what riches there are in it, and so he was a great help to me. He commanded me on no account to abandon my plan. Once I had his opinion and backing, I decided to go no further in search of advice, which no one was better fitted to give than he, since he possessed knowledge based on long experience.

One day, when I was earnestly commending my project to God, the Lord told me to let nothing dissuade me from my purpose of founding the convent in poverty, for that was His Father's will and His own, and He would help me. I was in a profound rapture at the time, the effects of which were so great that I could not doubt its divine origin. On another occasion He told me that money led to confusion and said other things in praise of poverty. He assured me that anyone who served Him would not go short of the necessities of life. But this was a danger that, as I have said, I never feared. The Lord also changed the heart of the licentiate[1] – I mean of the Dominican friar – who, as I have said, had written counselling me to make no foundation without the necessary money. I was delighted to hear this, and with the opinions in my favour. Once I had decided to live on the love of God, it seemed to me that I possessed all the riches in the world.

About this time my Provincial[2] revoked his order, and released me from the obedience which had compelled me to stay in that place. He now left it to me to do as I liked. I could depart if I wished, and if I wished to stay I could do so for a certain time. But during that time elections would be held in my convent, and I was warned that many of the sisters wanted to confer on me the onerous office of Superior. The mere thought of this was such a torment to me that, though I was re-solved cheerfully to undergo any martyrdom for God's sake, I could not possibly persuade myself to accept this. For apart from such reasons as the heavy labour involved, owing to the large number of nuns, I had always disliked such work and had never wanted any office – indeed I had always refused such posts as were offered me – since I thought that it would put my conscience in great danger. So I praised God that I was not there, and wrote to my friends asking them not to vote for me.

Just as I was feeling delighted at not being mixed up in this turmoil, the Lord told me that I must on no account fail to go. If I wanted a

1. Brother Ibáñez.   2. Father Angel de Salazar.

cross, He said, here was a good one ready for me, which I must not reject. On the contrary, I must take courage, for He would help me, and so I must depart. I was very much upset and did nothing but weep, for I thought that my cross was to be the office of Superior and, as I have said, I could not convince myself that it would be of the least good to my soul, or see any way in which it might be. I talked to my confessor, and he told me to prepare for my immediate departure, since this was clearly the way of greatest perfection. But he added that it would be enough if I arrived there in time for the election and that, as the weather was very hot, I might stay for a few more days longer, so as not to fall ill on the road. But the Lord had disposed otherwise, and I had to leave forthwith. For I was afflicted with a great inner disquiet, and was unable to pray. I felt that I was failing the Lord's command, and that I was too easy and comfortable where I was to be willing to go and offer myself for the work. I feared that I was giving God only lip-service. How could I neglect a chance like this to lead a life of greater perfection? If I had to die, so be it. With these thoughts an oppression fell on my soul, and the Lord robbed me of all my pleasure in prayer. In fact I was in such a torment that I begged my hostess kindly to let me go, which was what my confessor advised me to do when he saw me in this state. For God moved him as He did me.

She was very sorry that I should go, and this was a further trial. For it had cost her considerable trouble and all kinds of importunities to win the Provincial's consent to my coming. Considering her feelings, I thought it a very great thing that she should agree to my departure. But she was a most God-fearing woman; and as I told her that my going might be a great service to God, and gave her other reasons of this kind, and as I also held out the hope that I might possibly come back and visit her again, she consented to my departure, though with great sorrow.

For myself, I was no longer sorry to go. I realized that this was the more perfect course, and would be the more serviceable to God; and so, as it always pleases me to please Him, I bore the pain of leaving my hostess, though I saw that she was suffering, and of leaving others to whom I was greatly indebted, my confessor in particular, a priest of the Society of Jesus with whom I was on very good terms. But the greater the comforts I gave up for the Lord's sake, the gladder I was to forego them. I could not understand how this was possible, for it was quite clear to me that I was moved by two contrary feelings; I was rejoicing, that is to say, and finding joy and comfort in something that was oppressing my soul. But I was calmed and consoled, and had opportunities for many hours of solitary prayer. I saw that I was about to plunge into a fire, for the Lord had told me this already when He said that I was to bear a heavy cross. But I never thought that it would be as heavy as it proved. Yet, despite everything, I set out gladly, only distressed that, since the Lord wished me to take part in the battle, He was not plunging me straight in. Thus His Majesty was sending me strength and founding it on my weakness.[1]

As I said, I could not understand how this was possible, but I thought of the following comparison. If I possess a jewel or something else that affords me great pleasure, and I happen to learn that it is desired by someone whom I love better than myself and whose pleasure I prefer to my own contentment, then I shall gain greater happiness by pleasing that person than ever I had in the possession of my jewel. Moreover, as my pleasure in pleasing that person will transcend my joy of possession, so my regret at not having this jewel, or some other object that I like, and at losing my original pleasure, will disappear. In the same way, although I wanted to be sorry when I found myself saying goodbye to people who were so sorry to see me go, and although I have a very grateful nature which would have been enough to upset me very much under other circumstances, on this occasion I could feel no sorrow at all, much though I wished to.

Another day's delay would have had such important effects on the affairs of this blessed house that I do not know how they would have been settled if I had stayed any longer. O how great God is! I am often astounded when I reflect on this, and think how particularly anxious His Majesty was to help me deal with the business of this little corner of God's kingdom – for such I think it is – or of this dwelling in which His Majesty takes His delight, as He once told me in prayer, when He spoke of this house as the paradise of His delight. So it seems that His Majesty has chosen the souls he has drawn to Himself, in whose company I live in very deep shame. For I could never have asked for better companions with whom to live this life of strict enclosure, poverty, and prayer. They live it so joyfully and contentedly that not one of them thinks herself deserving of her place in this house; and this is especially true of some whom the Lord has called from all the show and vanity of the world, whose customs they might have followed and in which they

1. A reference to 2 Corinthians xii, 9.

might have been happy. But here the Lord has so multiplied their happiness that, as they clearly recognize, in exchange for one thing forsaken He has rewarded them a hundredfold, and they can never give His Majesty enough thanks. Others who were good, He has made better. To those who are young He gives fortitude and knowledge, so that they may desire nothing else and understand that to live apart from all the things of this life is to live in greater peace, even here upon earth. To those who are older and poor in health, He has given – and continues to give – strength to endure the same austerities and penances as the rest.

O my Lord, how abundantly You display Your power! There is no need to seek reasons for Your will, for You transcend all natural reason and make all things possible. Thus You show us that we need do no more than truly love You, and truly forsake everything for You, and that You, my Lord, will then make everything easy. Here the saying is apposite that You pretend to make Your law difficult,[1] for I do not see and I cannot understand how the way that leads to You can be narrow. It is no path but a royal road, and when anyone seriously sets out along it he travels in safety. Mountain passes and rocks that might fall on him – by which I mean occasions for sin – are far away. What I call a path – a wretched path and a very narrow road – is one that has a deep gorge into which one may fall on one side, and a precipice on the other. A single careless step, and one falls and is dashed to pieces. Anyone who loves You truly, O my Lord, walks in safety along the broad, royal road, far away from the precipice. If he makes the slightest stumble, You put Your hand upon Him. One fall – indeed many falls – will not be enough to destroy him. If he loves You and not the things of this world, he will be walking along the valley of humility. I cannot understand what makes people afraid of setting out on the way of perfection. May the Lord, of His mercy, make us see how unsafe we are among the manifest perils that beset us when we walk with the crowd, and that our true safety lies in trying to press far ahead on God's road. We must fix our eyes on Him, and have no fear that this Sun of Justice will set, or that He will allow us to travel by night and lose ourselves, unless we first forsake Him.

People are not afraid of going among lions, each one of which seems eager to tear them to pieces – I mean among honours and delights and suchlike pleasures, as the world calls them. The devil seems to be

1. A reference to Psalm xliv 20, which reads to this effect in the Vulgate version.

frightening us with bogeys here. This has astounded me a thousand times, and ten thousand times I long to weep till I have no more tears, and to cry aloud to everyone, telling them of my great blindness and wickedness, in the hope that this may do something to open their eyes. May He open them, as in His goodness He can, and may He never allow mine to become blind again. Amen.

CHAPTER 36

*She continues with the previous subject, and describes how the founda-
tion of this convent of the glorious St Joseph was concluded. She speaks
of the great opposition and many persecutions which the nuns had to
endure after taking the habit, of the great trials and temptations
which she herself underwent, and of how the Lord delivered her
victoriously from them all, to His own praise and glory*

AFTER leaving that city, I made a very happy journey, resolved to
suffer most willingly all that the Lord might be pleased to send
me. On the very night of my arrival in these parts, our patent for the
convent was delivered together with the Brief from Rome. I was
astonished, and so were those who knew how the Lord had hastened
my coming and now saw how very necessary it had been; in fact the
Lord had brought me back at the vital moment. For I found here the
Bishop and that saintly friar, Peter of Alcántara, and another gentleman,[1] a great servant of God, in whose house that good man was staying, and who habitually gave hospitality to God's servants.

Together they succeeded in persuading the Bishop to sanction the
foundation. This was far from easy, because it was to be founded in
poverty, but he was such a friend to all whom he saw thus determined
to serve God that he at once felt impelled to help us. All our success was
due to the backing of this saintly old man, and to his persuasion of one
after another to come to our aid. If, as I have said, I had not arrived at
this juncture, I do not see how all this could have been done, for that
saintly man was only here a few days – I think no longer than a week.
He was extremely ill all the time, and very shortly afterwards the Lord
took him to Himself. Indeed, His Majesty seems purposely to have preserved him until this business was over, for he had been a very sick man
for some time – I think for more than two years.

It was all done in great secrecy; otherwise I do not think anything
could have been managed at all, for the people were against it, as afterwards appeared. The Lord ordained that one of my brothers-in-law[2]
should fall ill while his wife was away, and that his state should be so
serious that I was given leave to remain with him. This prevented anything from leaking out, though a few people must have suspected

1. Probably Don Juan Blásquez.   2. Don Juan de Ovalle.

something, without, however, trusting their suspicions. The remarkable thing is that my brother-in-law's illness only lasted so long as was useful for the negotiations. When it was necessary for him to be better, so that I might be free again and he might leave the house empty, the Lord, to his great wonderment, restored him to health.

I had a great deal of trouble in persuading one person and another to sanction the foundation. Then there was the sick man, and the workmen – for the house had to be converted very quickly for its use as a convent, and there was still a great deal to be done. My friend was not there, for it seemed to us that, for the better preservation of our secret, she ought to remain away. I saw that for many reasons everything depended on speed; and one of them was that I was in hourly fear of being sent back to my convent. I was subjected to so many trials that I wondered if these were not my cross, though it seemed a light one to me in comparison with the heavy one which I had understood from God I must bear.

When everything had been arranged, the Lord was pleased that some of the sisters should take the habit on St Bartholomew's Day, and on that day too the Most Holy Sacrament was brought to the convent. So with full sanction and authority, this convent of our most glorious father St Joseph was founded in the year 1562. I was there myself to give the habit, with two other nuns of our own house who happened to be absent from it. As the house which thus became a convent belonged to my brother-in-law – for as I have said, it was he who purchased it in order to keep things secret – my special permission allowed me to be there. I did nothing without the approval of some learned men, so as in no way to infringe my obedience. But as they saw what a benefit this was in so many ways to the whole Order, they told me to follow my wishes, even though everything was being done in secret and was being kept from my superiors' knowledge. Had they pointed to a single imperfection in all this, I would, I believe, have willingly given up a thousand convents, let alone one. I am certain of this; for although I desired the foundation to be made in order to withdraw more completely from activities and to fulfil my profession and vocation more perfectly under conditions of greater enclosure, I desired it only in so far as I believed the Lord would not be better served by my abandoning it. If I had thought that He would, I should have given it up with complete peace and tranquillity, as I had done before.

Well, it was like heaven to me to see the Blessed Sacrament in its place, and for us to be supporting four poor orphans, who were taken without dowry and were great servants of God. It was our aim from the beginning to accept only persons whose examples would be a basis on which we could effectively develop our scheme for a community of great perfection and true prayer, and perform a work which I believed would be for God's service, and would honour the habit of His glorious Mother. This is what I yearned for. But I was greatly comforted also, to have done what the Lord had so firmly commanded me, and that there was now one more church in the town than there had been, dedicated to my glorious father, St Joseph. It was not that I thought I had done any part of all this myself. I never thought that, and do not think so now. I have always known that it was done by the Lord. My share in the business was so full of imperfections that I clearly deserved more blame than thanks. But it was a great joy to me to see how the Lord had made me, wicked though I was, his instrument in this grand design. I was so happy, therefore, that I was quite carried away with the strength of my prayer.

When it was all finished – it must have been some three or four hours later – the devil plunged me into a spiritual battle once more, as I shall now relate. He suggested to me that what I had done might have been wrong, and that I might have been violating my obedience by bringing it all about without a mandate from the Provincial. It certainly occurred to me that he would be somewhat displeased at my having placed the convent under the Ordinary's jurisdiction, without previously informing him of my intention; though, on the other hand, as he had refused me his sanction and I had not changed my plans, I had imagined that he would not care a great deal. The devil also asked me whether the sisters would be happy, living under so strict a rule, whether they might not go short of food, indeed whether the whole venture was not ridiculous – for who had made it my business, seeing that I was in a convent already? All that the Lord had commanded me, all the opinions I had been seeking and the prayers I had been making almost unceasingly for over two years – all these things were as completely blotted from my memory as if they had never been. All I remembered now was my own opinion; faith and all the virtues were suspended within me, and I had not the strength to put any of them to use or to defend myself from all these blows.

The devil also made me ask myself how I could think of shutting myself up in so strict a house, subject as I was to frequent illnesses, and how

I should endure so many penances. He asked me why I had left that large and pleasant house, where I had always been so happy and had so many friends, and suggested that I might not like the nuns in the new house. He then suggested that I had taken on a big task, and might perhaps find my hopes deceived, indeed that it might have been the devil himself who had put it into my head in order to rob me of my peace and quiet. Then, once I was disturbed, I should lose all power of prayer and should forfeit my soul. He suggested thoughts of this kind to me all together, and it was beyond my powers to think of anything else. At the same time my soul was plunged into such affliction, darkness and gloom that I can find no words to describe it. When I found myself in this state, even though I could not commend myself to God, I went to visit the most Holy Sacrament. I was in such anguish that I think it was like the agony of death. I did not dare to speak of it to anyone, for as yet no confessor had been appointed. O God help me, what a miserable life this is! No happiness is secure, all things are subject to change. Only such a short time ago I had thought that I would not exchange my happiness with anyone on earth, and now its very cause was so tormenting me that I did not know what to do with myself. If only we were to think carefully over the events of our lives, we should all learn by experience how little happiness or unhappiness we really derive from it. This was certainly one of the worst periods I have ever known; my soul seems to have had a premonition of all the sufferings that were in store for me; yet, bad though these were, a prolongation of the state that I was then in would have been worse. But the Lord did not allow His poor servant to suffer long; in none of my tribulations has He ever failed to come to my aid. He did so in this one, by casting me a ray of light which showed me that this was the devil's work. Then I recognized the truth and knew that it was all an attempt to scare me with lies. Then I began to remember my grand resolutions to serve the Lord and my desires to suffer for Him. I realized that if I meant to carry them out I must not go about looking for repose, that to withstand trials was the way to win merit, and that unhappiness endured in God's service would serve me for purgatory. I asked myself what I was afraid of. I had demanded trials, and now I had them; and the greater the opposition the greater the gain. Why did I lack courage then to serve Him to whom I owed so much? Having gained control over myself with the help of these and other reflections, I vowed before the Most Holy Sacrament that I would do everything in my power to obtain permission to enter the new house and that, if I could do so with a good conscience, I would make a vow of enclosure.

The moment I had made this vow, the devil fled, leaving me quiet and happy; and so I remained, as I have done ever since. I find all the rules of enclosure, penance, and the rest that we observe in this house extremely sweet and easy. Indeed, I am so very happy that I sometimes wonder whether I could possibly have chosen any place on earth more delightful. I do not know whether this may not have played some part in the improvement of my health, which has been better here than ever before; perhaps, since it is right and necessary that I should do all that the others do, the Lord has been pleased to make this possible for me as a consolation that costs me some effort. But all those who know of my infirmities are astonished that I can keep the Rule. Blessed be He who gives everything, and by whose power this can be done.

This conflict left me quite exhausted, but I laughed at the devil, for I clearly saw that it was his doing. Since I have never known what it is to be discontented with the religious life even for one moment in the twenty-eight years and more that I have been a nun, I believe that the Lord permitted this trial in order to show me what a great favour He had done me in this, and from what tortures He had delivered me, also in order that if ever I were to see anyone in this state, I should be sorry for her and know how to console her. After dinner, when this turmoil was over, I tried to get a little rest. I had scarcely had any peace all night, and for several nights previously I had been continuously worried and disturbed, so that I had been tired every day. When what we had done became known in the convent and about the town, there was, for the reasons I have already given, a considerable commotion – not, as I thought, without some cause. Then the Superior sent for me to appear before her immediately; and when I received her order, I went at once, leaving my nuns in a great upset. I knew well enough that there was plenty of trouble awaiting me, but as the thing was done now I did not care much about that. I offered up a prayer, imploring the Lord to help me, and begged my father, St Joseph, to bring me back to his house. I offered what I should have to suffer to God, very happy that I had some suffering to offer Him and some way in which to serve Him. I went in the belief that they would immediately put me in the prison cell; which would, I think, have been a great joy to me, since I should have had nobody to speak to and should have been able to rest for a while alone.

For I needed some solitude very badly and all this dealing with people had quite worn me out.

When I arrived and gave the Superior my account of the affair, she was a little mollified, and they all sent for the Provincial,[1] to put the case before him. When he came, I went to receive the judgement, very happy to find myself suffering for the Lord. I did not believe that I had offended in any way either against His Majesty or against the Order. On the contrary, I had been trying with all my might to strengthen the Order, and would gladly have given my life for that cause. All my desire was that its Rule should be observed with all perfection. But I remembered Christ's trial, and realized the triviality of my own. I acknowledged my fault as if I had been very much to blame, and I must have appeared guilty to anyone who did not know all my reasons. The Provincial gave me a severe rebuke, but he was not so sharp as my crime deserved according to the report of it that many people had given him. I did not care to excuse myself; I had already resolved not to do so. I merely begged him to forgive me and punish me, but to be angry with me no longer. I saw quite well that in some respects they were condemning me unjustly. For they told me that I had done everything in order to be well thought of, and to make a name for myself, and so on. But I was well aware that in other respects they were in the right when they said that I was wickeder than the other nuns, and when they asked me how, having failed to observe the many rules that were kept in my own house, I could consider keeping a stricter discipline in another. They said that I was scandalizing the people, and introducing new ideas. None of this disturbed or troubled me in any way, though I made a show of feeling it for fear that I might appear to be taking what they said to me lightly. Finally I was commanded to put my version of the case before the nuns, and I had to do so.

As I was inwardly quiet and the Lord helped me, I put up such a defence that neither the Provincial nor the nuns who were present saw any reason to condemn me. Afterwards, when I was alone with him, I explained things to him more plainly, and he was quite satisfied. He promised me that, if my foundation succeeded, he would give me permission to move, once the town was quiet. For there had been a great commotion in the place, as I shall now relate.

Two or three days before there had been a meeting between the Mayor and some of the Councillors and the Chapter, and they had all

1. Father Ángel de Salazar.

agreed that the new convent must on no account be sanctioned. They decided that it would do notable harm to the community, that the Most Holy Sacrament must be removed from it and that things must on no account go any further. They called together representatives of the Orders – two learned men from each – to give their opinions. Some said nothing, others condemned the foundation, and finally they decided that it must be broken up immediately. One alone, a Prior of the Order of St Dominic,[1] was not opposed to the convent, though he objected to its poverty. He said that there was no reason for a dissolution, that the question should be carefully examined, that there was plenty of time for that, that it was the Bishop's business, and other things of this kind. This did a great deal of good; for, to judge by their fury, we were lucky that they did not dissolve us out of hand. But the fact was that the convent was destined to be; its foundation was the Lord's will and, all together, they could do very little against that. They stated their arguments and showed great zeal; and so, without committing any offence against God, they made me suffer – and all those who favoured our project as well. There were many of them now, and they all sustained a good deal of persecution.

The town was in such a turmoil that people were talking of nothing else. Everyone condemned me, and went to see the Provincial, and visited my convent. I felt no more distressed by all that they said about me than if they had said nothing at all, but I was afraid that the dissolution might take place. This fear did distress me, and so did the fact that the people who were helping me were losing credit and suffering great trials. I think that what they said about me made me rather glad. If I had had a little faith, I should not have wavered at all, but the slightest failing in a single virtue is enough to benumb all the rest. I was very much troubled during those two days when they were holding the meetings I have spoken of in the town, and once when I was quite exhausted the Lord asked me, 'Do you not know that I am powerful? What are you afraid of?' and He assured me that the foundation would not be dissolved. I was greatly comforted by this. The information taken was sent to the Royal Council, and an order came back for a full account of the whole matter.

Here we were at the beginning of a grand lawsuit. The city sent representatives to the Capital, and the convent would have to do so as well. But there was no money, and I did not know what to do.

1. Father Domingo Báñez.

However, the Lord provided, and my Father Provincial never ordered me to withdraw. He was such a lover of every good cause that, though he did not help us, he would not stand in our way. But he did not give me permission to move here until he saw what the outcome was going to be. So these servants of God were left on their own. But they did more with their prayers than I with all my negotiations, though the affair demanded my utmost diligence. Sometimes everything seemed to be going wrong; particularly on a certain day before the arrival of the Provincial, when the Prioress ordered me to give the whole project up and to have nothing more to do with it. I turned to God and said: 'Lord, this house is not mine; it was made for You. Now there is no one to manage its business, so Your Majesty must do it.' After this I was as calm and untroubled as if I had the whole world conducting my negotiations for me. From that moment I felt quite sure of the outcome.

A priest, who was a very great servant of God and a lover of all perfection,[1] and who had always helped me, went to the Capital to undertake the negotiations and worked very hard for us. That saintly gentleman whom I have already spoken of did a great deal in the matter also, and helped us in every way. This cost him great trials and persecutions. But he always behaved like a father to me, as he does still. The Lord implanted such fervour in our helpers that each one of them regarded the cause as if it were his own and as if his own life and honour were at stake, though it really had nothing to do with them except in so far as they believed it to be of service to God. It seemed clear that His Majesty was assisting that priest whom I have mentioned before,[2] and who was another of my principal helpers. It was he whom the Bishop sent as his representative to one of the great meetings that were called. Here he stood alone against all the rest, and eventually mollified them by suggesting certain measures which could have formed the basis of an agreement. But this was not enough to bring them round immediately; they had staked their all, as they say, on breaking us up. It was this servant of God who had given us the habit and reserved the Most Holy Sacrament for us, and he was sorely persecuted for it. This attack upon us lasted for almost six months, and to relate in detail all the heavy trials we endured would be a long business.

I was astonished at all the trouble the devil was taking about a few poor women, and at the universal belief that a mere dozen sisters and a Prioress – for I must remind those who opposed us that this was to be

1. Gonzalo de Aranda.   2. Master Gaspar Daza.

our number – would do such harm to the town whilst living so strictly. If there had been anything wrong or mistaken about the plan, it would have affected them alone. There was no possible way in which the town could be damaged, and yet our opponents saw all sorts of dangers in it, and so fought us with a good conscience. Eventually they said that they would allow the scheme to go forward if we would accept an endowment. By now I was worn out, less by my own trials than by all those that I saw our helpers to be enduring. It did not seem to me a bad idea, therefore, to accept some money until things calmed down, and to give it up afterwards. At other times I would wonder, wicked and imperfect woman that I am, whether it was not the Lord's wish that we should have an endowment, seeing that we could not go ahead without one. So in the end I agreed to this arrangement.

The discussion of the terms had already begun, and a settlement was to be made next day, when the Lord told me during my night prayers that I must agree to no such thing. He said, amongst other things, that once we had an endowment we should never be allowed to give it up. On the same night that blessed friar Peter of Alcántara, who was now dead, appeared to me. Knowing what great resistance and persecution we were encountering, he had written to me before his death to say how pleased he was that the foundation was being heavily opposed, since all these efforts that the devil was making to prevent the foundation were a sign that great service would be rendered to the Lord in the new convent. He had added that I must on no account accept any revenue, and had stressed this two or three times in the course of his letter, assuring me that if I insisted on this point, everything would turn out as I wished. I had seen him twice already since his death in a state of great glory, and so I was not afraid. Indeed his appearance made me very happy, for he always came in his glorified body, full of great bliss, and it made me most blissful to see him. I remember that the first time I saw him he told me, amongst other things, of the greatness of his joy, and said how fortunate it had been that he had performed the penances he had, since they had won him so great a reward.

As I think I have already said something about this, I will only observe here that this time he spoke to me with some severity, saying that I must on no account accept an endowment, and asking why I would not take his advice. Then he immediately disappeared, leaving me astounded. Next day I told that gentleman what had happened, for I used always to resort to him as the person who had helped us most. I instructed him on no account to agree to the endowment, but to let the suit continue. He had been much stronger on this point than I, and was highly delighted; he afterwards told me how reluctantly he had agreed to the compromise.

Then another person came forward, a great and most zealous servant of God, who suggested that, the issue now being clear, it should be referred to some learned men. This caused a good deal of uneasiness. Some of my helpers agreed to the idea, but this new tangle in which the devil had involved us was the most difficult of all to unravel. The Lord helped me throughout, but it is impossible in this short narrative to describe all that happened between the beginning of the foundation and its completion. The last half-year and the first were the most difficult.

When the city was somewhat calm, the Dominican prior who was helping us[1] acted very skilfully on our behalf. He had not been here before, but the Lord brought him at a most opportune time for us, and His Majesty seems to have done so for this purpose alone, since, as he told me afterwards, he had had no reason for coming and had only by chance heard of our plight. He stayed here as long as was necessary, and when he left he somehow managed – impossible though it may seem that he could have done so in so short a time – to get our Father Provincial to give me leave to come to this house. I was permitted to bring some other nuns with me also, so that we might recite the Office and instruct the sisters who were already there. The day of our coming was a most joyful day for me. While I was praying in the church before entering the convent, I fell into an almost complete rapture and saw Christ, who seemed to receive me with great love, place a crown on my head, and thank me for what I had done for His mother. On another occasion, after Compline, when we were all praying in the choir, I saw Our Lady in the greatest glory, clothed in a white robe, beneath which she seemed to be sheltering us all. I saw this as a sign of the high degree of glory to which the Lord would raise the nuns of this house.

Once we began to recite the Office in our convent, the people began to be very devoted to the place. More nuns were received, and the Lord began to move those who had persecuted us most to show us great favour and give us alms. In this way they marked their approval of what they had hitherto condemned so strongly, and gradually they let the lawsuit lapse, saying that now they realized this was a work of God,

1. Brother Ibáñez, whom Teresa had hitherto known only by correspondence.

since His Majesty had been pleased to make it prosper in the teeth of so much opposition. Now there is no one who thinks it would have been right to abandon the scheme, and so they make a great point of providing us with alms. We make no appeals and ask nobody for anything, but the Lord inspires them to send us money. So we get along very well, and do not lack for necessities; and I trust in the Lord that we never shall. As the sisters are few I am sure His Majesty will never fail them so long as they do their duty, as at present He is giving them the grace to do. I am sure they will never need to be a burden or a bother to anyone, for His Majesty will continue to take care of them as He does at present. It is the greatest joy to me to find myself among such detached souls.

Their occupation is to learn how to advance in God's service. Solitude is their delight and they dislike the mere thought of seeing anyone, even a close relative, unless the meeting will help to kindle their love of the Bridegroom. So no one comes to this house except for that purpose, and it would be no pleasure to themselves or to the sisters if they did. Their sole conversation is of God, and they understand no one who speaks of anything else, nor do those others understand them. We observe the Rule of Our Lady of Carmel, and it is kept without any relaxation, in the form drawn up by Friar Hugo, Cardinal of Santa Sabina, and published in 1248, the fifth year of the reign of Pope Innocent IV.

All the trials that we have suffered will, I believe, have been to good purpose. True, the Rule is rather strict; meat is never eaten except in cases of necessity, there is an eight months' fast, and there are other ascetic practices, as can be seen from the primitive Rule. Yet this comes very easily to the sisters, and we follow certain other practices in addition, which we have thought it necessary to make for the more perfect observance of our Rule. I trust in the Lord that what we have begun will prosper, as He told me it will.

The Lord also showed favour to that other house which was established by the holy woman of whom I have spoken.[1] It was founded in Alcalá, where it had no lack of heavy opposition, nor did it escape severe trials. I know that all religious observances are kept there, in accordance with this primitive rule of ours. God grant that all may be to His own glory and praise, and to that of the glorious Virgin whose habit we wear. Amen.

I think that your Reverence will be weary of this long history of our

1. María de Jesús.

convent, though when you think of the many trials and marvels that I have described, it may well seem short. For the Lord has been at work here, as many witnesses will be able to testify. So I beg you, sir, even if you think fit to tear up all the rest of these writings, at least to preserve this part which concerns our convent. Then, after my death, it should be given to the sisters here, for it will be a great encouragement to our successors. It will stimulate them in the service of God, and prevent this work that we have begun from falling into decay. In fact when they see what importance His Majesty must have attached to its foundation, since He was willing to use such a poor and wicked creature as myself as His instrument, it will go steadily forward. The particular favour which the Lord has graciously shown to our house convinces me that any attempt to relax the perfect Rule that He has initiated here will not only be a great wrong but will be severely punished by God. For He has countenanced its introduction and it works smoothly. In fact it is quite plain that it is not only tolerable but pleasant to carry out, and most suitable for perpetual observance by those who wish to enjoy the company of their Bridegroom, Christ, in solitude. For this must always be the sole aim of our nuns: to be alone with Him. They will never be more than thirteen, for after collecting many opinions I have come to the conclusion that this is the best number. Moreover I have learnt by experience that if we are to preserve our present spirituality, live on alms, and make no appeals, we can admit no more. May they always believe one who with great labour, and with the help of many people's prayers, contrived to arrange things for the best. That this is the best arrangement is proved by our great joy and gladness and the rareness of our trials during the years that we have been in this house, also by our health, which is much better than before. If any nun thinks our Rule harsh, she should blame her own lack of spirituality and not our observance. It can be borne with ease by people who are not at all strong but really delicate, so long as they have the necessary spirituality. Those who have not should go to some other convent, where they will find salvation according to their own spiritual natures.

CHAPTER 37

She describes the effects that remained with her after the Lord had
granted her a favour, and gives much sound teaching as well. She
speaks of the efforts that we must make to attain one more degree of
glory, and of the high value we must set on it, allowing no trial to
deprive us of a blessing that is eternal

IT is painful to me to say more than I have said already about the graces
which the Lord has granted me. Even these are so many that people
will find it hard to believe they have been granted to anyone as wicked
as I. But in obedience to the Lord, who has commanded me to do so,
and also to your Reverences, I will describe some more events, to His
greater glory. May it please the Lord that it shall benefit some soul to
see that His Majesty has been gracious to such a miserable creature as
myself. How much more will He do for one who has served Him truly!
Let everyone strive to please His Majesty, since he gives such pledges
as these even in this life.

The first thing to understand is that in these graces which God
grants to the soul, there are greater and lesser degrees of glory. For the
glory, joy, and comfort conveyed by some visions so exceeds that of
others that I am astonished at the diversities of bliss, even in this life.
The joys and consolations granted by God in a vision or a rapture can be
so various in scale that it seems impossible to desire anything in this life
higher than the highest of them. Indeed the soul does not desire, and
would never ask for, any greater happiness. Nevertheless, now that the
Lord has informed me that there is a difference in heaven between the
joys experienced by one and by another, and of the extent of it, I
clearly see that here too, when it is the Lord's pleasure, there is no
measure in His giving. I wish that the same were true of my service to
His Majesty, and that I devoted my whole life and strength and health
to it; I would not wish by a single fault to lose one grain of my reward. I
can say then that if I were asked whether I should prefer to endure all
the trials in the world until the world itself ends and gain a little more
glory afterwards, or to have no trials but one degree less of glory, I
would willingly accept every trial in exchange for a little more of the
blissful contemplation of God's greatness. For I see that he who best
understands Him loves and praises Him best.

I do not mean that I should not be glad and count myself lucky to be in heaven, even if I were in the lowest place there. For since I have earned an equivalent place in hell, the Lord would be granting me a great favour in admitting me to heaven at all. May it please His Majesty to do so, and to disregard my grievous sins. What I really mean is that if the choice were mine and the Lord were pleased to offer me great trials to endure, whatever the cost to myself I should not care to lose anything at all by my own fault. Wretch that I am, by my many faults I have lost everything already!

It should also be observed that after each favour which the Lord granted me, whether vision or revelation, some great gain accrued to my soul; and from some visions the gain was very great. A vision of Christ left with me an impression of His very great beauty, which is with me still; and if a single vision was enough to effect this, how much more deeply must it have been imprinted by all the visions with which the Lord favoured me! I received one very great benefit, which was this. A very serious fault of mine which led me into great trouble was that if I began to see that someone liked me, and I happened to take to that person myself, I would become very fond of him. Then my memory would be drawn to dwell on that person, although I had no intention of offending God. But I would delight in seeing him and thinking of him, and in considering the good qualities that I saw in him; and this was such a harmful thing that it was ruining my soul. But once I had seen the Lord's great beauty, I could find no one who seemed handsome to me in comparison, and no one to occupy my thoughts. For merely by turning the eyes of my mind on to the image that I carry in my soul, I become so entirely free that from that time forward everything I see has appeared nauseating to me in comparison with the excellencies and glories that I have glimpsed in the Lord. There is no knowledge and no kind of consolation that I value in the very least in comparison with the joy of hearing a single word from those divine lips – and how much more joyful I am when I hear many! Unless, for my sins, the Lord allows this memory to fade I do not think I shall ever be so deeply absorbed in anything that I shall not immediately regain my freedom by turning my thoughts back, even for a moment, to the Lord.

This fault of mine has troubled me in my relations with some of my confessors. I always feel a great affection for those who direct my soul. I think of them as so truly taking the place of God that my mind is largely taken up with them. I have always felt perfectly safe, however, and have therefore always behaved warmly towards them. But they, being God-fearing servants of God, have been afraid that I might become attached to them and bound up with them – in a spiritual way, of course – and have treated me curtly. This has happened after I have acquired the habit of obeying them; I have not felt this affection for them before. I used to laugh to myself when I saw what a mistake they had made. I did not always tell them outright how little I was attached to anybody, though I knew it myself. But I always reassured them, and when they had become more used to me, they realized the extent of my debt to the Lord. For these suspicions of theirs always came at the beginning of their dealings with me.

Once I had seen my Lord, I was in such continuous converse with Him that my love for Him and my confidence in Him greatly increased. I saw that, although He was God, He was also man, and that the weaknesses of men do not surprise Him. He understands our miserable nature, which is subject to frequent falls on account of that first sin for which He came to make reparation. Although He is the Lord, I can speak to Him as to a friend, because He is not, as I believe, like those whom we call lords on earth, whose entire lordship is conferred on them by others. Such lords have times of audience and chosen people who may speak with them. If a poor man has business with them, he must use roundabout methods, beg for favours and take all sorts of trouble. But supposing that his business is with a king! Then no one who is poor and not well-born can get near him. He has to find out who the king's favourites are, and you can be sure that they are not people who despise the world. People who do so speak the truth, fear nothing, and have no need to. They are not at home in palaces, because they cannot act naturally there, but must keep quiet about what they dislike, and dare not even think about it for fear of falling from favour.

O King of glory and Lord of all kings, Your kingdom is not hedged about by trifles, for it is infinite. We have no need of third parties through whom to approach You. We have only to look at Your person to realize that You alone deserve the name of Lord. When You reveal Your majesty, You need no retinue or guard to convince us that You are a king. An earthly king cannot be recognized as such by his mere presence. Try though he may, no one will know that he is a king so long as he looks no different from the rest. The difference must be visible if it is to be recognized. So it is reasonable that kings should preserve their artificial authority. If they did not, no one would respect them. Their appearance of power does not spring from themselves; their authority must be conferred on them by others. O my Lord, O my King, who now could picture Your majesty? It is impossible not to see from Your presence that You are a mighty Emperor, for the sight of Your majesty strikes awe. But I am more awe-struck, O my Lord, to see how You combine majesty with humility, and by the love that You show to a miserable creature like me.

Once we have lost our first awe and terror at the sight of Your majesty, we can talk and converse with You about anything. But by then we have acquired a deeper fear of offending You, though not of the resulting punishment, for punishment is nothing compared with the loss of You. Here then are the benefits of this vision. But the soul is also greatly benefited by the results that it leaves behind. If the vision is of God, that will be clear from its effects when the soul receives light. But, as I have often said, the Lord often wishes it to remain in darkness and not to see the light. So it is not surprising that one who knows her own wickedness, as I do, should be afraid.

It happened only recently that for a whole week I was in such a condition that I seemed to have lost all sense of my obligations to God, and could not regain it. I did not remember His mercies, and my soul had become quite stupefied. It was busy all the time, though I do not know with what or how. I had no wicked thoughts, but I was so incapable of thinking good ones that I positively laughed at myself, and was amused to see how low a soul can sink when God is not continuously working in it. It realizes that in this state it is not without God; this is not like one of those great trials which, as I have said, I experience at times. But although the soul lays on wood and does all that it can by itself, it cannot kindle the fire of the love of God. He does it a great mercy merely by allowing the smoke to be seen, as a sign that the fire is not altogether dead. Then the Lord returns to kindle it, for though the soul is driving itself crazy with blowing on the fuel and rearranging it, it only seems to be stifling the flames more and more. I think that the best thing it can do is to accept with complete resignation its inability to do anything for itself, and to engage, as I have said, in other meritorious activities. It may be that the Lord is depriving it of the power to pray only so that it may direct its attention to these other matters and discover by experience how little it can do of itself.

It is true that while in conversation with the Lord to-day I have dared to complain to His Majesy. 'How is it, O Lord, that You are not satisfied to keep me in this miserable life, which I endure for the love of You, resigned to live where obstacles of every sort prevent my enjoying You? Why do I have to eat, sleep, conduct business, and talk to everyone as well, and all this for the love of You also? You know very well, Lord, that this is a very great torture to me, yet even in the few moments that still remain for You, You hide from me. How is this consistent with Your compassion? How can Your love for me allow it? If it were possible for me to hide from You as You hide from me, such is Your love for me that I do not believe You would endure it. That is what I think and believe. But You are with me and see me always. O Lord, this must not be. Consider, I beg of You, what a wrong You are doing to one who loves You so much.'

These and other words came to my lips, while all the time I realized how merciful was my place in hell, considering my deserts. But sometimes I am so crazed with love that I do not know what I am saying. With such sense as I have I make these complaints, and the Lord bears with it all. Praised be so good a King! Should we be so bold in our approach to the kings of this world? It is not surprising that we dare not even speak to an earthly king, for it is only right that men should be afraid of him, and of the lords who are his representatives as well. As the world is at present, our lives would have to be a great deal longer if we were to learn all the world's new customs and procedures and rules of correct behaviour, and yet have some time left for the service of God. When I see what goes on, I cross myself in dismay. The fact is that when I came to this house I did not know how I was going to live. One's failure to treat people much better than they deserve is not taken lightly, but considered a serious affront; and if one has been careless, as I have said, one has to satisfy people that one's intentions were good – and please God they believe it!

Really, I repeat, I did not know how I was going to live. My poor soul was quite worn out. It hears when it is told that it must devote all its thoughts to God and that, unless it keeps them fixed on Him, it will never escape from dangers of every sort. On the other hand, it sees that it must not fail to observe every point of worldly etiquette, for fear of giving offence to people who think these observances essential to their honour. All this simply exhausted me; my offers of apology were never-ending. For, try though I might to please, I could not help making mistakes; and these, as I have said, are not passed over in the world as unimportant. Is it true that no such explanations are necessary in religious houses? It might be thought reasonable that we should be excused from these observances. But people say that convents should be courts and schools of good breeding. For myself, I really cannot understand this. Possibly some holy person may have said that they should be courts for the instruction of those who wish to be courtiers of heaven, and that people have misunderstood his meaning. For if we take care, as we rightly should, always to please God and hate the world, I do not see how at the same time we can be equally careful to please those who live in the world in matters that are continually changing. If this etiquette could be learnt once and for all, it might be tolerable. But even the correct addressing of letters demands the establishment of a University chair; there ought to be lectures in the art – or whatever you call it. In one case one corner of the paper has to be left blank, and in another case another; and suddenly a man who was not even a 'Magnificence', has to be described as 'Illustrious'.

I cannot think where this will stop. Though I am not yet fifty, I have seen so many changes in my lifetime that I do not know how to go on. What will it be like for those who are born to-day and who have long lives before them? I am really sorry for those spiritual people who for certain pious reasons are obliged to live in the world; they have a heavy cross to bear. If they could all agree to remain ignorant of this science, and insist on being considered so, they would be free from a great deal of trouble. But what nonsense I have started talking! From speaking of the greatness of God, I have descended to the pettinesses of the world. But as the Lord has graciously allowed me to renounce it, I will leave the subject. Let those who devote so much labour to these trifles settle them to their own satisfaction. Pray God that in the next life, which is unchanging, we may not have to pay for all this. Amen.

CHAPTER 38

She describes certain great favours that the Lord bestowed on her, by graciously revealing to her some of the secrets of heaven, and by vouchsafing her further great visions and revelations. She speaks of the effects which these had upon her and of the great benefit that they did to her soul

ONE night when I was so ill that I intended to excuse myself from mental prayer, I took up a rosary, so as at least to occupy myself with vocal recitation. At the same time I tried not to be recollected in mind, though I was so outwardly since I was in an oratory. But such precautions are of no avail when the Lord wills otherwise. I had been there only a few moments when I was seized by a rapture so violent that I could offer no resistance. I seemed to be raised to Heaven, and the first persons I saw there were my father and my mother. Such mighty things happened in so short a time – it can have been no longer than it would take to recite an *Ave Maria* – that I was quite lifted out of myself, finding it altogether too great a favour. As to the question of time, it may have been longer than I say, but it all passed in a very short space.

I was afraid that this might be an illusion, though it did not seem like one. I could not think what to do, since I felt ashamed to go to my confessor about it – not, I think, out of humility, but because I was afraid he might laugh at me and say: 'What a St Paul she is with her heavenly visions, or another St Jerome!' The fact that these glorious saints had similar visions made me the more afraid, and all I could do was to weep copious tears, for I did not think I could possibly have seen what they saw. In the end, though feeling even more upset, I went to my confessor. I never dared keep such things to myself, however much it pained me to speak of them; I was too much afraid of being deceived. When he saw me in this distressed state, he comforted me a great deal, and gave me plenty of sound reasons why I need not worry.

In the course of time, the Lord showed me other great secrets, and He sometimes does so still. The soul may wish to see more than is put before it, but this is impossible; there is no way in which it may do so. I never saw more on any occasion, therefore, than the Lord was pleased to show me. But what I saw was so great that the least part of it was enough to leave the soul amazed, and so to benefit it that it considers all the things of this life as of small account. I wish that I could describe at least some small part of what I learnt, but when I consider how to do so I find that it is impossible. The mere difference between the light we see here and the light of vision is inexpressible. Both are alike light, but the brightness of the sun seems dull in comparison with that other. In fact, however skilful the imagination may be, it will not succeed in describing or indicating the nature of this light, or any of the other things that the Lord revealed to me. This revelation is accompanied by a joy so sublime as to be indescribable. All the senses are filled with such a profound bliss and sweetness that no description is possible. It is better, therefore, to say no more about this.

On one occasion, when I had been in this state for more than an hour and the Lord had been showing me the most wonderful things, just as He seemed on the point of leaving me, He said: 'Daughter, see what they lose who are against me. Do not fail to tell them of it.' Ah, Lord, how little good will my words do to people blinded by their own actions, unless Your Majesty gives them light! There are some to whom You have given it who have profited by the knowledge of Your wonders. But when they see them, Lord, revealed to such a poor and base creature as myself, I think it is remarkable if anyone believes me. Blessed be Your name and Your mercy, for at least I have seen a notable improvement in my soul. After that vision I wished it had stayed in that state for ever, and never returned to life, for I was left with a great contempt for all earthly things. They seemed to me like so much dross, and I see the meanness of our occupations, while we are detained here below.

When I was staying with the lady of whom I have spoken, I happened on one occasion to have pains in my heart – as I have said, I used to suffer severely from these, though I do so less now. Being a very kind person, she had some precious golden jewels and stones brought out for me, one set of diamonds in particular which she valued most highly. She thought that these would cheer me. But I only laughed to myself, and felt sorry that people should value such things, when I remembered what the Lord has in store for us. I thought how impossible it would be for me to attach any value to such objects, even if I tried, unless the Lord were to expunge other things from my memory.

A soul in this state has so great a dominion over itself that I do not think anyone can understand it who does not possess it. It is a real, natural detachment, achieved without any labour of our own, and it is all of God's doing. For when His Majesty reveals these truths to us, the very deep impression that they make upon our souls clearly shows us that we could not possibly acquire them for ourselves in this very short time. With that experience, I lost almost all my fear of death, which had always terrified me. Now it seems to me a very easy thing for a servant of God that in a single moment the soul should find itself freed from this prison and at rest. This moment in which God raises and transports the soul to show it things of such a sublime excellence seems to me very like that in which the soul leaves the body. In just such a single instant it finds itself in possession of all its blessings. Let us, therefore, leave out of account the agonies at the moment of parting, to which no great importance need be attached, because to those who really love God and have put aside the things of this world death must come very gently.

I think that this experience also helped me greatly to recognize my true home and to realize that here we are but pilgrims. It is a great thing to see what awaits us there, and to know where we shall live hereafter. For if someone has to go and settle in another country, it makes the hardships of the journey much lighter for him if he has evidence that he is going to a place where he will live in great comfort. It also makes death easier if we turn our minds to heavenly things and try to hold conversation with heaven. This is a great gain; merely to glance up to heaven makes the soul recollected, for as the Lord has graciously revealed some part of what is there, the thoughts turn to it. It sometimes happens that my companions and those who give me the greatest comfort are amongst those whom I know to dwell there; they are, as I see it, the people who are truly alive, whilst those who are on earth are so dead that I seem unable to find a companion in the whole world, especially when these raptures come upon me.

Everything seems to me like a dream. That which I see with the eyes of the body is a mockery, and that which I have seen with the eyes of the soul is what the soul desires. Finding itself so far from all such things is for it death. In brief it is a very great favour that the Lord is granting when He gives people such visions. He is helping them greatly, while at the same time he gives them a heavy cross to bear, for then nothing on earth is pleasing, everything is an impediment. I do not know how one could live if the Lord did not sometimes allow His high mysteries to be forgotten – though they are soon remembered again. Blessed and

praised be He for ever and ever! May His Majesty grant, by the blood
which His Son spilt for me, that since He has been pleased to give me
some understanding of these great blessings and since I have now begun
in some degree to enjoy them, I may not share the fate of Lucifer, who
lost everything through his own fault. May He not permit this, for His
own sake. Sometimes I am afraid that He will, although at other times,
and more generally, I am comforted by the thought of God's mercy.
Since He has rescued me from so many sins, He will not let me slip from
His hand and be lost. I implore you, your Reverence, always to beg this
of Him for me.

The favours of which I have spoken so far are less great, in my
opinion, than the one that I shall now describe. There are many reasons
for this, including the great benefits with which it left me, and the great
strengthening that it brought to my soul. But each favour, considered
by itself, is so great as to be beyond comparison. One day – it was on
the eve of Pentecost – I went after Mass to a very lonely spot where I
used often to pray, and began to read about this festival in the Carthusian
book.[1] I read about the signs by which beginners, improvers, and the
perfect may know if the Holy Spirit is with them; and when I had read
of these three states, it seemed to me, in so far as I could understand it,
that God, of His goodness, was certainly with me. I praised Him for
this, and remembered another occasion when I had read this passage,
and when I had lacked much that I have now. I saw the difference very
clearly and, as I grew aware of how radically I had altered, I realized
what a great favour God had done me. Then I began to meditate on the
place in hell that I had earned by my sins, and gave great praise to God,
for I did not seem to recognize my own soul, so great was the change
that had come over it. While I was meditating in this way, a great impulse swept over me, without my seeing the manner of it; my soul
seemed to be on the point of leaving my body, because it could no
longer contain itself and was incapable of waiting for its great blessing.
The impulse was so strong that I could do nothing against it; it did not
seem the same as on other occasions, and my soul was so changed that
I did not understand what had happened to it, or what it desired. I
leaned for support, because even seated I could not stay upright; my
natural strength entirely failed me.

While in this condition, I saw above my head a dove very different

1. *The Life of Christ*, by Ludolf of Saxony, translated into Spanish by
Ambrosio de Montesinos at the beginning of the sixteenth century.

from the doves of this world. It was not feathered like them, but its wings were made of little shells which shone with a great brilliance. It was bigger than a dove, and I seemed to hear the rustling of its wings. It must have been hovering like this for the space of an *Ave Maria*. But my soul was in such a state that, as it became lost to itself, so it lost sight of the dove. My spirit was calmed by the goodness of its guest, though I think that this marvellous favour disturbed and alarmed it. But once it began to rejoice in the vision, all fear left it and, as this rapture continued, with joy came tranquillity.

The glory of this rapture was very great; for the remaining days of the feast I was so bewildered and foolish that I did not know what to do, or how I could have received this great favour and grace. Such was my inward rejoicing that, as you might say, I could neither hear nor see. From that day I realized the very great progress that I had made in the highest love of God, and the great increase in the strength of my virtues. May He be blessed and praised for ever. Amen.

On another occasion I saw this same dove above the head of a Father of the Order of St Dominic.[1] But the rays and the brightness of the wings seemed to extend much further. I understood by this that he was to bring souls to God.

On yet another occasion I saw Our Lady putting a pure white cope on a Licentiate of this same Order,[1] of whom I have spoken several times. She told me that she was giving him that vestment as a reward for the services he had rendered her in helping towards the foundation of this house. She meant it as a sign that his soul would remain pure from that time onwards, and that he would not fall into mortal sin. I am quite sure that he never did. He passed the remainder of his life in penitence and sanctity, and a few years later died so holy and contrite a death that, so far as anything can be known, there can be no doubt about his freedom from sin. A friar who had been present at his death-bed told me that before he breathed his last he said that St Thomas was beside him. He then died with great joy, fervently desiring to depart from this exile. He has appeared to me several times since his death in very great glory, and has informed me of certain things. He was so given to prayer that when, on the point of death, he was so weak that he would have liked to cease praying, he was too continuously enraptured to be able to do so. Some time before he died, he had written to ask me what he ought to do, for as soon as he finished saying Mass he would

1. Santa Teresa appears to be referring to Brother Ibáñez in both cases.

go into a long rapture and could not avoid doing so. At the last, God gave him the reward for the many services he had rendered Him throughout his life.

As for the Rector of the Society of Jesus,[1] whom I have mentioned many times, I had several visions of the great favours that the Lord was granting him, but for fear of being too long I will say nothing of them here. There was an occasion when he was in great trouble, being very sorely persecuted and suffering great distress. One day when I was hearing Mass, at the elevation of the Host I saw Christ on the Cross, and He gave me a message of comfort for the Rector, together with a warning of what was to come. He wished him to remember what He had suffered on his behalf and to prepare himself to suffer also. This gave the Rector great consolation and courage, and everything has since fallen out as the Lord told me it would.

I have seen great things concerning other members of the Society of Jesus to which this Father belonged, and concerning the Order as a whole. I have several times seen them in Heaven with white banners in their hands and, as I say, I have seen other visions of them that are truly wonderful. I have a great veneration, therefore, for the Order, with which I have had many dealings. I see too that their lives conform to what the Lord has told me about them.

One night when I was at prayer, the Lord began to speak to me. He reminded me of the wickedness of my past life, and filled me with shame and distress. Although He did not speak severely, He roused a consuming grief and sorrow within me. But a single word of this kind makes one more conscious of one's progress in self-knowledge than many days spent in the contemplation of one's wretchedness, since it bears the undeniable stamp of truth. He set before me the former bent of my will towards vanities, and told me that I must set great store by my present desire to fix my will, which had hitherto been so ill-employed, upon Him. He promised to accept this desire, and He told me to remember how I had once thought it honourable to oppose His honour. At other times, He said, I must remember my debt to Him, for when I was dealing Him the harshest blows He was all the time bestowing favours on me. Now, when I am doing anything wrong – and my wrong-doings are many – His Majesty makes me so conscious of it that I become entirely dissolved with shame – and as my faults are frequent the occasions for this are numerous. Sometimes I have been rebuked by

1. Probably Father Gaspar de Salazar.

my confessor, and when I have tried to find consolation in prayer, I have received a real reprimand there.

To return to what I was saying, when the Lord began to remind me of the wickedness of my past life, I wept to think that until then I had achieved nothing. But in the midst of my tears, I would wonder if He was not just about to grant me some favour. For quite often when I receive some particular favour from the Lord, it follows after a moment of complete humiliation. I think that His purpose in treating me like this is to show me how little I deserve His favours.

Soon after this my spirit was so transported that I felt it to be almost entirely out of the body, or at least I had no realization that it was still in it. I saw the most sacred Humanity in far greater glory than ever before. I saw Him with amazing clarity in the bosom of the Father. I cannot possibly say how it was, but without seeing, I seemed to see myself in the presence of that Divine Being. I was so amazed that I think it must have been several days before I came to myself again. All the time I seemed to have that majesty of the Son of God present with me, although not in the same way as in the original vision. I understood this well enough, but it remained so impressed on my imagination that, quickly though it passed, for some time I could not be rid of it. It has been a great comfort to me, and also a great blessing.

I have seen this same vision on three subsequent occasions. I think it is the most sublime vision that the Lord has ever given me the grace to see. It brings great benefits with it, and seems to have a most purifying effect upon the soul, almost entirely taking the strength out of our sensual nature. It is a great flame that seems to burn up and annihilate all worldly desires. For though – glory be to God! – I had no desires for the usual vanities, it was plainly shown to me here how all things are vain, and how absolutely vain are the dignities of this world. This is a great incentive towards raising the desires to pure truth. It impresses on the soul a sense of reverence of which I can say little except that it is very different from anything that we can acquire on earth. The soul is overwhelmed with amazement to think that it has dared offend His Supreme Majesty, or indeed that anyone should have the temerity to do so.

I must have spoken several times of the effects left by visions and other such experiences. As I have already said, they may bring greater or lesser benefits; this kind of vision brings the greatest benefits of all. When I came up to take Communion, and remembered that tremendous majesty that I had seen, and reflected that it was He that was in the most holy Sacrament, and that the Lord often graciously appeared to me in the Host, my hair would stand on end and I would seem to be utterly annihilated. O my Lord, if You did not veil Your greatness, who would dare, being so foul and wretched, to bring himself into such frequent contact with Your great majesty? May You be blessed, O Lord, and may the angels and all creatures praise You, who measure all things by our weakness. Otherwise, when we are receiving Your sovereign favours, we might be so alarmed by Your great power as not to dare enjoy them, because we are weak and miserable creatures. The same thing might happen to us as happened, to my positive knowledge, to a certain peasant, who found a treasure far more precious than his poor mind could grasp. The mere possession of it made him so sad that little by little he wasted away to death out of pure grief and perturbation, because he did not know what to do with it. If he had not found it all at once, but had been given it bit by bit, so that he could have lived on it, he would have been happier than when he was poor and it would not have cost him his life.

O Treasure of the poor, how wonderfully You can nourish souls, by revealing Your great riches to them gradually, and not allowing them to be seen all at once! Since that vision I have never seen so great a majesty hidden in anything so small as the Host without marvelling at Your great wisdom. I do not know how the Lord gives me the courage and strength to approach Him. I only know that they were – and still are – bestowed on me by Him who grants me these great favours, and that I could not possibly conceal this, or refrain from proclaiming it aloud. What must be the feelings of a wretch like myself, weighed down by abominations, who has spent her life with so little fear of God, when she finds herself approaching that majestic Lord? It is His will that my soul shall see Him. But how can I open my mouth, that has spoken so many words against this same Lord, to receive that most glorious Body, which is all purity and compassion? For the soul, conscious that it has not served Him, is far more pained and grieved by the love that shines in that most beautiful, kind, and tender face than frightened by the majesty that it sees there.

Think then what my feelings must have been on the two occasions when I saw what I shall now describe. I feel impelled to say, O my Lord and my Glory, that my soul has performed some sort of service for You by suffering the great afflictions that it did. But I do not know what I am saying. I am writing this as if it were not myself that speaks. I find myself confused and almost beside myself when I recall these things to my memory. If my feelings really emanated from me, I should have a right to say that I have done something for You, my Lord. But since there can be no good thought unless You give it, I have nothing to thank myself for. I am the debtor, Lord, and it is You who have been offended.

Once when I was about to take Communion, I saw with the eyes of my soul, more clearly than ever I could with my bodily eyes, two most hideous devils. Their horns seemed to be about the poor priest's throat; and when I saw my Lord, in all His majesty, held in those hands, in the form of the Host that he was about to present to me, I knew for certain that they had offended against Him, and that here was a man in mortal sin. How terrible, O my Lord, to see that beauty of Yours between two such hideous shapes! They seemed so cowed and alarmed in Your presence that I think they would gladly have fled if You had let them go. I was so upset, Lord, that I do not know how I was able to receive the Host; and afterwards I was afraid, for I thought that if the visions had been of God, His Majesty would not have allowed me to see the evil that was in that soul. Then the Lord Himself told me to pray for him, and said that he had allowed this in order that I might realize what power there was in the words of consecration, and that God never fails to be present however wicked the priest who pronounces them. He also wanted me to realize His great goodness in placing Himself in the hands of His enemy, only for the good of myself and of all men. This clearly showed me that priests are under an even greater obligation to be good than other men, and what a terrible thing it is to receive this Most Holy Sacrament when one is unworthy, also how completely the devil is master of a soul that is in mortal sin. This vision was a very great help to me, and made me fully understand what I owe to God. Blessed be He for ever and ever.

On another occasion I saw something else of a similar kind, which greatly alarmed me. I was in a certain place where someone had died who, as I knew, had lived a very evil life for many years. But for the last two he had been ill and seemed in some respects to have improved his ways. He died without confessing, but I did not think, all the same, that he would be damned. While his body was being laid in its shroud, I saw a number of devils lay hold of it. They seemed to be playing with it and tearing at it, tossing it from one to another with great hooks. I was utterly horrified. But when I saw it carried to the grave with all the honour and ceremony that is paid to the dead, I kept thinking of God's great goodness in not allowing that soul to be dishonoured, or the fact that it had been His enemy to be revealed.

What I had seen drove me half out of my mind. But during the funeral service I saw no more devils. Afterwards, however, when they laid the body in the grave, there was such a multitude of them waiting there to seize it that I was beside myself at the sight, and needed no small presence of mind to conceal the fact. I thought of what they would do to his soul, if they could take possession of his body in this manner. Would to God that everyone who is in an evil state could see that hideous spectacle that I saw. I think it would be a great incentive towards the reformation of their lives. All this makes me more conscious of what I owe to God and of what He has delivered me from. Until I had talked to my confessor, I was in a state of great fear, for although this man had no great reputation for piety I wondered whether this was not a trick of the devil's intended simply to discredit him. The truth is that, illusion or no, every time I remember it I am afraid.

Now that I have begun to speak of visions of the dead, I will refer to some matters which Our Lord has been pleased to reveal to me concerning certain souls. For the sake of brevity, and because such tales are unnecessary – for our profit, I mean – I will relate only a few. I was told that a former Provincial[1] of ours had died – at the time of his death he was Provincial of another province – a man with whom I had had dealings and to whom I was grateful for various kindnesses, and a person of many virtues. I was very much upset when I heard that he had died, because I feared for his salvation. He had been a superior for twenty years, and this always makes me afraid, for I think it is a most dangerous thing to have charge of souls. I went in some distress to an oratory and offered on his behalf all the good that I had done in my whole life, which must have been very little. Then I begged the Lord to make up the deficiency from His own merits, so as to deliver that soul from purgatory.

Whilst I was offering the Lord the best prayers that I could on his behalf, he seemed to rise out of the depths of the earth on my right, and I saw him ascend into Heaven with the greatest joy. He had been very old, but as I saw him he appeared to be thirty or even less, and his face was bright. This vision was quickly over, but I was so comforted that I could never grieve for his death again, although I found people much

1. Father Gregorio Fernández.

distressed by it, for he was very well liked. My soul felt so much comfort that nothing disturbed it and I could have no doubt that this was a genuine vision – I mean, that it was no illusion. He had not been dead more than a fortnight at the time. Nevertheless I was tireless in getting people to commend him to God and in doing so myself, though I could not pray with as much earnestness as if I had not seen that vision. For once the Lord gives me a demonstration like that, I cannot help thinking that attempts to commend a soul to His Majesty are like gifts of alms to the rich. He died a long way away. So it was not till afterwards that I learnt what kind of death the Lord gave him. It was one of great edification; everyone was astounded by the consciousness, the tears, and the humility with which he died.

It was about a day and a half after the death, in our house, of a nun who had been a great servant of God, that the following incident occurred. The service for the dead was being recited for her in the choir. A sister was reading the lesson, and I was standing there to assist her with the response. Half way through, I seemed to see the dead woman's soul rising on my right, as in my earlier vision, and ascending to Heaven. This was not an imaginary vision, like the last, but was similar to the others of which I have spoken. But there was no more doubt about it than about those visions that are seen.

Another nun died in this same house, at the age of eighteen or twenty. She had always been in poor health, but was a great servant of God, dutiful in the choir and extremely virtuous. I certainly thought she would be excused purgatory, for not only had she suffered from severe illness but she had a superfluity of merits. About four hours after her death, while the Office was being said preparatory to her burial, I saw her rise on that same side and ascend into Heaven.

Once I was in a College of the Company of Jesus, suffering severely both in my body and soul as I have said I sometimes used to and still do, I was in such a state that I do not think I was capable of thinking a single good thought. A member of the Company, who belonged to that house, had died that night and I was endeavouring to commend his soul to God, while listening to a Mass said for him by another Father of the Company. Suddenly I became deeply recollected and saw him ascend to Heaven in great glory; and the Lord ascended with him. I understood that it was by a special favour that His Majesty rose with him.

Another friar of our Order, a very good man, was extremely ill. I was at Mass and became recollected. Then I saw that he was dead and was ascending into Heaven without passing through purgatory. He had died, as I afterwards learnt, at the hour when I had seen him. It amazed me that he had not gone to purgatory. But I realized that as he had been a friar who had carefully kept the Rule, the Bulls of the Order had been efficacious in saving him from a sojourn there. I do not know why this was revealed to me. I think it must have been to teach me that a habit – I mean the wearing of a habit – is not enough to make a man a friar, and does not imply that state of great perfection which is proper to a friar.

I will say no more on this subject, although the Lord has graciously allowed me to see many such things. For, as I have said, it is unnecessary. But from all the visions I have seen I have never learnt that any soul escaped purgatory, except those of this father, of the saintly friar, Peter of Alcántara, and of the Dominican father whom I have mentioned. It has pleased the Lord to show me the degrees of glory to which some souls have been raised, and He has shown them to me in the places assigned to them. There is a great difference between some of these places and others.

CHAPTER 39

*She continues with the same subject, and recounts the great mercies
which the Lord has shown her. She tells of His promises to help those
persons for whom she might pray, and some outstanding instances in
which His Majesty has favoured her in this way*

I WAS once earnestly importuning the Lord to restore the sight of a
person who was almost blind, and to whom I had a certain obligation; I was very sorry for him, and feared that the Lord would not hear
me on account of my sins. But He appeared to me as on previous occasions, and began to show me the wound in His left hand. Then with
His right He drew out a long nail that had been driven through it, and
as He pulled at it, He seemed to tear His flesh. It was clear how painful
this must be, and it distressed me greatly. 'Seeing that I have done this
for you,' He said, 'you need have no doubt that I will even more readily
do what you have asked Me. Anything that you ask of Me I promise
you to do, for I know that you will never ask for anything that will not
redound to My glory. Therefore I will do what you ask of Me now.
Even when you did not serve Me, you never asked for anything that I
did not grant you in a better form than ever you were able to imagine.
Do not doubt, therefore, that I shall do so now, when I know that you
love Me.'

I do not think a week passed before the Lord restored that person's
sight. My confessor heard of it at once. It may be, of course, that this was
not owing to my prayer. But as I had seen this vision, I felt quite certain
that it was a mercy granted to me, and I thanked His Majesty for it.

Once there was someone who was extremely ill with a very painful
disease which I shall not describe here since I do not know its nature.
For two months his sufferings had been intolerable, and he was in such
agony that he tore at his flesh. My confessor – the Rector of whom I
have spoken – went to see him and was very sorry for him. He said that
I must certainly pay him a visit – and this was possible because he was a
relative of mine. I went and was moved to such pity for him that I began
to beg the Lord most importunately to cure him. Here I saw a clear
proof, as I believe, of the favours which He grants me, for on the very
next day my relative was free from that pain.

On another occasion, I was in the deepest distress because I had learned that someone to whom I was under a deep obligation was about to commit an act highly offensive to God and dishonourable to himself, and that he was quite resolved to do so. I was greatly agitated, for I did not know of any way in which I could dissuade him; there did not seem to be one. I besought God from the bottom of my heart to show me some way, and until I saw one I could find no relief from my distress. In this state, I went to a very lonely hermitage, of which our convent has several, in which there is a picture of Christ bound to the Column; and there I begged Him to grant me this favour. Then I heard a very soft voice speaking to me, as it were, in a whisper. All my hair stood on end with terror. I tried to hear what He said to me, but I could not, and it was quickly over. When my fear left me, which it very soon did, I felt a calm, a joy and an inward delight; it amazed me that the mere hearing of a voice – for this I heard with my physical ears – should have such an effect on my soul, even though I did not understand a word. I saw by this that my request was going to be granted, and so it was. But even before that my distress was as completely dispelled as if it had never been. I told my confessors about this – for I had two[1] at that time, very learned men and great servants of God.

There was someone I knew who had resolved to serve God in real earnest, and who had been engaged in prayer for some days, during which time His Majesty had granted him many favours. But certain occasions for sin had presented themselves, which were very dangerous, and instead of avoiding them he had given up prayer. This caused me the greatest distress, for he was a person of whom I was very fond and to whom I was indebted. I believe that for more than a month I did nothing but pray God to turn this soul back to Himself. One day when I was at prayer, I saw a devil beside me, tearing up some papers that he held in his hand in a wild fury. This gave me great comfort, for it seemed to show that my prayer had been granted; and so it was, as I afterwards learnt. This man had made a very contrite confess: , and so genuinely turned back to God that I trust in His Majesty he will make continuous progress. Blessed be He for all things! Amen.

In answer to my prayers, the Lord has very often delivered souls from grave sins and brought others to great perfection. As for rescuing souls from purgatory and such notable acts, the Lord has granted me so many favours of this kind that I should exhaust myself and my readers if I were to describe them all. But he has done more through me for the salvation

1. Father Báñez and García de Toledo.

of the soul than for the health of the body; all this is very well known, and there are many witnesses to it. It used to cause me very great scruples, for I could not help believing that the Lord was doing this because of my prayers. I say nothing of His principal reason, which is His pure goodness. But these favours are now so numerous and have been observed by so many people that it no longer distresses me to believe this. I praise His Majesty, and am ashamed when I see that I am more deeply in His debt than ever. Indeed, I believe that even now He is increasing my desire to serve Him, and quickening my love for Him. But what most astonishes me is that when the Lord sees my requests to be unsuitable I cannot ask for them; when I try to, my prayers have no strength, spirituality, or concentration. However hard I try to force myself, I can do no better. Yet when it comes to other petitions that His Majesty means to grant, I find that I can make them very often and with great importunity, and although I am not concentrating on them they frequently come into my mind.

There is a wide difference between these two ways of praying, which I do not know how to explain. As for the first, when I pray for the kind of favours that the Lord does not mean to grant, I resolutely persist, yet even if it is a request that touches me closely, I do not feel the same fervour as when I am praying for favours of the other kind. I am like a person whose tongue is tied, and who cannot speak even though he wants to, or if he does so cannot make himself understood. But in the second case I am like someone who is speaking clearly and readily to a person whom he sees is a willing listener. The first, we might say, is like vocal prayer, and the second like that high contemplation in which the Lord reveals Himself. We know that His Majesty has heard us, that He approves of what we are asking of Him, and that He will grant us the favour. May He be blessed for ever, who gives so much when I give so little. For what can one accomplish, Lord, unless one utterly abases oneself for You? How far, how far, how far – I could repeat this a thousand times – do I fall short of doing so! For this reason – though there are many others – I cannot desire to live at all, since in my way of life I do not fulfil my obligations to You. What imperfections I find in myself! How slack I am in Your service! Sometimes I could really wish that I had no sense at all, for then I should not know how much evil is in me. May He who can do so come to my aid!

When I was staying in the house of that lady whom I have mentioned, I had to keep a watch on my behaviour, and constantly to bear in mind the vanity that is inseparable from all the things of this life. For I was greatly valued there and highly praised, and there were many things there to which I might have become attached if I had only considered my own interests. But He who sees things in their true light looked after me and did not let me escape from His hand.

When I speak of seeing things in their true light, I am reminded of the great difficulties encountered by those to whom God has given some knowledge of the truth about earthly things, when they have to deal with others. For on earth there is so much concealment, as the Lord once said to me. Indeed many of the things that I am writing here do not come out of my own head, but were said to me by this Heavenly Master of mine; and so in places where I expressly say 'I was told this' or 'The Lord said this to me', I am most scrupulous not to add or subtract a single syllable. But when I do not remember every detail exactly, then it must be understood to come from me, and some things also come from me altogether. But I do not attribute to myself anything that is good, for I know that there is no good in me except what the Lord has given me without my deserving it. When I say that something is from me, I mean only that it was not given to me in a revelation.

But, O my God, how is it that even in spiritual matters we often try to interpret things in our own way, as if they were things of this world, and so distort the truth? We think that we can measure our progress by the number of years during which we have been practising prayer. We even think that we can find a measure for Him who bestows immeasurable gifts on us at His own pleasure, and who can give more to one person in six months than to another in many years. I have seen this so often and in so many cases that I am surprised we can fail to see it.

I am quite sure that no one who has a gift for spiritual discernment, and to whom the Lord has given true humility, will remain under this delusion for long. He will judge things by their fruits, and by the good resolutions and love to which they give rise; and the Lord will give him the light by which to recognize these. God considers a soul's advancement and progress, but takes no account of time. One soul may have achieved more in six months than another in twenty years, since, as I have said, the Lord gives at His own pleasure, and to him who is readiest to receive. Many of the girls who come to this house at present are quite young. But God touches their hearts and gives them a little light and love – for that brief period, I mean, in which He gives them sweetness in prayer. They have not been expecting this, but they put everything else aside, not even remembering to eat, and enclose themselves for ever in a convent that is unendowed. They seem to ignore their own lives for the sake of Him whose love for them they know. They give up everything, want no will of their own, and never think that they may become discontented within such narrow bounds. They offer themselves entire, as a sacrifice to God.

I admit most willingly that they are better than I, and I ought indeed to be ashamed of myself when I enter God's presence. For what His Majesty has not achieved in me in the very many years since I began to pray and He began to grant me favours, He has achieved in them in three months – and in one case, in three days – though He gives them far fewer favours than He gives me. But His Majesty rewards them well, and they certainly have no reason to be dissatisfied with what they have done for Him.

I wish therefore that we could remind ourselves of how long it is since we made our profession, or since we began to pray, though not for the purpose of distressing those who have made greater progress in a shorter time, and making them turn back to travel at our pace, or forcing those who are soaring like eagles, thanks to the favours that God has given them, to move like tethered hens. Let us rather fix our eyes on His Majesty and, if we see these souls to be humble, give them the reins. The Lord, who is showing them so many favours, will not let them fling themselves into the abyss. They themselves put their trust in God, and so the truth that their faith has taught them can be of assistance to them. Shall we not trust them too, therefore, and not try to measure them by our measure, which is fixed by our own meanness of spirit? We must never do that. If we cannot achieve results and resolutions equal to theirs, which are difficult to understand without experience, let us humble ourselves and not condemn them. Otherwise our apparent concern for their profit will impede our own, and we shall be losing a God-given opportunity for humbling ourselves and understanding our own faults – also for realizing how much more detached and how much closer to God their souls must be than ours, since His Majesty is drawing so near to them.

My sole purpose here – and I do not wish to suggest that I have any other – is to explain my reasons for valuing prayer which has lasted only for a short time, yet produces results so notable and so speedily apparent; for we cannot resolve to give up everything for the love of God without very strong love. I had rather have this than prayer which has lasted over many years but which has produced no more resolution to do anything for Him at the end than at the beginning, except perhaps some tiny actions. For these weigh no more than a grain of salt which a bird could carry in its beak, and cannot be considered as fruits of prayer or signs of mortification. Sometimes we attach a pitiful importance to things we do for the Lord which could not really be considered important even if we did them very often. I am like that myself, and I forget His favours at every turn. I do not say that His Majesty will not value such services as I do Him, for He is good. But I should not like to make much of them myself, or even to notice that I do them, since they are nothing at all. But pardon me, my Lord, and do not blame me if I try to comfort myself with the little that I do, seeing that I do not serve You at all. If I served You in great things, I should not think anything of these trifles. Blessed are they who serve You by great deeds. If envying them and desiring to emulate them would help me, I should not be backward in pleasing You. But I am worth nothing, O Lord. Put value into what I do, since You love me so.

One day, after I had received the Brief from Rome, empowering me to found this convent without an endowment, and after all the business – which I really think had cost me some labour – had been concluded, I was feeling glad that everything had turned out as it had, and thinking of the difficutlies I had met with, and praising the Lord for having graciously made some use of me. Then I began to think of what I had gone through, and in every action of mine which had seemed to me of some value I began to find numberless faults and imperfections. In some of them too I could see a lack of courage, and in many of them a lack of faith. Until now, when I see that everything which the Lord prophesied to me in regard to this house has been accomplished, I have never resolutely managed to believe in His promise, nor ever been able really to mistrust it. I cannot explain this. The fact is that, on the one hand, it often seemed to me impossible, while on the other, I could not doubt it – I mean I could not believe that it would not be fulfilled. Eventually I found that the Lord had done all the good things, and I all the bad, and so I stopped thinking about the matter, and I would rather not remember it for fear of recalling all my faults. Blessed be He who turns every one of them to good, when it is His pleasure. Amen.

As I say, it is dangerous to keep counting the years that we have practised prayer. For even though it may be done in humility, it always seems liable to leave us with the feeling that we have earned some merit by our service. I do not say that we deserve nothing or that we shall not be well rewarded. But any spiritual person who believes that by the mere number of years during which he has practised prayer he has earned these spiritual consolations, will, I am sure, fail to reach the peak of spirituality. Is it not enough that God has thought him worthy of being guided by His hand and prevented from committing those offences into which he fell before he began to pray? Must he also, as they say, sue God for his money's worth? This does not seem to me profound humility. It may be so, of course, though I look on it as presumption. I have little enough humility, but I do not think that I have ever dared to think like that. It may be because I have never served Him that I have never asked for a reward; if I had, perhaps I should have been more anxious than anybody for the Lord to give me my due.

I do not say that if a soul has prayed humbly, it does not steadily advance, or that God will not grant us progress. But we must forget this number of years, for all that we can do is as nothing compared with one drop of that blood which the Lord shed for us. And what are we asking for, if the more we serve Him the deeper we are in His debt? If we pay a farthing of it, He gives us a thousand pounds in return. For the love of God, let us leave this for Him to judge, for judgement is His. Comparisons of this kind are always bad, even in earthly matters. What must they be then, when applied to what only God has knowledge of? His Majesty clearly showed this when He paid the last labourers in the field as much as the first.[1]

It has taken me so long to write all this – the last three sheets have taken me as many days, for, as I have said, I have had, and still have, few opportunities for writing – that I had forgotten what I had begun to describe, which was this vision. Whilst I was at prayer, I saw myself in a large field alone, and around me was a crowd of all sorts of people that hedged me in on every side. They all seemed to be carrying weapons with which to attack me; some had lances, others swords, others daggers, and yet others very long rapiers. In fact, I could not escape in any direction without running the risk of death, and I was quite alone, without anyone to take my part. I was in great spiritual distress and did not know what to do, when I raised my eyes to the sky and saw Christ – not in Heaven, but far above me in the air – holding out His hand towards me and encouraging me in such a way that I no longer feared all these people, and they could not harm me, try though they might.

1. Matthew xx, 10.

This vision will seem to lead nowhere, but it has since been of the greatest profit to me, because its meaning was explained to me, and soon afterwards I found myself attacked in almost that way. I realized then that this vision was a picture of the world, the whole of whose inhabitants seem to take up arms and fall on the poor soul. Not to mention those who are no great servants of God, or honours, possessions, delights, and all such things, there are clearly other agents who will ensnare, or at least try to ensnare, the soul when it is not on the look-out: its friends, its relatives, and, what surprises me most, some very good people. I found myself hard pressed by all these; they thought that what they did was right, and I did not know how to protect myself or what to do.

God help me! If I were to describe all the different trials and tribulations that I suffered at that time, in addition to those I have already spoken of, what a warning it would be to people that they must loathe all worldly things entirely! Of all the persecutions I endured, I think this was the worst. As I have said, sometimes I found myself so hard pressed from all sides that I could only find relief by raising my eyes to Heaven and calling upon God, keeping a clear memory of what I had seen in that vision. This greatly helped me not to put much trust in anybody, since no one can be relied on except God. The Lord showed me how, in these great trials, He always sent someone to hold out a hand to me on His behalf, just as He had promised He would in that vision, so that I had no need to cling to anything, but had only to please Him. This has served to sustain that little virtue that there was in my desire to serve You. May You be blessed for ever.

On one occasion I was very restless and disturbed, and quite unable to recollect myself. I was fighting and struggling in my mind, and my thoughts were straying to subjects that had nothing to do with perfection. Moreover I felt that I had lost my former detachment. I saw my own wickedness, and was afraid that the favours which the Lord had granted me might be illusions. In short, my soul was in great darkness. But in the midst of this distress, the Lord began to speak to me, telling me not to be troubled, but to learn, from the consideration of my misery, what a state I should be in if He were to withdraw from me, and to realize that we are never safe so long as we live in this flesh. I was shown how profitable our warring and struggling are to us, seeing that it is for such a prize, and the Lord seemed to me to be sorry for those of us who live in the world. He told me not to consider myself forgotten, for He would never abandon me, but that I must do everything in my power to help myself. The Lord said this to me with tenderness and compassion, and other things as well that were most gracious, and that there is no need to repeat.

The Lord often says to me, as a sign of His great love: 'Now you are Mine and I am yours'. There are some words that I habitually repeat to myself at these times, and I believe that I mean them. They are: 'What do I care about myself, Lord, or about anything but You?' When I remember what I am, these words and tokens of love make me deeply ashamed. For, as I believe I have said on other occasions, and as I sometimes say at present to my confessor, I think one needs more courage for receiving these favours than for undergoing the sorest trials. When they come, I almost forget all I have done, my reason ceases to work, and I can only see a picture of my wickedness. I sometimes think that this too is a supernatural experience.

At times I feel such a longing for Communion that I cannot express it in words. One morning it happened to be raining so heavily that I was afraid I should not be able to leave the house. But once I had set out I was so mastered by my desire that I think I should have gone on even if spears had been levelled against my breast instead of raindrops. When I came to the church, I fell into a deep rapture. I seemed to see not just a door into the heavens such as I have seen on other occasions, but the whole heavens thrown wide open. I beheld the throne, which, as I have told your Reverence, I have seen at other times, and above it another throne, on which I understood, in a way that I cannot explain, the Godhead sat. It seemed to be supported by some beasts, about which I think I have heard something, and I wondered if they were the Evangelists.[1] But I did not see what the throne was like, or who was on it, only a great multitude of angels, who seemed incomparably more beautiful than those I have seen in heaven. I wondered whether they were seraphim or cherubim, for they were very different in their glory and seemingly all on fire; the differences are very great, as I have said. The glory that I felt within me cannot be expressed in writing, nor yet in words; it is inconceivable to anyone who has not experienced it. I knew that everything one can desire was there at once, yet I saw nothing. I was told – I do not know by whom – that all I could do was to understand that I could understand nothing, and to consider that all things were as nothing in comparison with that. Afterwards my soul was

1. Apocalypse, iv, 6–8.

ashamed to find that it could rest on any created thing, and still more that it could feel affection for it. For the whole world seemed to me just an ant-hill.

I took Communion and attended Mass, but I do not know how I did so. I thought that my rapture had only lasted a very short time, and was surprised when the clock struck. I saw that I had been in that state of bliss for two hours. Afterwards I was amazed at having experienced this fire, which seemed to come from on high, from the true love of God. For however much I desire and strive for it, and annihilate myself to get it, it is only when His Majesty pleases, as I have said on other occasions, that I can obtain even a single spark of it. It seems to consume the old man, with his faults, his tepidness and his misery; and then, it is like the phoenix-bird, of which I have read; when he is burnt there rises from the ashes a new man. Thus the soul is transformed; its desires are changed, and its fortitude is increased. It seems not to be the same as before, but begins to follow the way of the Lord with a new purity. When I prayed the Lord that this might be so with me, and that I might begin to serve Him afresh, He said to me: 'You have made a good comparison. See that you do not forget it, and you will always try to improve.'

Once when I was afflicted with the doubt of which I have spoken, as to whether these visions were of God, the Lord appeared to me and said to me sternly: 'O children of men, how long will you be hard of heart!' He told me to examine myself carefully on one question, whether I had totally surrendered myself to Him or not. If I had and was His, then I must believe that He would never let me be lost. I was greatly troubled by this rebuke. So, very tenderly and consolingly, He told me once more not to worry, for He well knew that I should never knowingly fail to devote myself entirely to His service. He promised that all I desired should be fulfilled; and in fact what I was then praying Him for was granted me. He told me to reflect on my love for Him, which was growing within me every day, and then I should see that my experiences were not of the devil; nor must I imagine that He would ever allow the devil to have such traffic with the souls of His servants as to give them the clarity of mind and the quiet that I had. He gave me to understand that when so many people of such quality had told me that my visions were of God, I should be wrong to disbelieve them.

Once when I was reciting the psalm[1] 'Whosoever will be saved' I was shown so clearly how it was possible that there was one God alone

1. Actually the Athanasian Creed.

and Three Persons, that I was both amazed and greatly comforted. This greatly helped me to increase my knowledge of God's greatness and of His marvels; and now when I think of the Most Holy Trinity or hear it spoken of, I seem to understand how it can be; which is a great joy to me.

Once, on the Feast of the Assumption of Our Lady, the Queen of the Angels, the Lord was pleased to grant me this favour. In a rapture, I saw a representation of her ascent into heaven, of the joy and solemnity with which she was received, and of the place where she now is. It would not be possible for me to explain how this happened. My spirit was filled with great bliss at the sight of such glory, and the vision had great fruits. For I was left with a strong desire to serve that Lady, because of her great merits.

Once when I was in a College of the Company of Jesus, as the brothers of that house were taking Communion, I saw a very rich canopy above their heads. Twice I saw this, but when others were at Communion I did not see it.

CHAPTER 40

*She continues her account of the great favours that God granted her,
from some of which excellent lessons can be obtained. For instruction,
as she says, after obedience and the recording of such favours as will be
of profit to souls, has been her principal motive in writing. With this
chapter the account of her life comes to an end. May it be for the glory
of the Lord. Amen*

ONCE when I was at prayer, I felt such a delight within me that,
being unworthy of such a blessing, I began to think how much
more I deserved to be in that place I had seen prepared for me in hell.
For, as I have said, I never forgot the vision of myself in that place. As I
meditated on this, my soul began to take more and more fire, and I was
seized with a spiritual rapture such as I cannot describe. My spirit
seemed to be plunged into that grandeur which I had felt before, and to
be filled with it. In that state a truth was revealed to me which is the fulfilment of all truths. I cannot tell how this was, for I saw nothing. I was
told, without seeing by whom, but I clearly understood that it was the
Truth itself: 'This is no small thing that I am doing for you, but one of
those things for which you are greatly indebted to Me. For all the harm
that befalls the world comes from a failure to understand the truths of
Scripture in all their true clarity, of which not one tittle shall fail.' I
thought that I had always believed this, and that all the faithful did so.
'Ah, daughter,' He said to me, 'how few there are that truly love Me,
for if they did so I would not hide My secrets from them! Do you know
what it is to love Me truly? It is to know that everything which is not
pleasing to Me is a lie. You do not realize this yet, but you will come to
see it clearly in the profit it brings to your soul.'

I have come to see it, the Lord be praised! For from that day onwards I have looked on everything that is not directed to God's service
as vanity and lies. I could not explain in what way I realize this, or express my pity for those whom I see living in darkness and ignorant of
this truth. I have derived other gains from this also, some that I shall
describe here and many others that I cannot. At the same time, the Lord
said one special thing to me of particular grace. I do not know the
manner of it, for I saw nothing. But it gave me a very great fortitude,
in a way that I am equally incapable of describing; and so I became

firmly resolved to carry out with all my might even the smallest injunction in Holy Scripture. I do not think any obstacle could have been presented to me that I would not have overcome to that end.

Of this divine Truth which was presented to me without my knowing what it was or how it came, one particular truth remains impressed on me, which conveyed to me some notion of God's majesty and power, and gave me a new reverence for Him. I can say nothing about its nature, but I know that it is something extremely high. After that I felt a very great desire never to speak of anything except the profoundest truths, which go far deeper than the subjects usually discussed in this world; and so living in the world began to be most painful to me. But at the same time I was filled with much tenderness, joy, and humility. It seemed to me that the Lord had granted me a great deal, though I did not understand how; I had not the least fear that it might be an illusion. I saw nothing, but I understood what a great benefit it is to set no store by anything that will not bring us nearer to God. Thus I came to know what it is for a soul to walk in truth, in the presence of Truth itself. What I understood was that the Lord had shown me He is Truth itself.

All that I have described I learned sometimes by locutions and sometimes not; and yet I understood some things that were unspoken more clearly than others that were conveyed in words. I understood very great truths concerning this Truth, and more than if I had been taught by many learned men. I do not think that learned men could possibly have impressed on me so strongly or have shown me so clearly the vanity of this world. This same truth that was taught me is the Truth itself, and is without beginning or end. All other truths depend on this truth, as all other loves depend on this love, and all other greatnesses on this greatness. But this is an obscure way of putting something which the Lord allowed me to be shown in the utmost clarity. How mighty must be the power of the Majesty that brings the soul such great gains in so short a time, and leaves such things imprinted upon it! O my grand Majesty! What are you doing, Almighty Lord? Consider upon whom You are conferring these sovereign mercies. Do You not remember that this soul has been an abyss of lies and an ocean of vanities, and all through my own fault? You gave me a natural hatred of lying, yet I allowed myself in many ways to traffic in lies. How can it appear right and proper that these great favours and mercies should be granted to one who has so ill deserved to receive them from You?

Once when I was reciting the Office with the community, my soul suddenly became recollected, and seemed to me like a clear mirror; there was no part of it – back, sides, top, or bottom – that was not completely bright; and in the middle was a picture of Christ Our Lord as I usually see Him. I seemed to see Him in every part of my soul as clearly as in a mirror, and this mirror – I cannot explain how – was entirely shaped to this same Lord, by a most loving communication which I could not describe. I know the very great benefit which that vision brought me each time that I recall it, and especially after I have taken Communion. It was explained to me that when a soul is in mortal sin this mirror is covered with a thick mist and remains so dark that the Lord cannot be reflected or seen in it, even though He is always present and gives us our being. In the case of heretics, the mirror is much worse than darkened; it has the appearance of being broken. There is a great difference between seeing this and describing it, for it cannot be properly explained. But it has been of great benefit to me, and has also caused me deep regrets when by my own fault I have darkened my soul and been unable to see the Lord.

This vision seems to me very profitable to recollected persons, for it teaches them to think of the Lord as being in the very innermost part of the soul. This is a meditation which penetrates most deeply and, as I have previously said, is much more fruitful than the thought of Him as outside us, which one finds in certain books about prayer that tell us where we are to seek God. The glorious St Augustine puts this particularly well[1] when he says that neither in the cities, nor in pleasures, nor in any other place where he sought Him, did he find Him as he did within himself. This is quite clearly the best way. There is no need to climb up to Heaven, nor to go any farther than to our own selves; to do so troubles the spirit, distracts the soul, and brings but little fruit.

Here I should like to give a warning to such as experience deep rapture of one thing that occurs in the course of it. When the time is over during which the soul has been in complete union and its faculties have been wholly absorbed – and this time, as I have said, is short – the soul is still recollected and unable, even in outward things, to return to itself. But the two faculties of memory and reason will be almost frenziedly distracted. This, as I say, happens at times, especially at the beginning. I think that it may arise from the inability of our weak natures to endure such vehemence of spirit, and from the enfeeblement of the imagina-

1. In the apocryphal *Soliloquies*, ch. xxxi.

tion. I know that it happens to some people. I think it would be a good thing if they were to force themselves to give up prayer for a time, and take it up again later, when they may recover what they have lost by being disunited. Otherwise they may come to great harm. I have experience of this, also of the wisdom of considering what our health will bear.

In all this we need experience and a master. For when the soul has reached this point, many things occur that need to be discussed with somebody. But if one seeks guidance and does not find it, then the Lord will not fail one. For even though I am what I am, He has not failed me. I believe there are few who have acquired experience of all these things, and without experience it is useless to treat a soul – one will only bring it trouble and distress. But the Lord will also take account of this; it is better, therefore, to refer one's experiences to a confessor. I have said this on other occasions. Indeed everything that I am saying now I have said before. But I do not remember it very well. I am certain, however, that the choice and character of a confessor is a very important matter, especially for a woman. The Lord grants these favours to many more women than men, as I have heard from the saintly friar Peter of Alcántara, and have also observed for myself. He used to say that women made much more progress on this path than men, and he gave excellent reasons for it, which there is no reason to repeat here, all in women's favour.

Once when I was at prayer, I saw for a brief moment, without distinctness of form but with complete clarity, how all things are seen in God and how He contains all things within Him. I have no idea how to express this vision in writing; but it remained deeply impressed in my soul, and is one of those great favours which God granted me and which make me confused and ashamed when I remember the sins I have committed. I believe that if the Lord had been pleased that I should see this vision earlier, and if it had been seen by those who sin against Him, we should have had neither the heart nor the boldness to offend. This vision appeared to me, I repeat, but I cannot affirm that I saw anything. I must have seen something, however, since I am able to make this comparison. But it came in such a subtle and delicate way that the intellect cannot touch it. It may be that I cannot understand these visions, which do not seem to be imaginary, though there must be an imaginary element in some of them. But as, during the rapture, the faculties are in suspense, they cannot afterwards reproduce the picture which the

Lord has revealed to them, and in which he wishes them to rejoice.

Let us say that the Divinity is like a very clear diamond, much larger than the whole world, or a mirror, according to my description of the soul in my former vision, except that it is of so sublime a kind that I cannot find words to express it. Then let us suppose that all we do is seen in this diamond, which is so formed as to contain everything within itself, for there is nothing that can lie outside its greatness. It was a terrifying thing for me to see so many things together and in so short a time in this diamond, and it is very distressing, each time I remember it, to think that I saw such ugly things as my own sins reflected in that clearness and purity. In fact when I remember it, I do not know how to bear it, and at that time I felt such a deep shame that I did not seem to know where to hide. If only someone could explain this to those who commit the most ugly and dishonourable sins, they might realize that such deeds are not hidden; that as they are committed in His Majesty's presence, He is justly grieved by them, and that we behave most ir-reverently before God! I saw the way in which hell is actually earned by a single mortal sin, and the impossibility of understanding what a very grave thing it is to commit such a sin before so exalted a Majesty, and I saw how alien to His nature such deeds are. All this gives an in-creasingly clear demonstration of His mercy, in that He knows we are behaving like this and bears with us all the same.

All this made me consider whether an experience of that nature may not fill the soul with such terror of the Judgement Day that it asks: 'How will it be on that day, when His Majesty will reveal Himself to us clearly and we shall see the offences we have committed?' God help me, I have indeed walked in blindness! I have often been surprised by what I have written, but your Reverence must only be surprised at one thing: at my still being alive when I see all this and consider what I am. May He who has borne with me for so l ong be blessed for ever.

Once when I was at prayer, deep in recollection, sweetness and quiet, I seemed to be surrounded by angels and very close to God. I began to pray to His Majesty for the Church. Then I was shown the great benefit that was to come to it in future days from a certain Order,[1] and from the fortitude with which its members would uphold the Faith.

Again, when I was praying beside the Most Holy Sacrament, there appeared to me a saint[2] whose Order has been in some decline. In his

1. This probably refers to the Jesuits.
2. St Dominic.

hands he held a book, which he opened, telling me to read a few words which were in large and very legible print. 'In times to come,' they said, 'this Order will flourish and have many martyrs.'

On another occasion, when I was in the choir at Matins, I saw standing before me six or seven figures, who seemed to be members of this same Order, with swords in their hands. The meaning of this is, I think, that they will defend the Faith. At another time, when I was at prayer and my spirit was carried away, I seemed to be in a great field where many people were fighting, and members of this Order were struggling most heatedly. Their faces were beautiful and all on fire. Many were thrown to the ground defeated, and others were killed. I thought that this was a battle against the heretics.

I have seen this glorious saint several times, and he has told me various things. He has thanked me for my prayers on behalf of his Order, and has promised to commend me to the Lord. I do not say what Orders I am speaking of. If the Lord wishes their names to be known, He will declare them, in which case the others will not be offended. Each Order, and every member of each Order, should endeavour to be an instrument of the Lord. Then He will bless the Order by allowing it to serve Him in the Church's present great need. Blessed are those whose lives are spent in this cause.

Someone once asked me to enquire of God whether He would be serving Him by accepting a bishopric. After Communion, the Lord said to me: 'Tell him that when he truly and clearly understands that true dominion consists in possessing nothing, then he can accept it.' By this he meant that anyone who is to assume authority must be very far from desiring to do so. At least he must never strive to obtain office.

These and many other favours the Lord has given, and continues to give to this sinner. But I do not think I need describe any more of them, because I have said enough to show the progress my soul is making, and the spirituality which the Lord has granted me. Blessed be He for ever who has taken such care of me.

Once He told me consolingly that I must not worry – he spoke most lovingly – for in this life we cannot always remain in the same state. Sometimes we are fervent, and at other times not; sometimes we are restless and at other times calm in spite of temptations. He told me to trust Him and not be afraid.

One day I asked myself whether it showed a lack of detachment in me to rejoice in the conversation of the people with whom I talk about my soul, and to love them. For I always find comfort in the company of those whom I see to be true servants of God. The Lord said to me in reply that if a man who had been in peril of death were to attribute his recovery to a physician, it would be no virtue in him to withhold his thanks and to refuse him his love. For what would have happened to me but for these persons? He told me that conversation with good people was never a bad thing, and that provided what I said was always well considered and virtuous I should not abstain from their company. It would do me more good than harm. This gave me a great deal of comfort, for sometimes I used to think that I was not sufficiently detached, and then I wanted to give up seeing these people altogether. The Lord always gave me advice about everything, even to the extent of telling me how to deal with certain weak persons and with others. He never ceases to take care of me. But I am sometimes distressed to see how little I do in His service, and how I am forced to spend so much more time than I would wish in a body as weak and miserable as mine.

One night I was at prayer when the time came for me to go to bed. I was in considerable pain, and my usual sickness was coming on. When I saw how bound I was to my body and how my spirit, on the other hand, demanded time for itself, I became so depressed that I burst into floods of tears and was thoroughly upset. This was not the only time that I felt exasperated with myself. It happens frequently, as I have said, and when it does I look on myself like this. But I never fail to do what I see to be necessary for my life. Pray God I do not often do more than is essential. No doubt I do. On the occasion of which I am speaking, when I was so distressed, the Lord appeared to me, comforted me greatly, and told me that I must do these things for love of Him, and endure everything since my life was at present necessary. I do not think I was ever distressed again, once I had resolved to serve my Lord and Consoler with all my strength. Although He has let me suffer a little, He has so comforted me that it is nothing to me to desire trials. I seem now to have no other reason for living, and it is for trials that I pray God most fervently. Sometimes I say to Him with my whole will: 'Death or suffering, Lord, that is all that I ask of You for myself'. It comforts me to hear the clock strike, for then another hour of my life has passed away, and I seem to be a little nearer to seeing God.

At other times I am in a state in which I do not feel I am alive and seem to have no longing for death. I am lukewarm and in complete darkness, as I have said I often am after great trials. When the Lord was pleased that these favours which He is granting me should be publicly known, as He told me some years ago they would be, I was greatly troubled; and to this day I have suffered quite a little on that account, as your Reverence knows, since everyone interprets them in his own way. It has been a comfort to me, however, that they have not become public through any fault of mine, for I have always been very careful and taken great pains never to speak of them to anyone but my confessors or those to whom I knew they had spoken about them. This was not out of humility but because, as I have said, it distressed me to discuss these matters even with my confessors. But now – glory be to God! – though many still speak ill of me out of their zeal for righteousness, and others are afraid to talk to me or to hear my confession, and others say all kinds of things to my face, I care very little, because I believe the Lord has chosen this means of benefiting some souls, and I clearly see and remember how much the Lord Himself would suffer on behalf of just one. I do not know whether it is for this reason that His Majesty has placed me in this retired place, where I am so strictly enclosed and where I am so much like a dead thing that I once thought no one would remember me again. But I am not as much forgotten as I wish, since there are certain persons to whom I am obliged to speak. As I am not in a place where I can be visited, however, it seems that the Lord has at last been pleased to bring me to a haven, which I trust in His Majesty will be secure. As I am now out of the world, and in a small and saintly society, I look down on things as from a height and care very little what people say or know about me. I care more about a single soul's slightest advancement than for all that people may say about me; and since I have been here, it has been the Lord's will that my desires shall be limited to this. He has given me a life that is a kind of sleep, for I almost always seem to be dreaming what I see. I find in myself no great happiness or unhappiness. If some things make me feel a little of either, it passes so swiftly that I am amazed, and the feeling that it leaves behind is as of something met with in a dream. It is really true that if afterwards I want to glory in that pleasure or to grieve for that pain, I am no more capable of doing so than an intelligent person would be either of grieving or glorying over something that occurred in a dream. For the Lord has awakened my soul from that state in which, being neither mortified nor dead to the things of this world, I used to have such feelings; and His Majesty will not let me become blind again.

This, my dear Father, is how I live now. Your Reverence must pray

God either to take me to Him or to give me the means of serving Him. May it please His Majesty that what is written here may be of some benefit to your Reverence, since my lack of opportunities for writing has made it a hard task for me. But it will have been a blessed task if I have succeeded in saying anything which will bring to the Lord even a single act of praise. With that I should feel myself amply rewarded, even if your Reverence were to burn my writings immediately.

I should not like them to be burnt, however, before they have been seen by three persons known to your Reverence, who are or have been my confessors.[1] For if what I say is wrong, it would be well that they should lose the good opinion they have of me; and if it is good, I know that, being pious and learned men, they will see whence it comes and praise Him who has spoken through me. May His Majesty always protect Your Reverence and make you so great a saint that your spirituality and light may be shed on this miserable creature, who is so lacking in humility and so presumptuous as to have ventured to write on these sublime subjects. May it please the Lord that I have fallen into no errors, for my intention and wish have been to be accurate and obedient, so that through me the Lord may receive some praise. This is what for many years I have been praying for. As the works I have performed are not sufficient to gain this end, I have ventured to put together this story of my unruly life, though I have wasted no more time or trouble on it than has been necessary for the writing of it. I have merely set down what has happened to me in all possible simplicity and truth.

May it please the Lord, since He is powerful and can do what He will, that I may succeed in doing His will in all things. May He not allow this soul to be lost which He has, by so many artifices, in so many ways and on so many occasions, rescued from hell and drawn to Himself. Amen.

1. Fathers Bañez, García de Toledo, and a third, who cannot be identified.

I H S

MAY the Holy Spirit be ever with your Reverence. Amen. It would be no bad thing, sir, if I were to exaggerate the difficulty of this task so that you might feel obliged to commend me most earnestly to Our Lord; and I might well do so, considering what I have suffered when I have found myself writing down and calling attention to all my miserable deeds. Still, I can truly say that I have felt worse when recording the favours that the Lord has done me than when noting down the offences that I have committed against His Majesty. In writing at some length, I have fulfilled your Reverence's commands, but I have done so on condition that you fulfil your promise to me and tear up any part that seems to you wrong. I had not finished reading through what I have written when your Reverence sent for it. Some things, therefore, may be badly expressed, and others put down twice, for I have had so little time for the task that I have not been able to re-read what I have written. I beg your Reverence to correct my mistakes and, if this is to be sent on to Father Ávila, to have a fresh copy made; otherwise someone may recognize my hand.

I very much hope that Father Ávila will be ordered to read this, since it was for this purpose that I began to write. Then if he thinks I am on the right road I shall be greatly comforted, for I have done all that it is in me to do. Your Reverence must act in all respects as you think best, and will realize your obligation to one who thus entrusts her soul to you.

I shall commend your Reverence's soul to Our Lord so long as I live. Be diligent, therefore, in serving His Majesty, in order to help me. For your Reverence will see from these writings how profitable it is to give oneself entirely, as you yourself have begun to do, to Him who gives Himself to us without stint.

May He be blessed for ever. I trust in His mercy that your Reverence and I will meet in a place where we shall see more clearly what great things He has done for us, and where we shall praise Him for ever and ever. Amen.

This book was finished in June of the year MDLXII.[1]

1. This date refers to the original version written by Mother Teresa de Jesús. which was not divided into chapters. To this version she afterwards added many things that happened after this date, among them the foundation of the convent of St Joseph at Ávila.

Note by Father Bañez

READ MORE IN PENGUIN

In every corner of the world, on every subject under the sun, Penguin represents quality and variety – the very best in publishing today.

For complete information about books available from Penguin – including Puffins, Penguin Classics and Arkana – and how to order them, write to us at the appropriate address below. Please note that for copyright reasons the selection of books varies from country to country.

In the United Kingdom: Please write to *Dept. EP, Penguin Books Ltd, Bath Road, Harmondsworth, West Drayton, Middlesex UB7 ODA*

In the United States: Please write to *Consumer Sales, Penguin USA, P.O. Box 999, Dept. 17109, Bergenfield, New Jersey 07621-0120.* VISA and MasterCard holders call 1-800-253-6476 to order Penguin titles

In Canada: Please write to *Penguin Books Canada Ltd, 10 Alcorn Avenue, Suite 300, Toronto, Ontario M4V 3B2*

In Australia: Please write to *Penguin Books Australia Ltd, P.O. Box 257, Ringwood, Victoria 3134*

In New Zealand: Please write to *Penguin Books (NZ) Ltd, Private Bag 102902, North Shore Mail Centre, Auckland 10*

In India: Please write to *Penguin Books India Pvt Ltd, 706 Eros Apartments, 56 Nehru Place, New Delhi 110 019*

In the Netherlands: Please write to *Penguin Books Netherlands bv, Postbus 3507, NL-1001 AH Amsterdam*

In Germany: Please write to *Penguin Books Deutschland GmbH, Metzlerstrasse 26, 60594 Frankfurt am Main*

In Spain: Please write to *Penguin Books S. A., Bravo Murillo 19, 1° B, 28015 Madrid*

In Italy: Please write to *Penguin Italia s.r.l., Via Felice Casati 20, I–20124 Milano*

In France: Please write to *Penguin France S. A., 17 rue Lejeune, F–31000 Toulouse*

In Japan: Please write to *Penguin Books Japan, Ishikiribashi Building, 2–5–4, Suido, Bunkyo-ku, Tokyo 112*

In South Africa: Please write to *Longman Penguin Southern Africa (Pty) Ltd, Private Bag X08, Bertsham 2013*

READ MORE IN PENGUIN

A CHOICE OF CLASSICS

Adomnan of Iona	**Life of St Columba**
St Anselm	**The Prayers and Meditations**
St Augustine	**Confessions**
	The City of God
Bede	**Ecclesiastical History of the English People**
Geoffrey Chaucer	**The Canterbury Tales**
	Love Visions
	Troilus and Criseyde
Marie de France	**The Lais of Marie de France**
Jean Froissart	**The Chronicles**
Geoffrey of Monmouth	**The History of the Kings of Britain**
Gerald of Wales	**History and Topography of Ireland**
	The Journey through Wales and **The Description of Wales**
Gregory of Tours	**The History of the Franks**
Robert Henryson	**The Testament of Cresseid and Other Poems**
Walter Hilton	**The Ladder of Perfection**
St Ignatius	**Personal Writings**
Julian of Norwich	**Revelations of Divine Love**
Thomas à Kempis	**The Imitation of Christ**
William Langland	**Piers the Ploughman**
Sir John Mandeville	**The Travels of Sir John Mandeville**
Marguerite de Navarre	**The Heptameron**
Christine de Pisan	**The Treasure of the City of Ladies**
Chrétien de Troyes	**Arthurian Romances**
Marco Polo	**The Travels**
Richard Rolle	**The Fire of Love**
François Villon	**Selected Poems**